BODIES OF WORSHIP

Bodies of Worship

Explorations in Theory and Practice

Bruce T. Morrill, S.J.
Editor

Bernard J. Cooke   Andrea Goodrich
Paul Covino   Colleen M. Griffith
James L. Empereur, S.J.   Leo Keegan
Margaret Mary Kelleher, O.S.U.
Bruce T. Morrill, S.J.

A Liturgical Press Book

THE LITURGICAL PRESS
Collegeville, Minnesota

Cover design by Greg Becker

Library of Congress Cataloging-in-Publication Data

Bodies of worship : explorations in theory and practice / Bruce T.
   Morrill ; Bernard J. Cooke ... [et al.].
        p.   cm.
   Includes bibliographical references and index.
   ISBN 0-8146-2529-0 (alk. paper)
   1. Public worship.   2. Catholic Church—Liturgy.   3. Catholic
Church—Doctrines.   4. Body, Human—Religious aspects—Catholic
Church.   I. Morrill, Bruce T.   II. Cooke, Bernard J.
BX1969.B63   1999
264—dc21   99-22610
                                                    CIP

Contents

Contributors

Bernard J. Cooke, Loyola Professor Emeritus, College of the Holy Cross, Worcester, Massachusetts.

Paul Covino, Associate Chaplain and Director of Liturgy, College of the Holy Cross, Worcester, Massachusetts.

James L. Empereur, S.J., Parochial Vicar, San Fernando Cathedral, San Antonio, Texas, and Lecturer, Our Lady of the Lake University, San Antonio.

Andrea Goodrich, formerly Director of Music Ministries, College of the Holy Cross, is presently Director of Music at St. Thomas Aquinas Church, Jamaica Plain, Massachusetts.

Colleen M. Griffith, Director of Formative Spirituality Program and Adjunct Assistant Professor of Theology, Institute of Religious Education and Pastoral Ministry, Boston College, Chestnut Hill, Massachusetts.

Leo Keegan, Director of Liturgy, St. Maria Goretti Roman Catholic Church, San Jose, California.

Margaret Mary Kelleher, O.S.U., Associate Professor of Liturgical Studies, Department of Religion and Religious Education, School of Religious Studies, The Catholic University of America, Washington, D.C.

Bruce T. Morrill, S.J., Assistant Professor of Liturgical Theology, Department of Theology and Institute of Religious Education and Pastoral Ministry, Boston College, Chestnut Hill, Massachusetts.

Preface

Without doubt, one of the hallmarks of late modern society has been a heightened awareness of human bodiliness as it features in all aspects of life—familial, sexual, economic, legal, religious, political, and ecological. The body has figured prominently, as well, in academia, especially as the body's resistance to abstraction serves the various philosophical and political objectives of post-modern scholarship. Amidst the academy and wider society, Christian theology and pastoral practice have sought to take human bodiliness more prominently into account. This has proven a challenging task, given the ambiguous "career" the body has known in Christian history and tradition, let alone the extent to which the teachings and practices of the Church concerning the body (with all their strengths and weaknesses) have come under serious criticism and even rejection in the modern marketplace, social media, and academy—often by Christians themselves. In such a complex, if not in some ways dangerous context, nevertheless, always arises the promise of the Gospel, the healing and transforming message that comes to life for the mission of human salvation in a given moment of history. In all its ritual bodiliness, the liturgy of the Church stands at the center of that mission.

That a more concerted reflection on the bodily aspects of liturgy might contribute to the theory and practice of both liturgical theology and pastoral ministry was the prospect taken up by theologians and pastoral ministers at the week-long "Liturgy and the Body" conference offered by the Institute of Religious Education and Pastoral Ministry at Boston College in July, 1998. The chapters of this present book, as well as the book's overall scheme, have their origins in the lectures and workshops presented at that conference.

The book's two main parts, while related, are nonetheless distinctive in their structure and content. Part One systematically explores the various bodies engaged in the Church's worship—ecclesial, ritual, personal, and cultural—all with a view to how this humanly sanctifying work continues Christ's mission in the power of the Holy Spirit. The five chapters are purposefully arranged so as to unfold the multivalency of bodies at worship. Thus, a certain theological coherence is the goal. In Part Two, on the other hand, the four chapters describe and analyze specific liturgical, physical, and spiritual practices in the pursuit of further insights into the irreducibly bodily nature of the celebration of the Christian life as worship of God. The differences in subject matter and experiences of the body are respected by not constricting the chapters into any forced thematic sequence. The entire book is introduced by means of a narrative describing an actual liturgy which took place a few years ago. A brief conclusion reflects back across the landscape of the chapters to the narrative and symbolic basis for liturgical theology insofar as it is, at origin and end, practical and pastoral.

In offering this book in service to Church and academy I owe at least some brief words of thanks to several among the many people who have helped bring it along its way. The idea for this project—both the summer conference and the book—came to me while hiking in the mountains of Vermont. Upon returning to the Institute of Religious Education and Pastoral Ministry my proposal for a "Liturgy and the Body" week was welcomed with immediate, enthusiastic support by the director, Claire Lowery, whose warm encouragement never failed throughout the project. Sandy Hurley, the Institute's business administrator, navigated numerous logistical and financial challenges with unflappable patience and grace. Kara Tierney-Trevor, one of the graduate assistants at the Institute, was of great help through all the phases of the conference week. To these and the other staff and faculty of the Institute, and on behalf of my fellow authors in this book, I give heartfelt thanks.

For my own part, I am grateful to these authors for taking on the specific tasks I proposed to each and seeing them through in presentation and print. I also thank Don and Jane Saliers for continuously making their second home in Vermont available to me as a writer's getaway, as well as Jim Collins, S.J., minister of the Jesuit Community at Boston College, who finds the wheels for me to get there. My brother Jesuits in the Barat House Jesuit Community are an invaluable source of companionship, wisdom, prayer, and laughter.

Bruce T. Morrill, S.J.
Boston College

INTRODUCTION

Initial Consideration: Theory and Practice of the Body in Liturgy Today

Bruce T. Morrill, S.J.

The basic premise of this book, the wager of its authors, is that an exploration of the various bodily characteristics of human living can heighten our awareness and deepen our insights into what we Christians do together when we celebrate the liturgy of the Church, the sacraments of our living in Christ. The term "body," of course, carries a number of connotations ranging from the physical to the metaphorical (e.g., the body of a human or animal, an assembled body of delegates or legislators, the body of a text, a body of knowledge). It is precisely this multivalence of the concept that can provide us several distinct but interrelated approaches to how it is that liturgy relates us to God and to one another as a church in this world.

The move away from thinking about the sacraments as objects that dispense grace to perceiving them as relational events, as personal encounters among God and people, has been the hallmark of sacramental theology in the second half of the twentieth century. In his classic text, *Christ the Sacrament of the Encounter With God,* Edward Schillebeeckx, through his constructive retrieval of ancient Christian sources and the work of Thomas Aquinas, helped us to discover the Church and its sacraments as genuine, human encounters with God in the Spirit of the Risen Christ. In so doing, Schillebeeckx, as well as Karl Rahner and numerous others who built on the monumental theologies of those two, opened the field of inquiry concerning sacramental liturgy to the profound range and depth of human experience, including the embodied, symbolic ways in which we meet God now through our relating with one another in the world. In returning to

1

Schillebeeckx's early text, one discovers that the concept of the body pervades the work, developed as integral to human salvation in Christ through not only the principle of the incarnation but also the resurrection. Arguing anthropologically that there is no such thing as a "free spiritual act" that is "achieved in pure interiority" prior to or independent of the body,[1] Schillebeeckx posited the entire Christian life as a sacrament of the encounter with God. The Church's official sacramental liturgies function as "markers, milestones on the way" of the believer's life becoming increasingly united with Christ; they are "flashes of light within the whole of Christian life" as it is engaged in wider society.[2] Schillebeeckx's concluding insistence that the credibility of the Church's liturgical reform depends on its members being in active solidarity with all peoples in their struggles, anticipated the turn in his later work, wherein his identification of the biblical God of Jesus as the God of suffering people shaped his description of the Christian life as fundamentally entailing both mystical and ethical (political) dimensions.[3]

There is something remarkable, even scandalous, about the Christian tradition's claim that God has in Christ Jesus taken on the human condition (body and soul) and, through Jesus' faithful mission to broken humanity unto death, raised our condition to a new convenantal relationship with the Divine, one another and all creation. The scandalousness arises in our only too persistent awareness of the sinfulness of our selves and societies, of the ambiguity and suffering we experience as bodily persons, and of death, which places the whole in question. Taking a different critical tack, feminist theologians have come to perceive the scandal precisely in the theological and practical Christian history of distrusting the ambiguities of bodily human existence and, more specifically, of associating the temptation to sin with women's bodies. Susan Ross has argued that while Schillebeeckx and Rahner are to be commended for asserting the embodied nature of the human person and developing the point in significant ways, "neither offer[ed] an alternative to the traditional application of em-

---

[1] Edward Schillebeeckx, *Christ the Sacrament of the Encounter with God* (New York: Sheed and Ward, 1963) 198.

[2] Ibid., 200, 214.

[3] Edward Schillebeeckx, *Church: The Human Story of God,* trans. John Bowden (New York: Crossroad, 1991) 66–98. The characterization of Christian faith as a praxis of mysticism and politics also figures prominently in the theology of Johann Baptist Metz. See his *Faith in History and Society: Toward a Fundamental Practical Theology,* trans. David Smith (New York: Seabury Press, 1980) 76–77, and *Followers of Christ: The Religious Life and the Church,* trans. Thomas Linton (New York: Paulist Press, 1978) 63, 80.

bodiment to sex difference."[4] Furthermore, Ross's evaluation of the subsequent generation of sacramental theologians found them committed to embodiment as a principle without considering its implications in depth.

While the shortcomings, unfortunate consequences, and even tragic results of historical attitudes towards the body have received a growing amount of documentation and reflection in recent theological literature (as shall be noted at times in this present book), we nonetheless can positively acknowledge that the Church has never ceased to be amazed by its tradition which proclaims that God saves humanity right in our very material actions and circumstances. French sacramental theologian Louis-Marie Chauvet develops the point philosophically and historically in his *magnum opus:* "Faithful to its biblical roots, ecclesial tradition has attempted to discern what is most 'spiritual' in God on the basis of what is most 'corporeal' in us. This is especially the case in the liturgy. But it is more widely the case in the whole of *Church life*."[5] Even when, for various reasons, the faithful have had little direct access to the symbols and actions of the sacramental rituals of the Church, other forms of "popular piety" have emerged and flourished. One has only to think of the pastoral effectiveness of St. Francis's creation of the Nativity scene (the "creche") and promotion of the Stations of the Cross, let alone the myriad cultural renditions of the crucifix. All of these symbols have flourished since the Middle Ages, for they represent and foster faith in God's identification with and presence to people in their very bodily experiences of joy and wonder, struggle and suffering. For Christians, the most spiritual of realities can only be experienced or known in and through the materiality of our bodies.

Contemporary sacramental theology's conceptualizing of the sacraments as dynamic relational events joining people with God has led over the past twenty years away from abstract discussions of the principles involved in a given sacrament to increasing attention to liturgical action itself. The methodological shift to liturgy itself as the theological source—the study of its texts and ritual actions and their relationship to other ecclesial and theological issues—has resulted in a further crucial stage in the development of the discipline: the emergence of liturgical theology in its own right.[6] This is a necessary consequence of the theological commitment to the embodied

---

[4] Susan A. Ross, "'Then Honor God in Your Body' (1 Cor 6:20): Feminist and Sacramental Theology on the Body," *Horizons,* vol. 16, no. 1 (1989) 17.

[5] Louis-Marie Chauvet, *Symbol and Sacrament: A Sacramental Reinterpretation of Christian Existence,* trans. Patrick Madigan and Madeleine Beaumont (Collegeville: The Liturgical Press, 1995) 523.

[6] See Peter E. Fink, "Sacramental Theology after Vatican II," *The New Dictionary of Sacramental Worship,* ed. Peter E. Fink (Collegeville: The Liturgical Press, 1990) 1111.

character of our sanctification, for there is no disembodied realm where we are being saved. Neither can we merely reason to our salvation as if it were, to borrow a phrase from Johann Baptist Metz, happening "behind the back of the human history of suffering."[7] The sharing of stories, symbols and rituals is essential to a life lived in the paradoxical yet promising concreteness of the Gospel. Nor can we romanticize that the Church possesses some perfect ritual enactments of its divine worship. Not only do clergy and laity often fumble in their efforts to appropriate the revised rites, but the actual local celebration of liturgy is always charged with bodily tensions encompassing gender, race, age, ethnicity, as well as the needs and gifts of the physically, intellectually, or emotionally challenged. The practical ways these questions and tensions are actually approached in real pastoral settings has everything to do with whether a given community is embracing the diverse complexity of our bodily living as opportunities for sacramentally encountering the gracious favor of God or suppressing the body as an obstacle to what is "truly" holy and spiritual.[8]

With a view to advancing the pastoral work of liturgy in the Church today, this book is an invitation to think about liturgy—its structures, content, participants, and performances—in terms of the various, interrelated types of bodies engaged in its practice. To introduce what is meant here by "types" of bodies in relation to liturgy, as well as the potential benefits for thinking in such terms, we can best begin by turning to one of the actual rites of the Roman Catholic Church: the Order of Christian Funerals. The funeral liturgy is helpful to consider because the body is so undeniably central to it. By this I am, obviously, referring to the corpse, the human body which has expired, and whose ex-spiration places into stark relief the mysterious relationship between body, mind, and spirit in all human persons.

When one considers the enactment of the funeral rites for any particular deceased person, however, one quickly becomes aware of what I am calling the multivalence of the body, of the fact that the body is never merely a physical body (although the irreducible importance of the physical body of each person is not to be dismissed). The description and analysis of any specific funeral leads to the recognition that what happens with and to the body of the individual deceased person is a function of that person's relationship

---

[7] Johann Baptist Metz, *A Passion for God: The Mystical-Political Dimension of Christianity,* ed. and trans. J. Matthew Ashley (New York: Paulist Press, 1998) 69.

[8] "The most powerful experience of the sacred is found in the celebration and the persons celebrating, that is, it is found in the action of the assembly: the living words, the living gestures, the living sacrifice, the living meal. This was at the heart of the earliest liturgies." *Environment and Art in Catholic Worship* (Washington, D.C.: United States Catholic Conference, 1978) n. 29.

to and location within a number of other bodies: the Church as the *body of Christ,* the ecclesial body which is at once social in its members, traditional in its beliefs and practices, and mystical in its relation to the Risen Christ; the *ritual body* of the assembled participants and ministers, who enact the liturgy by entering into its symbolic mode of word and gestures; and the *cultural body,* which entails familial and other social relationships, customs and practices concerning dress, deportment, the expression of emotions, age and gender roles, as well as economic decisions. The participants in the funeral rites must negotiate all of these aspects of bodiliness or corporality in the process of their finding meaning (or not) in this human event.

What I have briefly outlined here about the body in relation to the church's funeral liturgy could, of course, be introduced in relation to any of the other rites of the Church. One might, for example, prefer looking to the beginning of the human life cycle and the rite for baptizing infants, starting from a recognition of the beautiful, vulnerable physicality of the baby to consideration of the social-cultural, ecclesial, and ritual bodies in which she or he now plays a part. I have chosen the funeral liturgy, however, because of a significant pastoral experience I had with it several years ago. A description and analysis of this particular instance of pastoral praxis is offered as a stimulus for the readers' theological imagination and thought, leading to the chapters that will follow.[9]

Theology as Practice: A Liturgical Narrative

The event I am about to describe took place when I was writing my doctoral dissertation. It was for me an experience of what Alexander Schmemann, about whom I was writing at the time, meant when he continuously and so passionately argued for the ongoing tradition and actual performance of the liturgy as the primary source for the Church's theology.[10] A

---

[9] Methodologically, this is an effort to perform theology according to the categories that Johann Baptist Metz has proposed as a critical corrective to the transcendental-idealism of modern theology: memory, narrative, and solidarity. With Metz, I share the conviction that Christian faith (the object of theology) is fundamentally a praxis. I am inviting the reader here to reflect upon the praxis of faith in liturgy so as to move into theoretical chapters that seek to elucidate and promote further practice of the Church's *leitourgia.* See Metz, *Faith in History and Society,* 184–237.

[10] See Alexander Schmemann, *Liturgy and Tradition: Theological Reflections of Alexander Schmemann,* ed. Thomas Fisch (Crestwood, N.Y.: St Vladimir's Seminary Press, 1990) 12, 39, 85. In a book dedicated to Schmemann's memory, Adain Kavanagh argues further for the liturgical event as *theologia prima.* See his *On Liturgical Theology* (New York: Pueblo Publishing, 1984) 73–95. Gordon Lathrop pursues this

telephone call summoned me away from the solitude of my desk and its realm of theoretical abstraction into the pastoral field, where I was privileged to witness what I perceived to be a glimpse of the reign of God.

The person calling was Sister Alice, the associate pastoral minister at Sts. Peter and Paul, a mostly black parish in southeast Atlanta. I presided at liturgies there from time to time, and knew the parish as one where the pastor and staff made a concerted effort to inculturate the liturgy in its African-American context through music, art and environment, and approaches to ministry. Sister Alice asked if I were willing and able to preside at a funeral on the day after next, as the pastor was out of town. The deceased was a forty-one-year-old woman named "Betty," who after years of struggle had finally succumbed to a debilitating disease, leaving orphaned her eight-year-old son, "Tommy."[11] With the exception of Tommy, Betty's last years had been spent in relative isolation. She was alienated in various degrees from some of her family. One of the sources of tension, it seemed, was her having left the Baptist Church many years ago to become a Roman Catholic.

Sister Alice explained that Betty held a special place in her heart in that Betty was one of the first people she had visited when she began her ministry at Sts. Peter and Paul some seven years ago and had continued to do so regularly over the years—more often still in the last months. Alice described Betty as a woman of courage who had suffered a great deal. Alice expected only a handful of family to attend the funeral and explained that she would be contacting parishioners who could be free on a weekday morning to come to the Mass. She hoped to recruit about a dozen, some of whom might remember Betty from years back when she was still able to attend services herself. There would thus be at least some small assembly of the faithful at the funeral liturgy. Listening to Sister Alice it became clear to me that she should speak at the funeral. Not only was she the pastoral minister amidst that community of faith but, given her clearly special relationship with Betty, she would be able to make the personal connection between the Christian story celebrated in the liturgy and the story of this poor woman. After a bit of coaxing, Alice agreed to provide a reflection at the close of the Communion Rite, as the Roman ritual allows, while I planned to keep my homily after the Gospel more brief. This raised, nonetheless, the question of the content of that homily and, given the integral role of the homily within the entire liturgy, it required my focusing on what I hoped for in this funeral mass.

---

trajectory of thought throughout his *Holy Things: A Liturgical Theology* (Minneapolis: Augsburg-Fortress, 1993).

[11] Out of respect for these individuals, I have changed their names in relating this story.

What I brought from my conversation with Sister Alice into the subsequent hours of preparation for the funeral liturgy was the conviction that I should allow the ritual of the Roman Rite to function at its fullest. This meant that I, in the office of presiding minister of the rite, wished to proceed in the confident desire of giving myself, the assembly, and the deceased over to the inherent power in the liturgy, the paschal mystery, so that it might *do us*.[12] Any death occasions a renewed awareness that we rely on the power and mercy of God. All the more in this situation of a painful, early death and, further still, the gathering of strangers across the omnipresent, if not conscious, lines of race, gender, generation, religion, and ethnicity. All of these aspects of human identity contribute to what Chauvet calls our *corporality,* the "triple body" of culture, tradition, and nature, in which each of us realizes ourselves as "person-bodies" through our decisions and desires.[13] Thus, the preparation and performance of the Church's liturgy carries with it the dual pastoral (and thereby, *theological*) commitments to, on the one hand, *confidence* in the liturgy as a privileged place where we may indeed expect God to "speak" in symbolic action[14] and, on the other hand, *sensitivity* to issues of human dignity and difference concretely operative in its enactment.

What this meant was that I would carefully let the ritual movement and gestures, the signs as well as the words, all together function as symbols into which the assembly might enter, creating a liturgical "space" that would serve the reality of the paschal mystery manifesting itself in that particular situation.[15] We would vary in or personal knowledge of Betty—

[12] See Schmemann, *Liturgy and Tradition,* 127.

[13] Chauvet, *Symbol and Sacrament,* 149–51.

[14] In addition to Chauvet's work, see David N. Power, *Unsearchable Riches: The Symbolic Nature of Liturgy* (New York: Pueblo Publishing, 1984) 144–71.

[15] To think here in terms of "liturgical space," as Chauvet has theorized, is to take into account all of the various material elements of the liturgy and how they function together in the actual celebration of a given rite. These physical, bodily elements include such stable features as the baptismal font, altar table, ambo, and presidential chair, each of which by its structure and placement symbolizes the irreducible roles of word, sacrament, and ministry in the life of the Church. There are, moreover, numerous elements whose selection vary according to particular rites, seasons, and pastoral occasions: music and chants, the placement of objects such as flowers or the paschal candle, the use of certain gestures, postures, or movements, as well as the roles of different ministers and the assembly. All of these—people, architectural fixtures, movable objects, sounds and actions—both relate in their own unique ways to various beliefs and values in the Christian tradition and relate within a particular liturgy to one another so as to create in that entire space a concrete experience of the tradition. See Louis-Marie Chauvet, "The Liturgy in its Symbolic Space," *Liturgy and the Body,* ed. Louis-Marie Chauvet and François Kabasele Lumbala, *Concilium* 1995/3 (London/Maryknoll: SCM Press/Orbis Books, 1995) 29–39.

I would number among those who knew her least of all—but we could all enter anew into an awareness, an experiential knowledge, of our lives as a participation in the mystery of Christ's dying and rising.[16]

More specifically, the preparation entailed my reviewing the ritual and choosing the scriptural readings in such a way that the two key elements of Christian liturgy, namely, word and sacrament, might mutually form each other, with the explicit and extended articulation of that relationship occurring in the homily. Turning to the Lectionary, Romans 6 (vv. 3-9) was the obvious choice for the first reading, as well as the primary source for the homily. It would afford the opportunity to preach on baptism, a sacrament that Betty's kin, as Baptists, could appreciate. The presence of the religious "other" in these Baptist sisters and brothers would, in turn, challenge me and my fellow Catholics to a greater awareness of the mystery of our having died with Christ in baptism as that which fundamentally identifies all Christians.[17] The common heritage of baptism needed to serve not only as a point of identity but also difference. Identity and difference *both* carry possibilities for comfort and challenge. While preaching could provide at least a basic ritual genre common to Catholic and Baptist, extensive liturgical symbolism was the tradition that could well be alien, if not distrusted, by the Baptists (but many modern Catholics, clergy and laity alike, distrust it too!).[18]

---

[16] A cogent presentation of the liturgical concept of the paschal mystery appears in Irénée H. Dalmais, "Theology of the Liturgical Celebration," Irénée H. Dalmais and others, *Principles of the Liturgy,* The Church at Prayer, vol. 1, ed. Aimé G. Martimort, trans. Matthew O'Connell, vol. 1, *The Church at Prayer* (Collegeville: The Liturgical Press, 1987) 262–66. For an exploration of the aesthetics involved in the inculturation of the paschal mystery in actual contexts, see Don E. Saliers, *Worship as Theology: Foretaste of Glory Divine* (Nashville: Abingdon Press, 1994) 191–202.

[17] While pursuing this Pauline theology of baptism as dying and rising with Christ, I am nonetheless aware that other theologies of baptism can be found in the New Testament and that some of these functioned more prominently in the earliest centuries of Christianity, especially in the East. See Mark Searle, "Infant Baptism Reconsidered," *Alternative Futures for Worship. Volume 2: Baptism and Confirmation,* ed. Mark Searle (Collegeville: The Liturgical Press, 1987) 30–32. See also Kilian McDonnell, "Jesus' Baptism in the Jordan," *Theological Studies,* vol. 56, no. 2 (June 1995) 209–36; and Adela Yarbro Collins, "The Origin of Christian Baptism," *Living Water, Sealing Spirit: Readings on Christian Initiation,* ed. Maxwell E. Johnson (Collegeville: The Liturgical Press, 1995) 35–57.

[18] Saliers offers insightful reflection on this point: "The more directly the body is involved, the more theological conflict there is likely to be between traditions. This is why, for example, conservative Protestants may have more trouble with the use of the Sign of the Cross or genuflection than with more explicitly doctrinal differences with Roman Catholics. The bodily signs carry theological convictions at a deeper cultural level than do rationally expressed 'beliefs.'" *Worship as Theology,* 164.

There were two ritual elements of the Mass of the Resurrection that I decided to exploit: structurally, the opening rite and, more pervasively, the use of incense. With its welcoming of the assembly gathered at the entrance of the church around the dead body of their loved one, the opening rite would be an opportunity to articulate from the start the baptismal hermeneutic of the entire Christian life now coming to poignant completion in this sister's bodily death. The articulation would come in the form of brief commentary in conjunction with covering the coffin with the white pall and then inviting the assembly to process behind crucifix and coffin so as to bring Betty's body for a final time into the church in a pattern reminiscent of the way those to be baptized are first welcomed therein.

The other ritual element I would exploit would press even more concertedly the difference in religious practice between Roman Catholics and Baptists. I chose to do so out of the conviction that the explicit recognition of difference, not merely in a passing word but in embodied performance, actually serves such an assembly better than seeking only ideas and gestures that are comfortable.[19] My decision was to use the ritual gesture of incense to the maximum extent in the liturgy—at the Gospel, Preparation of the Table, and the Concluding Rite of Farewell. This would need to be done purposefully and beautifully. The homily would be the place to link baptismal images and the purpose of the incensing—the dignity of Betty, who in life and death shares the very dignity of Jesus, the Christ to whom she belongs, the very child of God.[20]

As for the actual performance of the liturgy, things went as I and Sister Alice had planned, but in ways that far exceeded what we could have imagined. As the hour for the funeral Mass arrived, the church space was

---

[19] In asserting this conviction about Christian ecumenism, I consider my concern analogous to Paul Knitter's argument that the success of inter-religious dialogue depends on the recognition by each participant of what is unique and distinctive to one's own religion's way of grasping divine truth. See his *No Other Name? A Critical Survey of Christian Attitudes Toward the World Religions* (Maryknoll, N.Y.: Orbis Books, 1985) 219–20.

[20] While my intention for using the incense was to communicate a sense of honor, dignity and reverence, this purpose hardly exhausts its range of meanings. Incense introduces fragrances and sights into ritual activity which have served any of several purposes in the history of religions: a perfume for enhancing the air and/or masking foul odors, a form of sacrifice to a deity or to the spirits of the dead, an exorcism of evil spirits (causing healing or purification), a veneration of living persons, or an accompaniment to a procession, providing festivity or dignity. See Richard N. Fragomeni, "Uses of Incense," *The New Dictionary of Sacramental Worship*, 594–96; and W. Jardine Grisbrooke, "Incense," *The New Westminster Dictionary of Liturgy and Worship*, ed. J. D. Davies (Philadelphia: The Westminster Press, 1986) 265–66.

indeed dotted by about ten parishioners who had responded to Alice's call. When the acolyte and I went, however, to the narthex of the church, where I had instructed the morticians to place the coffin, I discovered a crowd of more than one hundred family members sharply dressed and lined up in single file out the door and along the sidewalk. I could see that they were lined up in expectation of their own religious custom of filing past the open coffin one last time before taking seats for the funeral service. I, however, decided to stick with the Roman liturgy of meeting the body in the coffin at the entryway, with family and friends assembled all around. I greeted the people warmly and expressed sympathy to them in their grief. I then moved into the opening ritual by making an explicit connection between Betty's death with Christ in baptism as her entry into the life of Christ in the Church and the entry now of Betty's body into this church for the community's ritual of commending her to God's promise of her sharing in the glorified body of the risen Christ. For this reason, I concluded, we blanket the coffin in white in reminiscence of her white baptismal garment, and we sprinkle the coffin with water symbolic of baptism. Having done that, I led coffin and congregation behind the symbol of the processional crucifix, carried by the acolyte.

I had done something different than this group of Baptist guests at a Catholic church had expected, but the responsiveness in many of their eyes and the nods of several heads assured me quickly that we were together in this liturgy. That sense of connection was confirmed in the people's vigorous participation in the music, led by the parish's young black cantor at a baby grand piano. The hymns were from the repertoire of the black gospel tradition, and the refrain of the responsorial psalm was of a genre in which these guests could and did readily join. Even more gratifying for me as a preacher and presider was the spontaneous responses of "Amen" and "Preach on" that welled up from the people during the first part of the homily, my exposition on Romans 6. All together, this responsiveness of Betty's family assured me that I was not, as I feared might be the case, off the mark in my pastoral planning, that I, a white Roman Catholic priest from the North, was able to serve and join these Southern black Christians in and through this act of worship. At that point in the homily, I drew confidence from my sense of connection with the people as I moved to my final and large point about the Roman ritual's use of incense.

I noted how I had used the thurible to incense the Book of the Gospels, which had been standing on the altar table from the start of the liturgy. I explained this gesture as a sign of deep reverence for the Word of God which comes alive in the proclamation of scripture in the liturgy. I went on to explain that I would once again avail myself of the thurible at the preparation of the gifts at the beginning of the Liturgy of the Eucharist. The gifts of bread and wine, brought forward by members of the community of faith, the Church which is the Body of Christ, hold a great dignity not only as products of the earth and human labor, and thus symbols of the people themselves, but also by the fact that they were now about to become the eucharistic body and blood of Christ.[21] That dual identity of the body of Christ would become explicit in a solemn ritual gesture. I would incense both the gift-laden table and the assembled people of the church, symbolically proclaiming the one dignity all share together in Christ. But finally, it is that very dignity that would be further manifested in the incensing of Betty's body in the coffin at the conclusion of the funeral Mass. The use of the very same gesture of reverence afforded the embodied presence of Christ in word, sacrament, and assembly would bespeak the reverence in which the church holds Betty, who had so faithfully shared in the Eucharist, and the confidence with which the Church now entrusts her to the eternal banquet with Christ and the saints in heaven.

The Liturgy of the Eucharist followed as I had explained in the homily, but Betty's loved ones surprised and moved me beyond my own expectations for how the Spirit of the Risen Christ might act in the Mass of the Resurrection. During the Sign of Peace I quickly reviewed with Sister Alice my intention to invite as many as would like to come forward in the Communion Rite to receive a blessing from me. Alice once again demonstrated her pastoral wisdom by suggesting, rather, that after I explained the opportunity and purpose of the blessing, she walk among the guests during Communion to ask who might wish to receive it. She would stand by each at their places, and I would come to them. This would not be difficult, since the church was furnished with amply spaced rows of chairs, allowing for flexibility and movement.

As the Communion Rite unfolded, several women and men did indeed ask for the blessing. Still holding the dish of consecrated bread in my left hand, I placed my right on each person's head, tracing the Sign of the Cross on the brow. When I did so with the first person, one of Betty's sisters, she raised her hands in prayer. We remained together in this posture for nearly a minute, with me praying silently while she voiced prayers and acclamations of praise. The others prayed in similar fashion, variously lifting up their arms, swaying rhythmically, speaking or singing their words of gratitude and praise. I was deeply moved as I realized that these Baptist sisters and brothers were entering into communion in a way consonant with their

---

[21] Robert Cabié describes the veneration of the gifts in the procession to the altar in the early churches. See his *The Eucharist,* trans. Matthew O'Connell, vol. 2, *The Church at Prayer* (Collegeville: The Liturgical Press, 1986) 78–80.

own tradition of ritual prayer. Communion was taking place for and among us in a way I had never experienced, and it was an embodied, incorporated and corporeal, form of communion, indeed.

After the Communion Rite, Alice delivered a reflection on Betty's life that was consoling in its honesty, directness, and graciousness. The Rite of Farewell went as planned. As I slowly circuited the coffin with incense, I sensed an intensity of prayer among us all that I do not think was merely a projection of highly invested emotions on my part.

The Narrative's Invitation:
Toward a Liturgical Theology of the Body

Betty's funeral was without doubt a powerful experience for us who participated in it. I am confident that readers of this text could also relate stories of liturgies—or even just moments of prayer and worship—that were and remain significant for them and, in many cases, their fellow participants. We may well find, however, that it is often difficult to explain why or how such liturgical experiences were so meaningful or, conversely, why a certain liturgy left us "cold," unengaged, uninspired.[22] One crucial factor, nonetheless, is the extent to which the participants in a liturgy find themselves personally engaged in the action. To speak of personal engagement, however, necessarily introduces consideration of the body, for each of us exists only as a "person-body." Here a further, albeit brief, rehearsal of Chauvet's theory of the body and its relation to sacramental worship may prove helpful.

As mentioned above, Chauvet conceptualizes each of us as an "I-body," a human subject whose corporality is, nonetheless, a "triple body" comprised of culture, tradition, and nature.[23] The key to this notion is recognizing that each of us does not have a body but, rather, *is* a body. The body is natural in its physicality, sharing in the rhythms and forces of the entire physical universe. In this sense, the human body is cosmic, for each person continuously projects oneself into the universe as a macrocosm of one's own physical bodiliness, while also introjecting that universe within oneself as a microcosm of the world. While there is a "givenness" to this ongoing dialogue of our physicality in the universe, the way in which people

[22] Indeed, the complexity and ambiguity of human ritualizing presents the burgeoning scholarly discipline of ritual studies with significant scholarly difficulties, as Margaret Mary Kelleher addresses in chapter 3 (below).

[23] See Chauvet, *Symbol and Sacrament*, 149–50. Colleen Griffith, in chapter 4 (below), proposes another threefold scheme for understanding the body as "vital organism," "socio-cultural site," and "product of consciousness and will."

consciously reflect upon and give meaning to themselves as a body in relation to the cosmos comes about through the mediation of culture and tradition.[24] Each human subject *as* body constructs meaning for one's life, uniquely according to one's own desires, through a myriad of symbols. Thus, the body is the fundamental functioning symbol of all human experience,[25] shaped through each one's participation with others in the symbol-systems of culture. Chauvet identifies culture with the network of current social customs, values, symbols, and practices of a people as these, for example, are inculcated by parents and other rearing figures to their children. Tradition is the term he uses for those elements of culture that situate a people in a historical relationship to a more or less mythic past, functioning as a living memory that connects them to their ancestors through symbol, story, and ritual.

If we return with Chauvet's theory of the human subject as a "triple body" to the narrative of Betty's funeral, we begin to have a way to understand something of how the participants in that liturgy found it personally meaningful. Each came to the liturgy with her or his own felt needs and desires, which were a function of each person's relationship with not only Betty but also God, the Church, and the other participants there. The unique experience of each participant, nonetheless, was only able to come about through our bodiliness, in its social, traditional, and cosmic aspects. The stark reality of the finitude of the physical body, both within its own cycle of aging, health, and illness and as part of the greater cycles of life and death in the universe, was undoubtedly evident to all in our awareness that the body of Betty now lay as a corpse in the coffin. Individuals' reflections on this natural reality might well have been conditioned by their own physical health or age. Awareness of one's body during the funeral liturgy could variably be heightened or numbed, depending on numerous factors, both internal and external to the given person. Different people clearly felt the need to be close to loved ones, even held by them, while others had less physical contact. The space and ritual entailed an array of sights, sounds (especially the music), and smells (notably, the incense), as well as movement and postures (including the raised hands in prayer). These and much more contributed to the physicality of the liturgical experience. They also point toward the roles of culture and tradition.

---

[24] Anthropologist Mary Douglas has made significant contributions to this line of inquiry. See *Natural Symbols: Explorations in Cosmology* (New York: Pantheon Books, 1982); and *Purity and Danger: An Analysis of the Concepts of Pollution and Taboo* (London: Routledge & Kegan Paul, 1969).

[25] Chauvet, following D. Dubarle, calls the body the "arch-symbol" of human experience. *Symbol and Sacrament,* 151.

As a group, we shared the common tradition of our Christian faith as mediated through the books of the Bible, the ancient and ongoing ecclesial
practice of assembling for worship, and the sacraments of baptism and Eucharist. Still, we cannot simply speak of tradition here, for Christianity has
long been comprised of numerous traditions, themselves conditioned by
cultural elements. Crucial to the black Baptist worshiping tradition of
Betty's siblings and wider circle of family and friends are practices of hospitality, dressing in one's "Sunday best," a vibrant style of preaching that
elicits verbal and gestural responses from the congregation and, perhaps of
greatest significance, the ample, full-bodied performance of a powerful
repertoire of gospel music. It may well be that the music at Betty's funeral
provided the deepest resonance (literally) with their own bodily ways of experiencing worship that is "done right." In my own desire as pastoral minister to honor Betty and serve her people well, I made conscious efforts
(along with the other ministers involved) to create an hospitable environment for these guests, one that connected at least in some ways with their
culture and traditions. On the other hand, in the initial preparations I realized that the ritual gesture from the Roman Catholic repertoire that I be-
lieved could powerfully "speak" in the funeral was the use of incense, an
action I considered at once to be most risky and most promising. The repeated incensing carried so much promise and risk precisely because it is
so bodily, because it leaves the liturgy's participants no choice but to be engaged on many bodily levels.[26] The use of incense during the Rite of Farewell at the conclusion of the Roman funeral Mass is optional. In order for it
not to have been merely an arcane decoration or a "Catholic" ritual curios-
ity, the incense had to be used at its appropriate places throughout the

---

[26] Pastoral experience has taught me that the use of incense, even on rare occasions,
in Roman Catholic parishes these days is often less than appreciated, if not directly opposed. Protesting coughs can arise at the sight of a thurible well in advance of any
grains touching charcoal. This discomfort with the smell of incense in the contemporary suburban parish seems a direct confirmation of an observation by Horkheimer and
Adorno in their criticism of modernity: "Of all the senses, that of smell—which is attracted without objectifying—bears clearest witness to the urge to lose oneself in and
become the 'other.' As perception and the perceived—both are united—smell is more
expressive than the other senses. When we see we remain what we are; but when we
smell we are taken over by otherness. Hence the sense of smell is considered a disgrace
in civilization, the sign of lower social strata, lesser races and base animals. The civi-
lized individual may only indulge in such pleasure if the prohibition is suspended by
rationalization in the service of real or apparent practical ends." Max Horkheimer and
Theodor W. Adorno, *Dialectic of Enlightenment,* trans. John Cumming (New York:
Continuum, 1972, 1991) 184.

liturgy, connecting the economy of Christian tradition through the Word of God, sacrament of the Eucharist, and lives of the believers assembled.

That latter reflection indicates how any one liturgical gesture can lead us to recognize the different aspects of bodiliness, the various "bodies of worship," that together constitute the practical sacramentality at the heart of living the faith of the Gospel. The work of liturgy entails our coming to know God, the world, and ourselves in the light of the One who has created and redeemed us. The assembled person-bodies together constitute the unique members of the body of Christ, the Church. The ritual body, in word and sacrament, obtains a knowledge of the Church and the world in relationship to God, but always within a body of culture, a social context wherein the story of salvation is mysteriously coming about. The Church takes confidence in a multiplicity of bodies and histories as the very "place" of humanity's redemption on the basis of the Gospel, wherein the Holy Spirit creates, guides, and raises up the body of Jesus as Christ, animates the Church as Christ's body for the life of the world, and sustains believers with the eucharistic body of the Lord at the center of all the ritual sacraments. A theological exploration of these bodies of worship is the task of the chapters that follow.

PART ONE

Exploring a Liturgical Theology of the Body

CHAPTER ONE

The Many Bodies of Worship:
Locating the Spirit's Work

Bruce T. Morrill, S.J.

To attend to the body in all its multivalency in the Church's liturgy is to attend to the persistently ambiguous condition of our humanity even in the definitive way God has saved us in Christ. It is ambiguous insofar as promise and threat, certitude and sheer hope against all evidence characterize our bodily human experiences of living by a faith grounded in the paschal mystery and empowered by the Spirit of the Risen Christ.[1] If indeed the Church today identifies its pastoral mission as one of embracing the "joy and hope, the grief and anguish of the [people] of our time, especially those who are poor or afflicted in any way,"[2] this conciliar language becomes a shared knowledge in the lives of believers when we bring our life-stories of practicing the Gospel, our ongoing experiences of the presence and absence of God, together as bodies of worship in our liturgical celebrations.[3] This is the reason why the Second Vatican Council placed such a high priority on the reform and renewal of the liturgy as the source and summit of the Church's life.[4]

[1] See Rom 8:9-11.

[2] *Gaudium et spes,* no. 1. In *Vatican Council II: The Conciliar and Post Conciliar Documents,* vol. 1, rev. ed., ed. Austin Flannery (Grand Rapids: Eerdmanns, 1992).

[3] See Don E. Saliers, *Worship as Theology: Foretaste of Glory Divine* (Nashville: Abingdon Press, 1994) 106–10; see also David N. Power, *The Eucharistic Mystery: Revitalizing the Tradition* (New York: Crossroad, 1992) 304–20.

[4] See *Sacrosanctum concilium,* no. 10. In *Vatican Council II* (full citation in note 2, above).

The practical mandate in this conciliar vision, of course, was the revision of all the liturgical rites of the Church, a work to be undertaken on the basis of "sound tradition."[5] The challenge for more than three decades has been for local communities of faith, under the leadership of their pastors and ministers, not merely to implement the rubrics of the new liturgical books but to grasp and be grasped by the practical theology they contain.[6] At the heart of this theology lies the belief and expectation that precisely in the bodily actions of Word and Sacrament, as enacted by the people and their ministers, believers personally encounter God in Christ.[7] The Church's assurance that this really takes place lies in its ancient liturgical experience, proclamation, and profession of the Holy Spirit as present and active in the various bodies comprising its acts of worship.[8]

The turn to the divine person and work of the Holy Spirit is proving to be a recovery of sound, ancient tradition for the Roman Catholic Church, not only in its liturgical texts but, to an increasing degree, in different areas of systematic theology. In their efforts to uncover the fundamentally economic reality and soteriological implications of the revelation of the Trinity, theologians (Catholic and Protestant) have highlighted the liturgical, doxological basis for the patristic arguments for and credal formulations of faith in God as Father, Son, and Spirit.[9] Part of the thrill in studying the various textual sources of the trinitarian controversies of the earliest Christian centuries is the discovery that, far from pursuing abstract, speculative debates, the different parties were concerned about the implications for *our* salvation in the questions of whether Jesus and the Spirit save as God. The bodily characteristics of creation and redemption were of no small concern in these questions. Indeed, it would seem that the more forceful the assertion that believers participate in the very life of God, that they are being *divinized* in the process of salvation,

---

[5] *Sacrosanctum concilium*, no. 4.

[6] A brief discussion of the practical nature of the liturgy as theology is offered in the concluding chapter of this book.

[7] See *Sacrosanctum concilium*, no. 7.

[8] See *Sacrosanctum concilium*, nos. 2, 5. Louis-Marie Chauvet notes that "a constant feature of ancient liturgies is their linking the Spirit and body." *Symbol and Sacrament: A Sacramental Reinterpretation of Christian Existence,* trans. Patrick Madigan and Madeleine Beaumont (Collegeville: The Liturgical Press, 1995) 525.

[9] See Catherine Mowry LaCugna, *God For Us: The Trinity and Christian Life* (San Francisco: Harper Collins, 1991) 319–75; see also Jürgen Moltmann, *History and the Triune God: Contributions to Trinitarian Theology,* trans. John Bowden (New York: Crossroad, 1992) 68–69; and Jürgen Moltmann, *The Spirit of Life: A Universal Affirmation,* trans. Margaret Kohl (Minneapolis: Fortress Press, 1992) 301–06.

the more forceful the need to recognize the person and work of God's Holy Spirit.[10]

Problems and Potential for the Spirit and the Body

The efforts of Western theologians to engage in a profitable recovery and appropriation of this ancient, more Eastern tradition of trinitarian soteriology has required their taking seriously the charge of "christomonism" that their Orthodox counterparts have leveled against Catholic and Protestant theologies alike. The criticism, while negative, is a helpful one that positively points toward theological sources that can contribute to a fuller appreciation, and therefore promotion, of the various bodily facets of the Church's worship in Spirit and Truth.

The French Dominican Yves Congar, a tireless servant of ecclesial renewal and ecumenism, was careful to discern the merits and excesses in the concept of christomonism. Orthodox theologians of the past century generated the term in their polemics over the *filioque* (the clause, "and the Son," which the Roman Catholic Church added to the Nicean-Constantinopolitan Creed's profession that the Spirit proceeds from the Father[11]). Congar recognized a validity in the Orthodox argument that the clause (however nuanced the theology supporting it) leads to theological thinking that not only subordinates the Holy Spirit to the Son but also grounds such further subordinations as charism to institution, mysticism to scholasticism, universal priesthood to ministerial hierarchy. On the other hand, Congar called to task those authors who seemed to construct artificial lists of what they liked or wanted in the Church and "call[ed] it pneumatology," while condemning all that they disliked as "Roman Catholic juridicism."[12]

At issue in the charge of christomonism is the general absence of any vital pneumatology in the theology and pastoral practice of the Western Church. As Congar points out, there has been a tendency from "the end of the apostolic period onwards . . . to lose sight of the Pauline teaching that

---

[10] See Athanasius of Alexandria, *Four Discourses Against the Arians.* In *The Nicene and Post-Nicene Fathers,* vol. 4, ed. Archibald Robertson (Edinburgh/Grand Rapids: T. & T. Clark/Eerdmans, 1891, 1987) bk. I, ch. 11, nos. 42–43, 330–31; and bk. III, ch. 25, nos. 24–25, 406–07.

[11] See Yves Congar, *I Believe in the Holy Spirit,* vol. 3, trans. David Smith (New York/London: Seabury Press/Geoffrey Chapman, 1983) 49, 53–59, 184–90.

[12] Yves Congar, *The Word and the Spirit,* trans. David Smith (London/San Francisco: Geoffrey Chapman/Harper & Row, 1986) 115, 117. See also Congar, *I Believe in the Holy Spirit,* vol. 3, 199–212.

the Holy Spirit is, through his gifts, present and active in all believers."[13] The problem is profoundly theological, affecting how we understand both the immanent and economic Trinity. A subordinationist view of the Holy Spirit not only depletes the Spirit's personhood and, thus, a genuine peri-choresis of persons in God, but also subverts the personal mission of the Spirit in the economy of salvation. The Spirit's function is merely added on to the ecclesial structures, authorities, and sacraments that Christ commissioned through the apostles and their successors.[14] Such an exclusive and "vertical" view of the relationship between Christ and the Church leaves little role for the genuinely different members of the body of Christ, clouds the recognition of ordained ministry's intrinsic link to the community of believers, and ignores the epicletic foundation of all the Church's sacramental actions. What Orthodox theologians desire, and what Congar argues Roman Catholic theology has gradually been realizing, is the creative and renewing function of the Holy Spirit in the Church, in all its ministries, liturgies, and other works.[15]

The shift to a more fully trinitarian soteriology, explains Protestant theologian Jürgen Moltmann, entails constructing a theology of God more concertedly based upon the history of salvation revealed in the Bible and inspired by the insights of the patristic writers. In both cases, notions of duality and subordination give way to images of relationality. Christology is necessarily pneumatological, and pneumatology is necessarily christological.[16]

Elaborating on Scripture, as well as Basil of Caeserea's *Treatise on the Holy Spirit,* Moltmann argues:

> [A]ll divine activity is pneumatic in its efficacy. It is always the Spirit who first brings the activity of the Father and the Son to its goal. . . . Through the energies and potentialities of the Spirit, the Creator is himself present in his creation. He does not merely confront it in his transcendence; entering into it, he is also immanent in it.[17]

The consequence of genuinely recognizing the presence of God in the world and ourselves, along with grasping the messianic character of Christ's

---

[13] Congar, *The Word and the Spirit,* 114. See also Bernard J. Cooke, *The Distancing of God: The Ambiguity of Symbol in History and Theology* (Minneapolis: Fortress Press, 1990) 37–56.

[14] See P. J. A. M. Schoonenberg, "Spirit Christology and Logos Christology," *Bijdragen* 38 (1977) 350–75, especially 353–55.

[15] See Congar, *The Word and the Spirit,* 115–17.

[16] See Moltmann, *History and the Triune God,* 82–84.

[17] Jürgen Moltmann, *God in Creation: A New Theology of Creation and the Spirit of God,* trans. Margaret Kohl (San Francisco: Harper, 1991) 9.

mission, is the dissolution of such theological dualities as "freedom and necessity, grace and nature, covenant and creation, being a Christian and being a human being." These are seen, rather, as "complementary aspects of a common process."[18] A perichoretic, social doctrine of the Trinity emboldens Moltmann to dismiss Karl Barth's theological doctrine of sovereignty. Since *in* God there are no relationships of superiority and subordination, all "analagously antithetical relationships" must likewise fall: "God and the world; heaven and earth; soul and body; and, not least, man and woman too."[19]

The way past the christomonism that has supported such shortcomings of Western Christianity as clericalism (at the extreme, Roman Catholics identifying salvation with the hierarchical structure of the Church) and biblical fundamentalism (at the extreme, Protestants restricting salvation to the intellectual assent of faith to the word revealed exclusively through Scripture) and various forms of spiritualism lies, according to Moltmann, in a biblically based doctrine of the Trinity. This is what Moltmann means by a salvation-historical approach, wherein the "historical interaction of Spirit and Christ, Christ and Spirit, brings salvation for the godless and godforsaken creation, because it takes it up into fellowship with the Father."[20] In terms of our present study, Moltmann's call for a recovery of the mutually dependent relationship of christology and pneumatology found in the New Testament and many of the writings in the early Church carries the promise of a genuine recognition of the body—physical, cosmic, social, and traditional—as the *locus* of salvation.

We would do well to take note of Congar's wisdom, as well, when he states:

> [T]he one place where Christology and pneumatology are united is undoubtedly the liturgy. In its contents, those who perform it and its whole context, in its combination of word and activity, spirit and form and finally as a celebration on the part of Christ as the great High Priest and the coming of the Holy Spirit in our hearts, it is instituted by Christ and constitutes an event of grace.[21]

Among the sources of early Christianity the writings of a fourth-century, West-Syrian pastor, Theodore of Mospuestia, provide a rich resource for responding to the call for a profitable appropriation of Scripture and tradition.

---

[18] Ibid., 8–9.
[19] Ibid., 17.
[20] Moltmann, *History and the Triune God,* 84.
[21] Congar, *The Word and the Spirit,* 116–17.

In his Catechetical Homilies, preached in the context of the liturgical initiation of Christian neophytes, Theodore melded the texts of Scripture and the
content of the Church's freshly minted trinitarian creed as he unfolded the
mysteries of salvation to his people. Among these homilies' several out-
standing theological features is the consistent manner in which Theodore
identifies the work of the Holy Spirit with the creation and redemption of
bodies—the bodiliness of Jesus, the Church, the Eucharist, and individual
believers. A survey of Theodore's homilies can attune us to the many bodies
of worship wherein the Spirit works, while also inviting a critique and some
suggestions for the pastoral theology of the church today.

Theodore's Catechesis of the Holy Spirit

Theodore served the church in Syria in the latter part of the fourth century, first as a presbyter in Antioch and then as bishop of the more obscure
town of Mopsuestia (d. 428). Theodore himself has remained a rather obscure figure in Christian history due to the lumping of his writings under
the heretical umbrella of Nestorianism in the sixth century. The present
century, however, has witnessed a renewed interest in Theodore's work.
Contemporary scholars have defended the viable and attractive qualities of
Theodore's christology, pointing out the injustice not only in holding him
accountable for doctrinal issues that had not yet been clearly defined in his
own day, but also in transferring a philosophical precision in concepts
from Nestorius's writings back into his own.[22]

Although the condemnation of Theodore's writings brought with it
their general destruction, we have today, in addition to fragments of his
commentaries on St. Paul and the Incarnation, the treasure of his sixteen
Catechetical Homilies in their entirety (albeit a Syriac translation of the
original Greek). Given by Theodore to neophytes during the Lenten and
Easter Season, the first ten concern the content of the creed, one gives
instruction on the Lord's Prayer, and the remaining five explain the
meaning of the sacraments of baptism and the Eucharist.[23] Before ex-

---

[22] See Edward Yarnold, *The Awe-Inspiring Rites of Initiation: The Origins of the
RCIA,* 2nd ed. (Collegeville: The Liturgical Press, 1994) 165–66; Rowan A. Greer,
Theodore of Mopsuestia; Exegete and Theologian (London: The Faith Press, 1961)
45–46; and Aloys Grillmeier, *Christ in Christian Tradition,* vol. 1, 2nd ed., trans. John
Bowden (Atlanta: John Knox Press, 1975) 421–22.

[23] Since I refer frequently to English translations of the Catechetical Homilies, a
system of citation within the body of my text seems preferable. The ten Homilies on
the Nicene Creed are in *Woodbrooke Studies V: The Commentary of Theodore of*

ploring those texts for what they teach about the relationship between the Holy Spirit and the body, it is worth noting some characteristics of Theodore's theology that make his work particularly attractive to contemporary theologians.

When we study the texts of Theodore we have the privilege of joining someone who desired to remain in the line of orthodox tradition while not shying away from difficult questions that needed to be asked. As an active participant in that tradition, he knew that orthodoxy can only be realized in right worship. Motivated as a pastor in a liturgical-catechetical context, Theodore recognized the irreducible value of the Church's liturgical activity as inspired by the word of God in Scripture and informing an entire way of life. Scripture was the touchstone for his theological thought. While he was indeed given to speculative reflection,[24] he (along with most of the Fathers) functioned primarily as an exegete, placing a close and prayerful reading of Scripture ahead of any philosophical system.[25] This is especially notable in his christology and soteriology.

Unlike the Alexandrians, who tended to develop their christologies in a Neo-Platonic framework that employed Scripture allegorically, Theodore stood in the Anitochene line (influenced heavily by Judaism), which interpreted Scripture in a historical and typological fashion and saw a salvific process in the real events of history.[26] While Theodore understood the soul as immortal and therefore essentially rational, he diverged from Platonism by treating reason not in the context of contemplating the realm of immutable forms but, rather, in the earthly realm of practical moral decisions

---

Mopsuestia on the Nicene Creed, trans. and ed. A. Mingana (Cambridge: Herder and Herder, 1932). These are cited as "NC" plus the number of the homily in roman numeral, followed by the page number in Mingana's text.

The Homily on the Lord's Prayer is cited as "LP," followed by the page number. This homily, as well as the first of the Baptismal Homilies, is in *Woodbrooke Studies VI: The Commentary of Theodore of Mopsuestia on the Lord's Prayer and the Sacraments of Baptism and Eucharist,* trans. and ed. A. Mingana (Cambridge: Herder and Herder, 1933).

The remaining four Baptismal Homilies are from Yarnold, *The Awe-Inspiring Rites of Initiation,* an English resource in print and, therefore, more readily available to readers (see note 22, above, for full citation). These are cited as "BH" plus the number of the homily in roman numeral, followed by the page number.

I am indebted to my colleague, E. Byron Anderson, for this system of citation and for assistance in obtaining the materials.

[24] See Yarnold, *The Awe-Inspiring Rites of Initiation,* 165.

[25] See Richard A. Norris, *Manhood and Christ* (Oxford: Clarendon Press, 1963), 125.

[26] See Greer, *Theodore of Mopsuestia,* 57–58.

and action.[27] The soul's primordial immortality, therefore, does not imply immutability; indeed, God chose to create souls with a mutable character so that humans could truly engage in the enterprise of choice and judgment.[28] Thus, Theodore refused to separate the human soul and will from the human body. On the contrary, he identified the integral living of the two as the challenging, difficult locus of salvation (see NC V, 55–58).

Given this anthropology, it is not difficult to see why Theodore placed such importance on the union of true divinity and full humanity (body and soul) in the one person Jesus Christ, as well as on the strong sense of human growth in virtue that he affirmed in Jesus. This is not to say that Theodore's view of the body in relation to the soul satisfies the full range of issues that contemporary critics of the Christian tradition have brought to bear on the topic. What matters, nonetheless, is the great value he placed on the process of personal growth in believers. His homilies have as their ultimate goal (and joy) the baptism of new Christians and their ongoing growth in the life of faith, strengthened and healed by the Eucharist. It is the Holy Spirit who makes this really possible in human bodies and wills. Thus, the Spirit, as well as the Spirit's relation to Christ, is no mere object of speculation but, rather, a practical, pastoral question concerning our experience of redemption.

As one reads Theodore's homilies in their entirety, a pattern in the triune God's activity in the world emerges. United as one Godhead in will and causality, God's actions nonetheless have their origin in the Father, proceed through the Son, and attain completion by the Holy Spirit.[29] Theodore identifies the distinctive role of the Holy Spirit in the economy

---

[27] Historian Peter Brown reports on this regional difference in philosophical theology and spirituality: "The purity of the body [in the Syrian tradition] was not, as it was for an Athanasius or a Gregory of Nyssa, a poignant, Platonic echo of an ever-distant spiritual reality. In Syrian thought, spiritual and physical lived side by side. Only a thin veil separated the world of the seen from the unseen realities that glowed beneath its surface. The ascetic could assert, through singulary austere self-mortification, the visible, physical freedom of the body from the restraints of normal human living. . . . Robed in the Holy Spirit, human flesh could do on earth what the angels did in heaven." Peter Brown, *The Body and Society: Men, Women, and Sexual Renunciation in Early Christianity* (New York: Columbia University Press, 1988) 330–31.

[28] See Norris, *Manhood and Christ,* 128–32.

[29] This pattern is consistent with Nicene-Constantinopolitan faith, as found explicitly in the work of Gregory of Nyssa, whose theology, along with that of his fellow Cappadocians, was employed at the Council of Constantinople in 381. See Gregory of Nyssa, "An Answer to Ablabius: That We Should Not Think of Saying There Are Three Gods," *Christology of the Later Fathers,* ed. Edward R. Hardy (Philadelphia: The Westminster Press, 1954) 266.

of salvation with a power that: effects bodily matter, is associated with birth and resurrection, and assures that God's plan of salvation—a venture undertaken with mortal bodies and corruptible wills—shall indeed be achieved. All of this is accomplished, nonetheless, through the Son, revealed in the pattern of Jesus' life as the very source of life for believers.

A crucial passage for inquiring into the Spirit's role in relation to Jesus Christ is found near the end of Theodore's fifth homily, concerning the incarnation:

> Our blessed Fathers said that He became incarnate so that you might understand that He assumed a complete man [sic], who was a man not only in appearance but a man in a true human nature, and that you might believe that He assumed not only the body but the whole man who is composed of body and of an immortal and rational soul. It is such a man that He assumed for our salvation and it is through him that He effected salvation for our life, because "He was justified in the Spirit," and again: "Who through the eternal Spirit offered Himself without spot to God." If he suffered death according to the law of men [sic], because He had no sin he rose from the dead by the power of the Holy Spirit and became worthy of a new life in which the wishes of the soul are immutable, and he made the body immortal and incorruptible. In this he made us all participants in His promises, and as an earnest of His promises He gave us the first-fruits of the Spirit so that we might possess a faith without doubts concerning future things; and "He established us with you in Christ and sealed us and gave the earnest of His Spirit in our hearts" (NC V, 60–61).

In this passage Theodore distinguishes the Spirit's activity as a power which (1) assures sinlessness in Jesus Christ, (2) raises him from the dead, and (3) assures Christians the promise of sinlessness and immortality, sealing them as participants in Christ's life. These three major points can guide our study.

(1) Theodore links Jesus Christ's resurrection to the condition of his having always remained sinless. Theodore argues extensively for the necessity of the Son's assuming a complete human being, that is, one composed of a body and of an immortal and rational soul. This was essential for humanity's salvation since "the majority of [sins] are not born of the passions of the body but exclusively of the will of the soul" (NC V, 57). In order to save us, Jesus Christ had to exercise his human will. The assurance that he would not falter and indeed achieve our salvation came from the activity of the Holy Spirit: "[Jesus Christ] was from us and from our human nature and was immune from death because of the greatness of His excellence and was always without stain by the power of the Holy Spirit" (NC VII, 80). Thus, the unique role of the Spirit's "power" in the life and

resurrection of Jesus Christ is the Spirit's assuring the success or completion of the entire operation which the Godhead had undertaken in assuming the human being for our salvation.

In his homilies on the second article of the creed, Theodore highlights
the Holy Spirit's distinctive part in the originating act of the incarnation as
well. While it is "God the Word" who "assumed [Christ] and united Him
to Himself" (NC VI, 64), the Spirit's role is to bring about this birth from
"a woman according to the law of nature" in a "novel way": "He alone, to
the exclusion of the rest of [human]kind, was fashioned in the womb by
the Holy Spirit without any marital intercourse" (NC VI, 69). Theodore,
ever attentive to Scripture, associates the Spirit with the initial creation of
Christ's body, the body with which the Son was in union. From there,
Theodore describes how Jesus grew up little by little according to the law
of humanity not only so as to become an example of genuine humanness
for us but also so as to become the source and exemplar of the new life that
awaits us fully in the future. Jesus' mission thus takes on both an eschatological and a practical character in its salvific import. Jesus "paid the debt
of the law, received baptism, and showed the new economy of the Gospel"
so that we who receive baptism might live according to that new economy
(NC VI, 70). This is possible because of Christ's gift of the Spirit to believers and the many gifts that flow therefrom.

(2) The key to understanding the Spirit's gifts Theodore locates in the
title that the third article of the creed ascribes to the Spirit, *"Giver of Life"*
(NC X, 110). The life which Theodore has in mind is the life of immortality and immutability. This gift the Spirit first conferred upon Jesus Christ.
Citing several Pauline passages Theodore proceeds to explain: "[Paul]
shows by his words that Christ our Lord was changed in His body, at the
resurrection from the dead, to immortality by the power of the Holy
Spirit" (NC X, 110).

Once raised from the dead and ascended into heaven, Christ is the one
who, in turn, has the power to confer the Spirit upon his disciples:

> [Our Lord] revealed in advance the gift of the grace of the Holy Spirit
> which was to be bestowed upon all the disciples after His ascension. In
> saying: 'When the Paraclete is come, whom I will send unto you' He
> refers to the grace of the Spirit which He was about to bestow on them
> (NC X, 108).

Theodore proceeds to draw upon titles from the Johannine passage. As
"Comforter" the Spirit provides for the disciples knowledge that will sus-
tain them through the many trials of the world. The title "Spirit of Truth"
denotes the Spirit's divine nature and ability to give "imperishable benefits." Theodore recognizes, then, a pattern to "the grace of the Spirit" or the

Spirit's activity in redemption. Just as the Spirit assured the constancy of Jesus Christ's will and the immortality of his body, so the Spirit sent by the ascended Jesus Christ enables Christians faithfully to endure the perishable and mortal evils of this world and promises the imperishable gifts of life in the world to come.

(3) In his Homily on the Lord's Prayer Theodore has Christ, speaking in the first person and drawing on Pauline texts, instruct the catechumens that he is the one who gives the Spirit of adoption to "those who believe in Me and choose My discipleship" (LP, 6). The unity of the Divine action—the grace—of adoption is, as we have come to expect, affirmed: "I do not wish you to say *my Father* but *our Father,* because He is a Father common to all in the same way as His grace, from which we received adoption of sons [and daughters] is common to all" (LP, 7). The grace of adoption is the grace of the Father, and of the Son, and of the Holy Spirit. Indeed, the pattern of this grace is from the Father, through the Son, and in the Spirit.

The adoption of believers, however, is not yet complete but, rather, will only be realized in heaven. During this present life Christians are to submit their wills to the Spirit's power. Christians thereby "increase in virtue and do the work of those who were found worthy to call God their Father" (LP, 8). The means whereby Christians first receive the adoptive grace of God and then are sustained in their exercise of virtue and rejection of sin are the sacraments of baptism and eucharist. To the remaining baptismal homilies, then, we now turn.

Awaiting the full reality of their adoption or "new birth," Christians presently live by faith in sacramental symbols. Theodore instructs the neophytes:

> Baptism contains the signs of the new birth which will be manifested in reality when you rise from the dead and recover all that death has stolen from you . . . but now you have faith in Christ our Lord, and while you are waiting for the resurrection you must be content with receiving symbols and signs of it in this awesome sacrament which affords you certainty of sharing in the blessings to come (BH III, 181).

Theodore closely links the power and effect of baptism to the work of the Holy Spirit. Commenting on John 3 and various Pauline texts, Theodore explains, "This second birth is the work of the Holy Spirit, whom you receive in the sacrament as a kind of guarantee . . . [Paul] calls this grace that the Holy Spirit gives us here on earth 'the Spirit of promise'" (BH III, 184). The grace of the Spirit makes the water "capable of begetting this awesome birth, making it a womb for sacramental birth" (BH III, 185). Theodore's teaching on the Spirit's role in baptism is consistent with his pneumatology in general. The Spirit's work effects bodily matter, is associated with birth and resurrection, and is the assurance or guarantee that God's plan of salvation will be completed.[30]

In his last two homilies, delivered in the wake of the neophytes' full initiation, Theodore teaches them to perceive in the present sacramental symbols of the eucharist the signs of the fullness of life yet to come: "When you have undergone the real resurrection, you will eat another kind of food which is wonderful beyond description; you will feed upon the grace of the Spirit, which will make your bodies immortal and your souls unchanging" (BH IV, 202). In their final heavenly existence, Christians will be sustained simply by divine grace. This grace Theodore identifies with the person of the Spirit, and it is (once again) characterized by constancy and completion. Theodore proceeds to explain the present grace which God gives to Christians as "the first-fruits of the grace of the Holy Spirit" which are "an advance payment of what we shall receive in full through the resurrection in the world to come" (BH IV, 202). "In that world believers' food will be the Spirit's grace, whereas the food suitable to the present life is a symbolic nourishing by that grace. The purpose of the eucharist's symbolic nourishment, the first-fruits of the Spirit's grace, is to preserve the new life they have received at baptism."[31] The Spirit's

---

[30] While I am concentrating on the pattern of the Trinity's economic activity, I should not neglect noting that in Baptismal Homily II Theodore directly identifies the Holy Spirit as God, a straightforward statement that was rare amidst the fourth century polemics between orthodox pastors and the "Pneumatomachians" ("Spirit-fighters"), who denied the Spirit's divinity. While Basil of Caesarea's pastoral desire to win over the Pneumatomachians led him to prescind from bluntly asserting the divine nature of the Spirit, Gregory of Nazianzus did rise to the occasion in his brilliant preaching. See Basil the Great, *On the Holy Spirit,* trans. David Anderson (Crestwood, N.Y.: St. Vladimir's Seminary Press, 1980) 10; and Gregory of Nazianzus, "The Fifth Theological Oration—On the Holy Spirit," *Christology of the Later Fathers,* ed. Edward R. Hardy (Philadelphia: The Westminster Press, 1954) 199.

[31] Here Theodore demonstrates an affinity with Athanasian eucharistic teaching. As Geoffrey Wainwright explains concerning *On the Incarnation of the Divine Word and against the Arians,* Athanasius interpets the "daily bread" petitioned in the Lord's Prayer "as 'heavenly bread'. . . which is both the Lord who is the living bread come down from heaven and also (since what is born of the Spirit is Spirit) the life-giving Holy Spirit. In the present age we pray for the 'future' bread . . . and have the first-fruits of it . . . as we receive the flesh of the Lord." Geoffrey Wainwright, *Eucharist and Eschatology,* rev. ed. (New York: Oxford University Press, 1981) 32.

For Gregory of Nyssa the digestion of the eucharistic elements begins the transformation of Christians' bodies into the immortal nature of the body of the risen Christ. The consecrated elements medicinally function as the antidote to sin, entering into the entrails and spreading through the body so as to "remove by counteraction the harmful effects of the poison that our body had taken in." *Catechetical Orations,* 37, quoted in translation in Wainwright, *Eucharist and Eschatology,* 112.

salvific action, then, completes the initial birth of Christians and assures their arrival at the second birth in which body and soul will enjoy their completion.

In the Eucharist the Spirit also continues to perform a unique task in relation to Christ's body:

> [Christ] wanted us to turn our attention from the nature of the bread and the chalice once they received the grace and the presence of the Holy Spirit, and to perceive them as the body and blood of our Lord. For even our Lord's body did not enjoy immortality and the power to confer immortality by its own nature, but by the gift of the Holy Spirit (BH IV, 205).

Given Theodore's theory of Christ's two distinct natures, one can easily understand why the Lord's *body* lacked the power to raise itself.[32] Still, one might wonder why the divine nature in the person of the Son (to which the human body and will are joined), is not the agent of his bodily transformation. Theodore's answer is, in effect: That is not what Scripture reveals to us. Exegeting the "Bread of Life" discourse (John 6), in which Christ describes the Son of Man's ascension, Theodore notes what immediately follows:

> And in order to show the source of this change, [our Lord] at once added: "It is the spirit that gives life, the flesh is of no avail." He would undergo this change, he meant, by the nature of the life-giving Spirit, which would transfer him to this state in which he would become immortal himself and confer immortality on others (BH IV, 206).

While Theodore's approach to doctrinal questions turns first and always to Scripture, what I am noting is the logic that emerges in his teaching that the Spirit's grace confers immortality. "For although it is not the nature of bread to produce this effect . . . [s]o too it is with our Lord's body, which the bread signifies: it received immortality and conferred it on others through the power of the Holy Spirit" (BH IV, 207). The salvific action of the Son is completed through the Spirit.

Theodore's teaching on the *epiclesis* in the eucharistic anaphora follows the same line of explanation:

> But *by virtue of the sacramental actions, this is the moment appointed for Christ our Lord to rise from the dead and pour out his grace upon us all.* This can take place only by the coming of the grace of the Holy Spirit, by which the Holy Spirit once raised Christ from the dead (BH V, 233).[33]

---

[32] For a treatment of Theodore's theory of the two natures (human and divine) in Christ, see Norris, *Manhood and Christ,* 156–57, 197–210.

[33] This passage demonstrates Theodore's method of allegorically identifying specific moments of the liturgy with events in the life, death, and resurrection of Jesus. Wainwright

Quoting Pauline and Johannine texts, Theodore demonstrates that Christ can now give what he received from the Spirit. The Antiochine epiclesis, moreover, is a twofold one in which the bishop also prays that the Spirit's grace come upon the assembly. Baptism has made these Christians "a single body." Now, by the Spirit's grace in the eucharistic Communion, "they are to be firmly established in the one body by sharing the body of our Lord, and form a single unity in harmony, peace and good works" (BH V, 234). The Spirit both completes the initial formation of the body and assures that its life continues joined to the body's head, namely, Christ.

Theodore's instruction on the words of invitation to Communion, *"What is holy for the holy,"* completes our study of the Spirit's gracious work in the Eucharist by connecting this symbolic, liturgical activity to the people's decision to live accordingly. First, Theodore provides an interpretation of the invitation: "For our Lord's body and blood, which are our food, are indeed holy and immortal and full of holiness, since the Holy Spirit has come down upon them" (BH V, 238). The Spirit's work is to sanctify Christ's body and blood, which is to say, to make them immortal. The medium of Christ's body and blood in this present age is symbolic, and the fully sanctified symbols of bread and wine are able to confer this holiness, this grace of sanctification, upon those who have been baptized. The life of holiness, however, is not a passive one for Christians: "You must lead good lives so as to strengthen in your own persons the gift which has been given you and to be worthy of the food you require" (BH V, 238). Since the exercise of one's will is bound up with one's salvation, Theodore explains that the Eucharist "feeds the soul as well as the body, and even more than the body" (BH V, 243). The Christian's body and soul are destined for heaven, where Christ's body and soul already are. Strengthened by the "Lord's body and blood and the grace of the Holy Spirit," Chris-

---

offers an insightful commentary on this aspect of Theodore's work, situating him in a larger historical trajectory: "[I]t was from the fourth century onwards, and beginning from the Jerusalem to which Etheria's *Travel Diary* bears witness, that a historicizing interest started to gain hold on the liturgy. To re-enact the events of Jesus's life round the holy sites in Palestine was a first step towards seeing the mass as a dramatic biography of the earthly life of the Lord. Looking upon the liturgical action in this way is not necessarily reprehensible, provided it is not considered necessary to give every minor detail of the liturgy its biographical significance, and provided also that the first coming of the Lord therein represented is understood as the promise of His final advent. Theodore of Mopsuestia, whose writings are the first evidence we have for this way of looking on the regular course of the eucharistic liturgy, met these requirements; but his successors in this line of interpretation, with few exceptions, did so less and less." Wainwright, *Eucharist and Eschatology,* 125.

tians "must all order our lives with a view to the world to come. This is our destiny which is in store for us and for which we hope" (BH V, 244).

A Constructive Critique: The Spirit in Creation and Redemption

The overarching concern of Theodore's pneumatology is the establishment and repeated affirmation of the Spirit's equal sharing in the one divine nature. That assertion of the Spirit's full divinity he bases predominantly (and characteristically) on Scripture, while also drawing upon the authority of the church's liturgical tradition and the decisions of ecumenical councils. Scripture also instructs Theodore about what is distinctive or unique to the person and work of the Spirit. Similarly to the trinitarian theology of Gregory of Nyssa, Theodore recognizes the Spirit's predominantly distinctive trait to be the bringing of God's salvific work to completion. For Theodore, this work of assurance and completion is primordially revealed through the Spirit's role in the life and resurrection of Jesus Christ. This work of the Spirit, moreover, Theodore identifies in relation to Christ's free exercise of his will and his bodily nature.

Theodore considers both human bodiliness and rationality (in the broadest sense, that is, including the affections) with utmost seriousness, for he recognizes the human need for the Spirit's power precisely in the challenges of exercising the will (i.e., the struggles of its mutability) as bodily (mortal) creatures. In the classic manner of a wide range of authors in the earliest Christian centuries, Theodore grasps the salvific import of the incarnation of the Word and the mission of Jesus unto death in terms of the immutability and immortality Christ has achieved for humanity. Believers enter into the mystery of this divinized life in baptism. They are given the grace and strength they need to embody the exemplary pattern of Christ's life through the power of the Spirit, especially as the Spirit nourishes them with Christ's body and blood and forms them as the body of Christ in the celebration of the Eucharist.

Perhaps the most appealing aspect of Theodore's catechetical work for contemporary pneumatology is his close association of the Spirit's power with the bodily condition of humanity and with the precarious but invaluable process of growth in freedom given to the children of God. His wedding of a strong pneumetology with a soteriologically sensitive christology invites believers to a knowledge of Jesus as not only the divine source but also the genuine human exemplar of the goodness inherent in pursuing the integration of body, mind, and spirit. The sanctification and salvation of people, in other words, does not occur on some "spiritual" plane, dualistically isolated from the body. The discarding of a body-soul dualism in theology, in turn, requires attention to human existence in all its aspects—

somatic, personal, interpersonal, social, ethical—without losing sight of
the memory and promise of what God has brought about in the person and
history of Jesus the Christ. The latter need establishes the irreducible role
of the Church's liturgical life. A systematic consideration of liturgy in relation to these various bodily aspects of human existence comprises the
work of the following four chapters of this book. By way of both transition
to those chapters and conclusion to this present one, we can critically review some aspects of Theodore's pneumatology that, although conditioned by his historical context, challenge us to further theological and
pastoral reflection today.

While Theodore instructs us with Scripture concerning the very presence and action of God, the Holy Spirit, in relationship to the full humanity of Jesus the Christ and the redemptive economy of the sacraments and
Christian life, he nonetheless does so with a measure of eschatological and
practical reserve that, in the end, still leaves us with a form of dualism. I
would argue that in Theodore's case, the dualism is not between the body
and the soul, but between the body and the body—or so, at least, it seems
to this late-twentieth-century reader. Theodore admirably insists on the
human freedom and growth in Jesus that led to the Spirit's raising him
from death to be the source or our life in the sacraments, but the process is
the unidirectional one of the body being conformed to the will. There does
not seem to be any evidence for the physical, human body being able to
teach or instruct Jesus in his growth through life, nor for our bodies doing
likewise for us.

The *good* case of physical bodiliness Theodore recognizes in the present time (between Christ's resurrection and return) resides in the physical
symbols of the ecclesial sacraments. The eschatology in Theodore's sacramental theology is pronounced: What we receive in the sacraments are the
symbols, the *tupoi,* which anticipate the full realization of their effects
which will take place through the final, general resurrection to life in
heaven. Theodore is not opposing the symbolic and the real (the Western
problem after the eighth century).[34] As firstfruits and guarantees of our salvation, the sacraments convey real grace to our bodies and souls, but so
that the latter might be fortified in virtuously directing the former.[35] While
there certainly is truth in such a view—indeed, Western Christianity needs

[34] Edward Kilmartin relays a fragment containing Theodore's commentary on Matt
26:26, wherein he teaches that the bread and wine undergo a change in being into the
body and blood of Christ through the act of thanksgiving. See Edward J. Kilmartin,
The Eucharist in the West: History and Theology, ed. Robert J. Daly (Collegeville: The
Liturgical Press, 1998) 39.

[35] See Yarnold, *The Awe-Inspiring Rites of Initiation,* 177, n. 25; 184, n. 15; 194, n. 47.

to recover an eschatological sense for the sacraments and ethics—Theodore nonetheless takes the pattern to the extreme. He contrasts our "vile bodies" to Christ's glorious one and, citing 2 Cor 5:6-8, states that our bodiliness keeps us remote from the Lord (NC VII, 77).

In all of this, Theodore does not dismiss the body as irrelevant to salvation—far from it. As historian Peter Brown demonstrates through his study of the Greco-Roman and Syrian social contexts of early Christianity, the persistent threat of starvation, the social restrictions of marriage, the mortal dangers of childbirth, and threats of various forms of illness all contributed to the ways in which early Christians in different periods and places developed their attitudes and practices concerning the body.[36] A "sense of the shared momentum of body and soul"[37] included an experience of freedom from being mastered by the viscitudes of bodily existence, especially the specter of death. Brown argues that the fourth century ascetics in both North Africa and Syria were the exemplars in this defiance of death's foreboding power. They practiced physical privation so as to "sweep the body into a desperate venture" whereby their severely ascetic transfigurations might signal to all believers "the eventual transformation of their own bodies on the day of the Resurrection."[38]

It is in this strange world, where heroes struggling in deserts and on tops of columns were icons of redeemed humanity, that Theodore instructed his neophytes to live according to another iconic form, the bodily and spiritual realities conveyed to them in the sacraments.[39] It would seem that for Theodore the latter comprised the bodily and spiritual evidence and encouragement for living by the gospel's vision. Given the fourth-century Syrian context, we can appreciate something of the sense in which Theodore identified the Spirit as "the Holy Spirit of promise" (see BH III, 184). Can

[36] See Brown, *Body and Society,* 5–17, 26, 218.

[37] Ibid., 235.

[38] Ibid., 222. For a captivating story that not only exemplifies this Syrian view of the ascetic but also demonstrates the ambivalent attitude toward sexuality and the feminine, see "Pelagia; Beauty Riding By," in Benedicta Ward, *Harlots of the Desert: A Study of Repentance in Early Monastic Sources* (Kalamazoo, Mich.: Cistercian Publications, 1987) 66–75.

[39] While the extraordinary asceticism of these ancient Syrians might strike us today as a strange practice of Christianity, we should nonetheless consider how our contemporary societies do not question the extremely ascetic lifestyle taken on by marathon runners, gymnasts, and various professional athletes. In fact, our societies glorify such people. In this light it is interesting to note that the fifth century Syrian pastor, Theodoret of Cyrrhus, characterized the desert ascetics as "athletes of virtue." Theodoret, Bishop of Cyrrhus, *A History of the Monks of Syria,* trans. R. M. Price (Kalamazoo, Mich.: Cistercian Publications, 1985) 3.

we not also, with due eschatological reserve, seek to recognize the "Holy Spirit of presence," the presence of the absent, ascended Christ not only in the Church's sacramental liturgies but also in the multivalent bodiliness of ordinary believers as they strive to live the Good News?[40] Moreover, might we not recognize in the beauty and aweful forces of the natural cosmos traces of the one true God—Father, Word, and Spirit—who creates and sustains all things?[41]

These last comments demonstrate both the necessary limits in criticizing the writings of a figure from a vastly different historical time and place and the care the contemporary theologian must take in using such a source in one's own constructive project. While it would be inaccurate, let alone anachronistic, to characterize Theodore's homilies as christomonist, still the exclusive degree to which he identifies the work of the Holy Spirit with the history and glorification of Jesus the Christ, and subsequently the Church (sacraments and believers), does limit the Spirit within a certain christocentrism. All of this is understandable on Theodore's part, given the fact that his homilies serve the specific pastoral needs of the Paschal Season and the initiation of the neophytes. Moreover, the difficult physical and social conditions of fourth-century Syria, as well as the extent to which most people's "worlds" were locally bound, help make sense of the way in which Theodore taught about the relationship between the human body and will, the human body of believers and the bodily symbols of the sacraments and, ultimately, the resurrected body.

The present context of the Church's work is, of course, significantly different. Indeed, one cannot think in terms of a context but, rather, many contexts. We recognize and celebrate numerous bodies of culture. Modern science and technology, as well as shifts in social philosophy, have led us to unprecedented abilities to heal, manipulate and, unfortunately, harm our natural bodies and the natural world around us. These historical realities have come to exercise no small impact upon the ways in which the Church goes about its pastoral and liturgical work, as well its ways of theologically reflecting upon and understanding the human and divine dimensions of that work. For theologians in both the Northern and Southern Hemispheres this has, among other things, entailed a rethinking of the

---

[40] See Moltmann, *The Spirit of Life*, 43–57, 177–79; and Elizabeth A. Johnson, *She Who Is: The Mystery of God in Feminist Theological Discourse* (New York: Crossroad, 1993) 124–28, 133–41.

[41] Consistent with one of the main agendas in his Catechetical Homilies, Theodore only discusses the topic of creation, in reference to the first article of the creed, in terms of the three divine persons acting as the one Creator, that is, equally sharing in the work of creation.

doctrine of creation in relation to the person of the Holy Spirit and the celebration of the eucharist.[42] The recent renewal in trinitarian theology has also supported a greater vision and role for women through a creative broadening of the use and gender specificity of different metaphors for God (including, of course, the Holy Spirit) in Judeo-Christian tradition.[43] In seeking the work of the Spirit and serving the many bodies of worship today, we would do well to learn from some of Theodore's theological insights and to embrace fully his pastoral zeal.

Suggestions for Further Reading

Brown, Peter. *The Body and Society: Men, Women, and Sexual Renunciation in Early Christianity.* New York: Columbia University Press, 1988.

Comblin, José. *The Holy Spirit and Liberation.* Trans. Paul Burns. Maryknoll, N.Y.: Orbis Books, 1989.

Congar, Yves. *I Believer in the Holy Spirit.* 3 vols./1 vol. Trans. David Smith. New York: Seabury Press/Crossroad Publishing, 1983/1998.

Johnson, Elizabeth A. *She Who Is: The Mystery of God in Feminist Theological Discourse.* New York: Crossroad Publishing, 1993.

Moltmann, Jürgen. *The Spirit of Life: A Universal Affirmation.* Trans. Margaret Kohl. Minneapolis: Fortress Press, 1992.

Yarnold, Edward. *The Awe-Inspiring Rites of Initiation: The Origins of the RCIA.* 2nd ed. Collegeville: The Liturgical Press, 1994.

---

[42] See Moltmann, *God in Creation,* 1–19, 94–103; and *History and the Triune God,* 70–79. See also, José Comblin, *The Holy Spirit and Liberation,* trans. Paul Burns (Maryknoll, N.Y.: Orbis Books, 1989) 43–51, 109–12; and Leonardo Boff, *Trinity and Society,* trans. Paul Burns (Maryknoll, N.Y.: Orbis Books, 1988) 219–31.

[43] See Johnson, *She Who Is,* 141–49; Moltmann, *The Spirit of Life,* 269–84; and Boff, *Trinity and Society,* 120–22, 170–71, 196–98.

CHAPTER TWO

Body and Mystical Body:
The Church as *Communio*

 *Bernard J. Cooke*

Commentators on Vatican II have remarked on the prominence in the documents of the council of the term *communio* and even more so of the allied notions of "sharing" and "communing."[1] Given a long preceding history of focus on the structural aspects of the Catholic Church, this shift towards a more dynamic understanding of the Christian community reflected a fundamental paradigm shift in Roman Catholic ecclesiology, a shift that was already in progress prior to the council. Influential as was the theological input into this changed mentality, not all the council's movement towards thinking of the Church in terms of "sharing," resulted from theological reflection. *Lumen gentium's* stress on the collegiality of the bishops, a key element in rethinking of the Church in terms of "sharing," was as much the result of a felt dissatisfaction with the power alignment resulting from Vatican I as it was the result of preceding scholarly research. And the role increasingly being played by lay persons in the twentieth century led up to the council's recognition of the baptized as "the people of God." This in turn raised the question of the manner in which the baptized shared in the life, mission and ministry of the Church.

However, biblical and historical study of *communio* as a characteristic of Christianity, especially in its origins, certainly contributed to preparation

---

[1] Throughout the chapter I use the Latin *communio* to preserve the active implication of the term, which can be lost by the translation "community."

for Vatican II and to its implementation in the decades since.[2] Biblical studies made it clear that God's salvific activity during the pre-Christian period occurred within the context of Israel *as a people*. Though Israel's history was marked by a movement towards increased recognition of the identity and responsibility of the individual, the vocation of the people as a people remained central to Israelite faith.

With the life and saving "passover" of Jesus and the advent of Christianity the shared characteristic of salvation continued, indeed was deepened. New Testament studies have noted the centrality of *koinonia* in the Christianity of those earliest decades, the sharing of goods, life, and ministries that was expected of those who accepted the gospel, a sharing that was rooted in the risen Christ's communication of the one Spirit.[3] Early communities honored hospitality as a key virtue, even as they began to develop limits beyond which "deviant" behavior excluded one from the community.[4] For a short period complete egalitarianism was advocated, even if not always translated into practice.[5] Even before the completion of the New Testament literature, one can notice in the texts a beginning stratification of the community, the marginalizing of women, and limits other than the Spirit's empowerment set on the sharing in mission and ministry.[6]

Though historical generalizations are often misleading and always require qualification, it does seem safe to say that over succeeding centuries the sharing by most Christians in the power of decision, exercise of ministry, and leadership in ritual diminished and gradually disappeared. Some sense of being the new people of God survived the patristic period and was translated culturally into the medieval identification of society as the *societas christiana*,[7] but as one comes closer to the modern period and the organizational model for the Church becomes even more dominant, most

---

[2] For an instance of post-conciliar study of the issue, see *The Church as Communion,* ed. James Provost (Washington, D.C.: Canon Law Society of America, 1984).

[3] See Joseph Bracken, "Community," in *The New Dictionary of Theology,* eds. Joseph Komonchak and others (Wilmington, Del.: Michael Glazier, 1989) 216–18; and Bernard Lee, "Community," in *The New Dictionary of Catholic Spirituality,* ed. Michael Downey (Collegeville: The Liturgical Press, 1993) 185–91.

[4] See Bernard Prusak, "Hospitality Extended or Denied," *The Church as Communion,* ed. James Provost (Washington, D.C.: Canon Law Society of America, 1984) 89–126.

[5] Gal 3:26.

[6] See Luise Schottroff, *Lydia's Impatient Sisters,* trans. Barbara and Martin Rumscheidt (Louisville: Westminster, 1995).

[7] See Bernard Cooke, *Ministry to Word and Sacrament* (Philadelphia: Fortress Press, 1976) 1–2.

Catholics' awareness of being Christian focused on "belonging to the Catholic Church" rather than to one or other Protestant denomination.

Stress on the institutional aspects of the Catholic Church, especially in official circles, continued into the twentieth century; but in the decades after World War I there was a slow rediscovery of a more organic, "mystery" understanding of Christianity. Patristic studies led to DeLubac's *Catholicism* and Mersch's *The Whole Christ;* Casel's mystery approach to Eucharist had widespread influence on the early liturgical movement; Rahner and Semmelroth drew attention to the sacramental dimension of the Church; and Congar's ecclesiology was a major voice in ecumenical discussion and in the emerging lay movement.[8] One could name any number of other historians, theologians and biblical scholars whose work was preparing the ground for Vatican II's largely unexpected turn towards a more dynamic view of the Catholic Church as a *communio.*[9]

Very briefly, then, what are some of the elements in Vatican II's documents, particularly in *Lumen gentium,* that reflect the emphasis on *communio?*

1) In what was probably their main concern in the Constitution on the Church, to rectify the relation between papacy and episcopate, the council fathers stressed the notion of *collegiality,* the idea that the bishops of the world, including the bishop of Rome, were a witnessing community within the life of the Church.[10] Without denying the proper authority of a bishop within his own diocese, nor denying the special prerogatives of the pope, Vatican II did recover the insight that the episcopacy was essentially a *group* whose responsibilities and functions and divine guidance were shared by individual bishops by virtue of their membership in the episcopal college.[11]

2) Extending the idea to the presbyterate, Vatican II reiterated the teaching that there is only the one priesthood of Christ which presbyters share

---

[8] Henri DeLubac, *Catholicism* (New York: Longmans, Green, 1950). Emile Mersch, *The Whole Christ,* trans. John Kelly (Milwaukee: Bruce Publishing, 1938). Odo Casel, *The Mystery of Christian Worship* (London: Darton, Ongmna & Todd, 1962). Karl Rahner, *The Church and the Sacraments* (New York: Herder and Herder, 1963). Otto Semmelroth, *Die Kirche als Ursakrament* (Frankfurt, 1953). Yves Congar, *The Mystery of the Church,* trans. A. V. Littledate (Baltimore: Helicon, 1960) and *Lay People in the Church,* trans. Donald Attwater (Westminster, Md.: Newman Press, 1965).

[9] See Dennis M. Doyle, "Mohler, Schleiermacher and the Roots of Communion Ecclesiology," *Theological Studies* 57 (1996) 467–80, and "Journet, Congar and the Roots of Communion Ecclesiology," *Theological Studies* 58 (1997) 461–79.

[10] *Lumen gentium,* nos. 22, 23.

[11] Ibid., no. 22.

with the bishop, though at a lower level. So, the ordained are exhorted to share in a *communio* of life, labor, and charity.[12]

3) Even prior, however, to its stress on the collegiality of the ordained, *Lumen gentium* insisted on the *communio* in faith, hope and charity that pertains to the whole Church as one body of Christ.[13] The entire people of God share in the prophetic office;[14] all the baptized are in communion with one another in the one Spirit. This *communio* extends in some fashion even to members of other Christian churches, since there is but one body and one Spirit.[15]

4) All the baptized share in the same holiness, though obviously to a greater or lesser extent. While the responsibility of "saintly" living may rest more heavily on some, like the bishops, all Christians in their respective ways of life share in the imitation of Christ and in the gifts of the Spirit.[16] All are meant to share in the *communio* of love, in the mind of Christ, and in the sacramental rituals.[17] Together, the baptized form one "communion of saints," one body of Christ; all are joined in the one eucharistic celebration.[18]

Vatican II's recognition of the communal dimension of the Church's life has profound implications for the activity and structuring of the Church. It points, not just to a readjustment of ecclesiastical power, but to a radical reassessment of *the nature of power* within the Church's life. It demands a recovery of the role of the *sensus fidelium* in the formulation and communication of belief. It reasserts, both in the Constitution on the Church and the Constitution on the Sacred Liturgy, the traditional teaching that the Eucharist is meant to be *the action of the entire assembly*.[19] In all these regards, while the insights drawn from the social and behavioral sciences contributed to the council's deliberations, it was basically a recovery of the mystery dimension of the Church as *body of Christ* that led to the focus on *communio* as central to the reality and life of the Church.

---

[12] Ibid., no. 28.

[13] Ibid., nos. 7, 8.

[14] Ibid., no. 12.

[15] Ibid., no. 15. On Vatican II's extension of *communio* to other churches, see James Provost, *Interecclesial Communion in the Light of the Second Vatican Council* (Rome, 1967).

[16] *Lumen gentium*, no. 15.

[17] Ibid., no. 42.

[18] Ibid., nos. 50, 51.

[19] On the historical process of gradually marginalizing the laity's role in Eucharist, see C. Howell, "From Trent to Vatican II," *The Study of Liturgy,* eds. Cheslyn Jones and others (New York: Oxford University Press, 1992) 285–93.

Body and Body of Christ

Among the paradigm shifts associated with "post-modernity," none is more basic and pervasive than the changed attitude to human bodiliness. And no place is this present-day changed view of the body more apparent and significant than in the religious attitudes of Euro-American Catholics. The change there is not simply from modern to post-modern, but a change from the body-spirit dualism and depreciation of bodiliness that marked centuries of Christian "spirituality" and continued into modern times.

Deeply touched as it was by the heritage of Platonism and even more by Neo-Platonism, a heritage channeled in large part through Augustine, Latin Christianity developed a suspicion that being bodily could not be integrated positively into being "spiritual." Instead, the spiritual quest was that of the soul's "ascent" to God, resisting and leaving behind the body's pull towards absorption in earthly pleasures. Negativity towards the human body could never be total or unchallenged in Christian understanding for the simple reason that *Genesis* spoke of God creating all things good and John's Gospel spoke of the Word becoming flesh. Still there persisted the notion that it was not good for a spiritual person to be too bodily, and "mortification" of the body became an accepted element in Christian asceticism.

Today that centuries-long reluctance to honor the body has noticeably diminished, to be replaced by a healthier acknowledgment that being bodily is a positive and indispensable aspect of being a whole person. Somewhat paradoxically, this has not been accompanied by any de-emphasis of the spiritual dimension of human existence. Just the opposite. For a variety of reasons, among them the emergence in the past century of psychology as a "science," and a growing reaction against the dehumanizing obsession with materialistic progress, more attention is being given to humans as spirit.[20] Along with this has been the subtle but important shift to emphasizing the *distinctive personhood* of each woman and man rather than seeing them as *individuals* within the species "human." This can be epitomized in the shift to describing humans as "embodied spirits" rather than "rational animals."[21] Without denying the link of humanity with the rest of created reality, human persons are more accurately thought of as a particular kind of spirit rather than as a particular kind of animal.

[20] One of the most notable instances of this "turn to spirit" was the *Esprit* movement in post-World War II France. See Emmanuel Mounier, *Personalism* (Notre Dame, Ind.: University of Notre Dame Press, 1952).

[21] On humans as spirit and their relation to nature, see *Spirit and Nature,* Eranos Jahrbuch (selections from 1937, 1945, and 1946 issues) ed. Joseph Campbell (Princeton: Princeton University Press, 1954).

Accompanying this acceptance of human bodiliness there has been a noticeable interest in the corporate dimension of human experience and existence. Increased anonymity connected with growing urbanization and the breakdown of traditional patterns of extended family and neighborhood have created a hunger for "community," for a relatedness to others that would support individual identity and worth.[22] Worldwide there has been dissatisfaction with collectivist social structures and oppressive economic processes, both of which impose impersonal organizational patterns that work against genuine human community. Indications seem clear that all this dis-ease will be increased with the apparently irreversible globalization of commerce, production, and culture.[23] Linked with these has been a heritage of "rugged individualism," an individualism that is particularly characteristic of the United States, which tended to downgrade community good.[24] An instance of this is the uncontrolled power of "the bottom line" which reflects the denial of responsibility for the common good or for the well-being or even survival of workers on the part of corporations.

It is an interesting paradox that "corporations" has such a different meaning in our world than does "corporate," when the latter is associated with shared experience and shared awareness. The paradox is rooted in a history that extends back to the Middle Ages: Congar (in his *Ecclesiologie d'Haut Moyen Age*), DeLubac (in *Corpus mysticum*) and Kantorowicz (in *The King's Two Bodies*) note the shift in the understanding of body *(corpus)* as applied to groups of people, the king, the Church and the Eucharist.[25] Along with the notion of "mystical body" shifting from Eucharist to Church and gradually losing its mystery connotation in the process, the understanding of Christian society as body moved from "body of Christ" to the "body" of the king and "the body politic." With the further application of *"corpus"* being applied to commercial and manufacturing associations, "corporation" began to take on an increasingly impersonal and organizational connotation.

The more communal and organic understanding of Church and civil society did not entirely dissipate, but the *organizational* model that had pre-

---

[22] See David Riesman, *The Lonely Crowd* (New Haven, Ct.: Yale University Press, 1950); William Whyte, *The Organization Man* (New York: Simon & Schuster, 1956).

[23] Pope John Paul II has drawn attention to the increasing threat to individual rights and development in his encyclicals, *Laborem exercens* in 1982, *Sollicitudo rei socialis* in 1987, and *Centesimus annus* in 1991.

[24] See Robert Bellah and others, *Habits of the Heart* (Berkeley: University of California Press, 1985).

[25] Henri DeLubac, *Corpus mysticum* (Paris: Aubier, 1944); Yves Congar, *L'ecclesiologie d'Haut Moyen Age* (Paris: Cerf, 1968). Ernst Kantorowicz, *The King's Two Bodies* (Princeton, N.J.: Princeton University Press, 1957).

viously been modified by the "organic" overtones of *corpus* became more and more dominant and "structural," reinforced by the emergence of legal studies and a legal mentality from the twelfth century onward and from the fourteenth century by the ascendancy of nominalist philosophy.

While it is not inevitable, and perhaps not even desirable, organizations (corporations) tend to develop bureaucratic structures. With bureaucracy comes the glorification of homogeneity as guaranteeing effectiveness, and diversity is seen as a problem rather than an enrichment. For the Roman Catholic Church the move to structured organization crystallized at the Council of Trent. Diversity as exemplified in the fracturing of Western Christianity in the Reformation appeared as an unmitigated threat, and Trent's response was to legislate homogeneity in structure, doctrine and ritual. In the post-Reformation Catholic Church homogeneity gained increased acceptance as the ideal and was identified with unity. Not only diversity but also the idea of an historical process of development were viewed as inimical to orthodoxy.[26]

Church as Body of Christ "Rediscovered"

Slowly, the forces of the modern world challenged the immobility and supposed "eternity" of ecclesiastical structures and teaching. Even before the 1930s, a decade which with the Spanish Civil War, Naziism, and then World War II was the watershed in European Catholic life, the re-surfacing of a more organic notion of the Church could be noticed. The appearance towards the end of the war (in 1943) of the encyclical *Mystici corporis* brought to general attention this ancient but long-neglected understanding of the Church, even though the encyclical itself, under the influence of Sebastian Tromp, opted for an interpretation of "mystical body" that stressed the institutional aspects of Christianity. By 1965, the momentum of historical, biblical, and liturgical studies had prepared for Vatican II's "remodeling" of the Church, so that *Lumen gentium* could once more raise up the vision of Christianity as the historical unfolding of the Christ-mystery and understand "mystical body" much more according to the *organic life* view espoused earlier by Emile Mersch and Yves Congar.[27]

---

[26] Until Vatican II, studies like Marin-Sola's *Evolucion homogenea del dogma catolico* (Fribourg: Librarie de L'oeuvre de saint-Paul, 1924) and even Newman's *Essay on the Development of Doctrine* (London: J. Toovey 1845) were suspect because they accepted the notion of historical development.

[27] See Yves Congar, *Diversity and Communion* (Mystic, Ct.: Twenty-Third Publications, 1985), which gathered ideas Congar had proposed for decades; and Emile Mersch, *Theology of the Mystical Body* (St. Louis: Herder, 1951).

So, what explanation can be given of the Church as *corpus Christi,* drawing from not only the Pauline epistles and centuries of Christian use of the term but also more recent social scientific and psychological insights into human community? Hopefully, the response will assist in understanding how Christian life in community can offset the worldwide control and shaping of human life by today's transnational corporations.

1) What is involved is *life,* life shared with the risen Christ who is now living with the fullness of risen life that flows from his obedience unto death on the cross.

2) It is *shared* life, expressed in many and diverse persons, but it is a common life. Using an organic model for the observable social community of the followers of Christ, we can argue, as Paul does in First Corinthians, to the diversity of exercised functions, acting together in complementary fashion to give implementation to the one pervading life and to translate into actions its teleology.

3) The kind of life process involved is *spirit-living,* i.e., personal awareness, thought and affectivity, consciously and freely chosen social identity. But because it is a human reality, the life is intrinsically bound up with human bodiliness. Indeed, the very function of the Christian community as body of Christ, situating and manifesting his own salvific work in history, demands the bodiliness of the Church. However, no more than my human body is a "container" for my spirit—for I am *embodied spirit*—the Spirit of Christ pervades and animates and creatively transforms the world in the bodiliness, the sacramentality, of the community.

New Testament theologies are explicit about the dynamic presence of God's Spirit to Jesus of Nazareth in his human living and his prophetic ministry. While that creative presence of Spirit to Jesus is not parallel to his embodiment of God's Word, it is inseparable from it and provides that dynamic eschatological thrust to achieving God's reign which Word proclaims. That creative divine Spirit working in Jesus continues in Christ now risen and in his body, the Christian community, to invite human history into its final fulfillment.

4) The Acts of the Apostles makes clear the role of Christ's Spirit as the Church's *principle of unity.* Without structures yet to order the incipient life of the early communities, it was the one Spirit that bound believers into a faith unity. This was a living unification, not simply an orderly arrangement. Just as a human body cannot be a body without its life principle, so the Christian Church can be nothing more than an organization without the abiding presence of Christ's Spirit.

Paul used the human body as a metaphor to assist in understanding the nature of the Christian community and was most likely thinking about a local church. It was a useful metaphor, but was it only that. Or is there some more intrinsic reason for describing the Christian Church, whether local or worldwide, as "body"? It seems quite clear that Paul viewed the Christian community as a sharing in life, as Christians bonded together by that life, and that the life in question is faith life unified ultimately by the one Spirit of Christ. Beyond that, there seems to be question of the nature of Jesus' "resurrection," a context of Spirit-existence in which in Christ's sharing his Spirit with those of faith a body-person bonding takes place in which the community of believers truly functions sacramentally for Christ, not too differently from the manner in which our human bodiliness locates and "translates" our spirit-person dimension.[28]

Being Bodily and Being Body of Christ

That means that in dealing with the Church as "body" we are not dealing with a reality that is *like* life. We are dealing with *life*, but a kind of life different from biological functioning. More precisely, we are dealing with the kind of life that is proper to humans as persons, i.e. spirit life, the life of thinking and imagining and loving and freedom. This life is intrinsically relational and therefore requires personal sharing in community in order to function and develop. As a result, individuals, in relating to one another through diverse forms of communication, do exist and act as parts of the whole which is human society, but in so doing do not lose their individual identity and importance. Exactly the opposite: in relating to others, a human person fulfills what it means to be "person," i.e., the subject of relationships.

In the actuality of being a person, two experiences, distinct but inseparable, occur. Even though we have long spoken about *"having a body,"* we are becoming more conscious today of the fact that we *are body;* our existing even as spirits is intertwined with being bodily. At the same time, we experience sharing in various forms of social life—in families, neighborhoods, nations, the Church. Or, if we are deprived of such corporate sharing, we experience this as a loss. This sharing is obviously grounded in communication of one sort or another, communication that can occur only because of our bodiliness, communication that is more or less effective dependent on the extent and manner of bodily involvement. It is precisely here that rituals of various forms are meant to play a key role in human life.

Dependent upon various kinds of sharing—of interests, goals, social location, gender identity, biological origin, common experiences—people

---

[28] See Alfred Wikenhauser, *Pauline Mysticism* (New York: Herder and Herder, 1960).

bond together in a variety of communities, and use rituals to express and nurture that bonding.[29] In the case of the Church, the Christian community, the bonding takes place—or at least should take place—on several levels. Shared commitment to and activity in ministries, participation in the life of parishes or small Christian communities, joining with others in prayer and worship and thus sharing faith in and devotion to Christ—all these can and should lead to experienced bonds of friendship and common identity as Christian. At the center is the bonding with the risen Christ that comes in sharing his Spirit.

Intrinsic to all we have said about the community's function as "body" is the role of our human bodiliness in communication. Were it not for the symbolic role our bodiliness plays in the various personal/spiritual relationships that make up our human experience, we would be able to experience one another neither as friends nor as Christians. Were it not for the fact that our bodiliness situates us in place and time, we could not as body of Christ situate Christ's continuing salvific activity in history. Apart from our bodiliness we could not communicate with one another and so form community, either as humans or as Christians. Rituals capable of expressing and shaping our faith identity as body of Christ would be impossible, for the fundamental sacramental symbol in all Christian rituals is the observable assembly.

Symbolic Function of Ecclesial Bodiliness in Eucharistic Celebration

Since the central Christian action of the Eucharist is a ritual and effects transformation in people's lives precisely as a ritual,[30] the symbolic role of human bodiliness in Eucharist is of obvious importance. What people see and hear and touch in the course of a liturgical celebration is basic to their experience of one another as an assembly of believers, basic therefore to any experience they might have of being body of Christ, any experience of

---

[29] There is a large body of literature dealing with the function of ritual. For three leading figures, see Victor Turner, *Dramas, Fields and Metaphors* (Ithaca, N.Y.: Cornell University Press, 1974) and *The Ritual Process* (Chicago: Adeline Publishing, 1969); Raymond Firth, *Symbols: Public and Private* (Ithaca, N.Y.: Cornell University Press, 1973); and Hugh Duncan, *Symbols in Society* (New York: Oxford University Press, 1968).

[30] See Aidan Kavanagh, *On Liturgical Theology* (New York: Pueblo Publishing, 1984); David Power, *Unsearchable Riches* (New York: Pueblo Publishing, 1984); *Liturgy and Human Passage,* eds. David Power and Luis Maldonado (New York: Seabury Press, 1979); Louis Bouyer, *Rite and Man* (Notre Dame, Ind.: University of Notre Dame Press, 1963).

corporately professing their faith. The challenge of creating liturgy that is appropriate to any gathered group lies in bringing into being a ritual act that truly expresses *their* Christian identity and commitment. But how can we encourage the bodily experiences that would activate the awareness of being "body of Christ" or the psychologically prior awareness of the presence of the risen Christ?

Central to any such consciousness-causing ritual activity must be *the action of the assembly,* people must *do* the ritual and they must be *aware* that they are doing it. This means that a group of Christians brought together for Eucharist must understand that they, gathered in the name of Christ and acting as his body, are co-celebrants with Christ present in their midst. While there is a distinctive and critically important role for a presider, that individual should function *within* the community's action— which is quite different from what had been the situation in which people "attended" Mass by watching the ordained presider perform.[31] People's theoretical understanding is not enough. Somehow they must *experience* Christ being present to them, which is the "flip-side" of their experiencing being body of Christ.

Admittedly, this introduces a note of great difficulty into liturgical planning and execution. People's awareness of their bodiliness in relating to one another is a factor in this ritual participation, so in any given situation people's cultural attitude toward bodiliness (for example, the normality of greeting one another with an embrace rather than a hand-shake) needs to be sensitively considered. Yet, without a certain ease in dealing with one another bodily, the kind of familiarity and intimacy that should characterize an assembly of Christians cannot exist. People will express a certain reserve and distance from one another, and the "naturalness" that is needed for open expression of faith will not characterize the eucharistic celebration. People will continue to wear their "prayer masks" as they attend Mass.

A great need, perhaps the greatest need, we have today in our efforts to achieve liturgical reform is *creative imagination.* It is in human imagining that our bodiliness impacts most profoundly upon the spiritual dimension of our being. We know this from our experience: it is by great poetry or art or theater that we are most deeply and lastingly affected as persons, for it is in such imaginative media that we are able to express, or at least discover with those who have the gift of artistic expression, what it means for each of us to be the person she or he is or can become. Liturgy is an art

---

[31] See no. 14 in Vatican II's Constitution on the Sacred Liturgy, where the council lays down what is probably the most fundamental principle of liturgical reform.

form, with its own proper artistic dynamism that flows from a creative, reverent and celebratory approach to our human bodiliness. The Word becoming flesh is not confined to the human Jesus of Nazareth, but is meant to find expression in the ecclesial body of the risen Christ.

Suggestions for Further Reading

Dulles, Avery. *Models of the Church*. 2nd ed., especially 47–75. New York: Image Books/Doubleday, 1987.

Kress, Robert. *The Church: Communion, Sacrament, Communication*. New York: Paulist Press, 1985.

Pelton, Robert, ed. *The Church as the Body of Christ*. Notre Dame: Notre Dame University Press, 1963.

Pelton, Robert. *From Power to Communion*. Notre Dame: Notre Dame University Press, 1994.

Rahner, Karl. "Church." *Encyclopedia of Theology: The Concise Sacramentum Mundi*. Ed. Karl Rahner, 210–19. New York: Crossroad Publishing, 1991.

CHAPTER THREE

The Liturgical Body: Symbol and Ritual

Margaret Mary Kelleher, O.S.U.

In one of the numerous statements in which Vatican II retrieved the principle that liturgy is an ecclesial event, the council identified every liturgical celebration "as an action of Christ the priest and of his Body, which is the Church."[1] Another significant move was made in those statements which affirmed that this Church, this body, is realized in local groups of Christians who gather to celebrate the liturgy.[2] Furthermore, the council made it clear that, in its liturgical celebrations, the Church discloses and effects itself.[3] In other words, the ecclesial body of Christ is manifested and shaped in its liturgical action which is carried out by local assemblies of baptized Christians. Statements such as these offer many possible topics for study, but the intent of this essay is to explore some of the biological, social, cultural and spiritual dimensions of a liturgical body in action.

Biological Roots of Liturgy

Imagine two beautiful white birds soaring in the air, making intricate patterns, as if they were dancing to the music of a ballet. The male leaves

---

[1] *Sacrosanctum concilium* 7. All references to conciliar documents are taken from the English translation in *Vatican Council II: The Conciliar and Post Conciliar Documents,* ed. Austin Flannery (New York: Costello Publishing Co., 1992).

[2] See SC 41, 42 and *Lumen gentium* 26.

[3] See SC 2 and 26.

to capture some prey and returns to feed the other, the female, in flight. It is a tricky maneuver but one carried out with grace. It is mating season and the male is trying to impress the female to join with him in building a nest and becoming a pair.[4] Does such activity have any remote connection with liturgy? Some would answer in the affirmative because liturgy is a form of ritual action and the roots of ritual are biological.

Ronald Grimes, a significant figure in the contemporary field of ritual studies, states that ritual begins with ritualization. This term has been used by ethologists "to designate the stylized, repeated gesturing and posturing of animals" which typically appears in mating behavior.[5] Grimes sees "no reason why we should not view ourselves as ritualizing animals" and is convinced that "there is no escaping ritualization—the stylized cultivation or suppression of biogenetic and psychosomatic rhythms and repetitions." Ritualization presupposes a process of interaction between people and an ecosystem and Grimes notes that "the rites that embody ritualization processes most fully are seasonal, agricultural, fertility, divinatory, funerary, and healing ones, because they make explicit the interdependence of people with their environments and bodies."[6]

Such ideas are compatible with the position taken by some neurobiologists who have suggested that the human capacity for ritual is based in our genetic makeup, in the very structures of our brains. This capacity is activated in diverse situations as people interact with their environment in different kinds of ritual activity. A group of theorists from varied disciplines have been working together for a number of years to study and synthesize neurobiological, anthropological, and phenomenological dimensions of human symbolic and ritual behavior. As an outcome of their collaborative research they have developed a complex body of theory called biogenetic structuralism.[7] From their perspective "ritual behavior is intricately coupled with the processes by which the human brain constitutes a world of experience and communicates knowledge about the world in symbolic ways."[8]

[4] David Attenborough, *The Trials of Life: Courting,* prod. BBC-TV with Turner Broadcasting System, Inc., 50 min., Time Life, 1991, videocassette.

[5] Ronald L. Grimes, *Beginnings in Ritual Studies* (Columbia, S.C.: University of South Carolina Press, 1995) 41.

[6] Ibid., 42–43. Grimes is presenting ritualization as the first and most basic of six "modes of ritual sensibility." The others are decorum, ceremony, magic, liturgy and celebration, but they all presuppose ritualization.

[7] For a summary of this theory and a helpful bibliography on the topic see Charles D. Laughlin, "Ritual and the Symbolic Function: A Summary of Biogenetic Structural theory," *Journal of Ritual Studies* 4:1 (1990) 15–39.

[8] Ibid., 15.

Biogenetic structuralism views the human being as an organism, a community of cells, and the nervous system as "a sub-community of cells that has evolved to facilitate communication between different body structures, regulation of these structures, and internal depiction of the self and its environment."[9] The symbolic function of the nervous system plays a central role in both internal communication and in the processes by which humans interact with their environments. Ritual symbolism may be quite complex and it can effect the coordination of certain internal processes within individual participants as well as external coordination among participants. The research of these scholars on ritual symbolism and the operations of the human brain has suggested that ritual can play a role in the processes of intentionality by controlling the context of perception, that ritual can engage the two cerebral hemispheres of the brain and promote an interaction between them, and that certain elements of ritual can even stimulate the endocrine and immune systems of the human body. Surely, there is much to be explored about the implications of the biological nature of the liturgical body.

Defining Ritual

People who approach liturgy as a form of ritual have an operative understanding of the meaning of the term and there are many possibilities to choose from. Those who have been influenced by Roy Rappaport's definition of ritual as "the performance of more or less invariant sequences of formal acts and utterances not encoded by the performers" will tend to focus their attention on activities that are handed down from generation to generation and remain constant.[10] Ronald Grimes resists offering a definition of ritual because he finds definitions too limiting. Furthermore, they can too easily give the impression that ritual is a thing when it is more like a quality. In place of a definition he offers a list of qualities that scholars have found to be characteristic of ritual action. No one ritual action will display all of them, but when some of the qualities become evident in association with an action, they indicate that it is becoming ritual action. Among the qualities he identifies are the following: ritual is performed, embodied, stylized, repetitive, rhythmic, collective, patterned, traditional, deeply felt, condensed, symbolic, dramatic, paradigmatic, transcendent, adaptive, and conscious.[11] While Grimes recognizes the traditional nature of much ritual, he focuses

[9] Ibid., 16.

[10] See Roy A. Rappaport, "Ritual, Time, and Eternity," *Zygon* 27:1 (1992) 5.

[11] See Ronald L. Grimes, *Ritual Criticism* (Columbia, S.C.: University of South Carolina Press, 1990) 13–14.

more attention on the phenomenon of ritualizing, activity in which ritual is created or generated. This process of inventing ritual can usually be expected to be found on the margins of a society rather than at its center.[12] He does offer what he designates as a "soft definition" for the phenomenon, noting that "ritualizing transpires as animated persons enact formative gestures in the face of receptivity during crucial times in founded places."[13]

Catherine Bell, another major figure in the contemporary field of ritual studies, is also wary of attempts to define ritual because they focus on universal qualities while ignoring the particular and tend either to isolate ritual as some kind of distinct and autonomous activity or to present ritual as an aspect of all activity. She prefers the term "ritualization" and uses it to refer to "a way of acting that is designed and orchestrated to distinguish and privilege what is being done in comparison to other, usually more quotidian, activities."[14] People in different particular contexts will employ specific strategies to set some activities off from others or to designate qualitative differences among activities. She is very interested in the impact of ritualization on the body and suggests that an outcome of ritualization is the production of a ritualized body, a body with a sense of ritual. Influenced by the work of Pierre Bourdieau, she suggests that "ritualization produces this ritualized body through the interaction of the body with a structured and structuring environment." The physical movements associated with ritual activity construct an environment which, in turn, acts to restructure those bodies engaged in ritualization. For example, required kneeling as part of ritual activity may produce a ritualized agent who is a subordinated kneeler.[15]

The Liturgical Body as a Social Body

My own approach to ritual views it as social, symbolic, and processual action in which meanings and values can be communicated, created, and transformed.[16] It is social because it emerges from within the life of a so-

---

[12] See Ronald L. Grimes, "Reinventing Ritual," *Soundings* 75:1 (1992) 21–41.

[13] See Grimes, *Beginnings in Ritual Studies,* 60. He contrasts a "hard" definition of ritual which is a "model of" properties of known rites with a "soft" definition which is a "model for" attending to what is yet relatively unknown about them.

[14] Catherine Bell, *Ritual Theory, Ritual Practice* (New York: Oxford University Press, 1992) 74.

[15] Ibid., 98–100.

[16] My understanding of liturgy as ritual action relies mainly on the work of Victor Turner. For a more extended presentation of my theory see Margaret Mary Kelleher, "Liturgy: An Ecclesial Act of Meaning," *Worship* 59 (1985) 482–97 and "Liturgical Theology: A Task and a Method," *Worship* 62 (1988) 2–25.

cial body, is performed by a social body, and participates in the life of that body. It is symbolic because its basic units are symbols and almost anything can serve as a ritual symbol—words, objects, gestures, actions, relationships established in the ritual, the arrangement of the ritual space. Ritual is processual in various ways. First, there is a dynamism within ritual action, a movement or rhythm, high and low points. Secondly, the symbolic components are dynamic, have histories in connection with one or more rituals. Finally, ritual is processual because it participates in the life and history of the social body which enacts it; it may change as the social body changes or it may promote change in that body.

A social body acts ritually within a field, both an immediate and extended field.[17] The immediate field is the place and space in which the activity occurs. The extended field may include the history of the social body and of the ritual itself as well as the political and cultural context in which the ritual is performed. Ronald Grimes offers six categories for mapping a ritual field and suggests numerous questions under each category for the purpose of eliciting information about the ritual.[18] Several of these categories are particularly appropriate for exploring the dynamics of a social body engaged in ritual activity. For example, under the category of ritual space he suggests looking for any indication of boundaries present in the ritual field and how they are defined. He also urges those studying a ritual to pay attention to the history of the use of the place and to notice whether there are any hierarchies facilitated by the use of the space. Under the category of ritual identity some of the suggested questions are as follows: What roles are involved and how are they determined? Who participates and how? What groups receive ritual recognition? Who is excluded by the rite? Who is marginal? Is identity hidden or changed through the use of masks, costumes, or face paint? Among the questions suggested for studying the ritual action are the following: What kinds of action are performed? What are the central gestures? What are the recurrent postures? What parts of the body are emphasized? What senses are used or avoided? Answers to such questions will provide interesting data for studying the relationship between physical and social bodies as they are engaged in ritual activity.

Imagine how these questions could be used to map the following entrance rites of two very different celebrations of a Roman Catholic Mass.

---

[17] For Turner's notion of the ritual field see Victor Turner, *The Forest of Symbols: Aspects of Ndembu Ritual* (Ithaca, N.Y.: Cornell University Press, 1967).

[18] The categories are ritual space, ritual objects, ritual time, ritual sound and language, ritual identity, and ritual action. See Grimes, "Mapping the Ritual Field," *Beginnings in Ritual Studies,* 24–39.

The first is a celebration of Solemn High Mass according to the 1962 *Missale Romanum*. It took place in 1986 in a church in London in accord with a papal indult issued in 1984.[19] Before Mass begins, the congregation is kneeling in pews which are divided by a middle aisle. The sanctuary area is set apart from the space in which the congregation is placed by a marble wall which is about one foot high and has an opening in the center with several steps which serve as a passageway into a rather large area which has an altar against the far wall. There is also a horizontal aisle between the congregational benches and the sanctuary area. An organ is playing in the background and, at the sound of a bell, the congregation stands in place as the procession begins. Emerging from a sacristy off to the right front side of the building and passing in front of that side of the congregation before entering the sanctuary area are more than a dozen male altar servers and clergy dressed in black cassocks and white surplices. They are followed by a priest, deacon, and subdeacon dressed in green vestments who proceed to the altar and kneel with their backs to the rest of the assembly for the intoning of the *Asperges me* by the priest. As the choir picks up the singing of the antiphon, the priest, deacon and subdeacon then rise and walk around sprinkling all those in the sanctuary area and the choir which is off to the side. They then leave the sanctuary and stand in the space in front of the pews as the priest sprinkles the congregation. They cross over from one side to the other but do not enter the middle aisle which is between the two sets of benches. They then return to the sanctuary and to the altar where the priest prays a prayer in Latin and proceeds with the rest of the entrance rite.

The second illustration is from a Mass celebrated during the 1980s in a church in Malawi.[20] It follows the 1969 *Ordo Missae* which was promulgated in accord with the principles set out by Vatican II. As in the previous example, the benches for the congregation are placed along a longitudinal axis with a central aisle dividing them. In this case there are no kneelers and the aisle is rather wide. There is also a horizontal aisle in front of the benches serving as a space between the congregation and the sanctuary area. One enters the latter by ascending four or five steps to a platform on which an altar is placed in the center and a lectern off to one side. The procession proceeds from the door of the church down the central aisle to the sanctuary area. It is led by young girls who are members of a parish dance

---

[19] The following description is based on a video entitled *Solemn High Mass and Low Mass Tridentine Rite, Missale Romanum 1962; Solemn Benediction of the Blessed Sacrament,* Promotone BV, 1986, videocassette.

[20] *The Dancing Church: Video Impressions of the Church in Africa,* prod. Thomas A. Kane, CSP, 58 min., Paulist Press, 1992, videocassette.

group. They are dressed in blue and yellow dresses and are followed by women in blue skirts and white blouses who are members of the Legion of Mary. Next come a group of men in slacks and shirts who are followed by a man in similar attire who is carrying the lectionary, a woman member of the Legion of Mary who is holding a candle, and two priests dressed in white vestments. During the procession a song is sung in the native language in call and response style and the procession is done as a slow, rhythmic dance which engages the whole body in movement. When the young girls reach the steps leading to the sanctuary, they do not proceed up the steps but move to the side. The women who follow remain standing in the space in front of the benches and the rest of the procession moves up the steps. The man serving as lector stands in front of the lectern with the book held high and the woman with the candle stands next to him. The men take up positions on three sides of the altar, facing the rest of the congregation and each other and they dance in place. Everyone continues singing and members of the congregation dance in place or sway to the music. Periodically the high pitched sound of a woman's voice is heard as she ululates in the midst of the song. At one point a woman dances up the stairs and enters the group of dancing men for a moment and then returns to her place. After a while, the lay men dance a cross over step behind the altar and dance their way back to the rest of the congregation and the Mass proceeds.

Grimes's categories and questions allow one to gather data but the task of interpreting that data is a complex one and will engage the interpreter in asking many more questions about the extended ritual field. What does the ritual disclose about the identity of the social body engaged in performing the ritual? My intent here is not to offer complete interpretations for the rituals that have been described but to suggest possible areas for exploration. Roland Delattre has offered a definition of ritual in which he presents it as "those carefully rehearsed symbolic motions and gestures through which we regularly go, in which we articulate the felt shape and rhythm of our own humanity and of reality as we experience it, and by means of which we negotiate the terms or conditions for our presence among and our participation in the plurality of realities through which our humanity makes its passage."[21] What he has to say about ritual as negotiation and passage are particularly relevant here.

Delattre suggests that ritual often plays a leading role as people negotiate a variety of relationships that are central to working out their passage through life. What are some of those relationships? The following appear

[21] Roland A. Delattre, "Ritual Resourcefulness and Cultural Pluralism," *Soundings* 61 (1978) 281–301.

among his examples: relationships between the sacred and secular, between thought and feeling, between physical and social bodies, between the sexes and generations, relations between different social classes or ethnic groups.[22] In both of the rituals described above one could explore aspects of ritual negotiation regarding relationships between the sacred and secular, clergy and laity, males and females, physical and social bodies. In other words, the identity of the liturgical assembly as a social body is itself being negotiated. Given the data that was described, it would not be surprising to discover two competing visions of what a liturgical assembly should be. Delattre notes that ritual action is always, in some aspects, political action because it "involves a mobilization of sentiment around a play for power in a field of alternative versions of things."[23] The fact that the assembly in London is celebrating according to the 1962 *Missale Romanum* rather than the 1969 Order of Mass already indicates a desire to distance themselves from the liturgical reforms of Vatican II. Since liturgical action discloses and shapes a vision of the Church, the rejection of the liturgical reforms is also a rejection of an ecclesial vision. Mapping the ritual field of these two assemblies may suggest two social bodies in conflict as they negotiate their passage through the post-Vatican II era of the Church's life.[24]

The Social Body Is a Cultural Body

Every social body engaged in ritual is immersed in a cultural context and one of the significant moves made at Vatican II was the recognition that culture is plural and dynamic.[25] Bernard Lonergan saw this as a shift from a classicist notion of culture which conceived it as an abstract set of norms applicable to all of humanity to an empirical notion which views culture as "simply the set of meanings and values that inform the way of life of a community."[26] Cultures, he says, are many and varied, each with good points and deficiencies. Cultures change and have histories but it "is

---

[22] Ibid., note 14, 299.

[23] Ibid., 288.

[24] William Dinges has suggested that disagreements over the liturgical reforms of Vatican II and resistance to them reveals an underlying social conflict within the Catholic Church, a conflict over Catholic identity. See William D. Dinges, "Ritual Conflict as Social Conflict: Liturgical Reform in the Roman Catholic Church," *Sociological Analysis* 48:2 (1987) 138–57.

[25] See *Gaudium et spes* 53.

[26] Bernard J. F. Lonergan, "Revolution in Catholic Theology," *A Second Collection*, ed. William F. J. Ryan and Bernard J. Tyrell (Philadelphia: Westminster, 1974) 232.

the culture as it is historically available that provides the matrix within which persons develop and that supplies the meanings and values that inform their lives."[27]

Theories of culture abound and Clifford Geertz is one among many anthropologists who have offered a definition. Culture, he says, "denotes an historically transmitted pattern of meanings embodied in symbols, a system of inherited conceptions expressed in symbolic forms by means of which men communicate, perpetuate, and develop their knowledge about and attitudes toward life."[28] Although Geertz speaks of conceptions and symbol systems, he is not among those anthropologists who hold that culture resides only in people's minds and hearts. No, he says, culture is public and human events, behavior must be studied in order to ascertain the meanings which inform human lives.[29] Theologian Robert Schreiter, also critical of culture theories that tend to focus only on the beliefs, values, attitudes and rules that guide human living, the ideational dimension of culture, notes that there are two other dimensions of culture that must be given equal attention. They are performance or behavior, and the material aspects of culture such as language, food, clothing, music and the organization of space.[30] Ritual is significant for both Geertz and Schreiter as a cultural performance.

People appropriate a culture in a process called enculturation and often do not realize they have done so until they encounter a different culture. Then all they took for granted as being "normal" is called into question. In the process of enculturation people learn the beliefs, memories, values and hopes that provide meaning for a society but these are found in diverse sources. In addition to learning in formal settings such as school, people assimilate a culture in everyday life as they learn such things as what and how to eat, what to wear, how to hold and move one's body in different settings, what is considered a proper emotional reaction, how to think and speak, how to interact with others.[31]

An example of behavior learned in the process of appropriating a culture would be modes of greeting people and parting from them. These would be classified within Ronald Grimes's schema as rituals of decorum,

---

[27] Ibid., 233.

[28] Clifford Geertz, *The Interpretation of Cultures* (New York: Basic Books, 1973) 89.

[29] Ibid., See 11–12 and 17.

[30] See Robert J. Schreiter, *The New Catholicity: Theology between the Global and the Local* (Maryknoll, N.Y.: Orbis Books, 1997) 29.

[31] For some interesting examples of enculturation see Louis J. Luzbetak, S.V.D., *The Church and Cultures: New Perspectives in Missiological Anthropology* (Maryknoll, N.Y.: Orbis Books, 1988) 182–88.

gestures and postures that facilitate face to face interaction.[32] These are culturally specific and what is standard behavior in one culture may be offensive in another. For example, in one culture it may be appropriate for two people to greet one another in public with a handshake or embrace whereas in another culture such bodily contact would not be acceptable and the greeting would take place in a mutual bowing to one another. Often, rituals of decorum are specified in accord with social status and/or gender. In such rituals we have examples of the interrelationship of physical and social bodies.

One of the fascinating dimensions of culture that is learned in a process of enculturation is the way people perceive and occupy space. Anthropologist Edward Hall wrote a book on the topic and coined the term "proxemics" to refer to "the interrelated observations and theories of man's use of space as a specialized elaboration of culture."[33] In his study of the dynamics of cross-cultural communication, he provides interesting examples of confusion that emerge from different understandings of what constitutes personal or private space, different perceptions of what is considered "inside" or "outside," and different expectations about how people should interact within a given space. Although he is not specifically writing about ritual behavior, much of what he says can be enlightening when trying to understand what occurs in any given ritual space.

Every culture that is learned is a human product. Geertz, using the image of a spider web, proposes that cultures are webs of significance spun by humans. Roger Keesing, another contemporary anthropologist writing on culture theories, brings a critical qualification to Geertz's statement. Although he is in agreement with the position that culture is produced by humans, he wants to call attention to the fact that not all members of a society play the same role in creating a culture. Quoting Scholte's comment on Geertz's use of the web image he notes that "one cannot merely define men and women in terms of the webs of significance they themselves spin, since . . . few do the actual spinning while the . . . majority is simply caught." He suggests that, in studying any culture, we need to find out who are involved in creating meanings and for what purposes.[34]

Anyone who studies ritual as a mediator of culture would do well to ask what role it plays in the process of enculturation and who is responsible for creating and shaping the meanings that are mediated in the ritual per-

---

[32] See Grimes, *Beginnings in Ritual Studies,* 44–47.

[33] Edward T. Hall, *The Hidden Dimension* (Garden City, N.Y.: Doubleday & Co., 1966; Anchor Books, 1969) 1.

[34] See Roger M. Keesing, "Anthropology as Interpretive Quest," *Current Anthropology* 28:2 (1987) 161–62.

formance. Catherine Bell shows a sensitivity to such concerns in her discussions of ritual and power.[35] Recognizing that ritual has the power to shape social reality, individual identities, and cultural realities, she seeks to know what is distinctive about the power exercised by ritual and focuses on the construction and deployment of the ritual body. I have already referred to her use of Bourdieau's work to suggest that the physical movements integral to a ritual construct an environment which plays a role in molding the bodies engaged in the ritual action. She also draws on the work of Michel Foucault and Jean Comaroff to suggest that ritual practices are "social practices that localize power relations within the social body, creating an economy or hierarchy of power relations inscribed as a whole within each person."[36] While very alert to the ways in which ritual power can be used for the domination of one group by another, she calls attention to another aspect of ritual power. Ritual practices can also be acts of resistance and, as such, exert a different kind of power.

A liturgical assembly engaged in ritual action is involved in mediating a culture. Ritual performances are complex events in which aspects of a culture can be appropriated, created, and criticized. *Sacrosanctum concilium* 37–40 provided a basis for what is now called liturgical inculturation and local churches throughout the world are in the process of exploring how their liturgical worship can employ language and symbols that are inherent to their local cultures. There are many definitions for the term inculturation, itself a neologism. Aylward Shorter suggests that "it is the creative and dynamic relationship between the Christian message and a culture or cultures."[37] All aspects of the Christian life are affected in a process of inculturation, liturgy among them. Anscar Chupungco has described liturgical inculturation "as the process whereby the texts and rites used in worship by the local church are so inserted in the framework of culture, that they absorb its thought, language, and ritual patterns."[38]

A church which operates with a classicist understanding of culture is not concerned about the task of inculturation. Such was the Roman Catholic Church in the years prior to Vatican II. In discussing the ecclesiology

---

[35] See, for example, Catherine Bell, "The Ritual Body and the Dynamics of Ritual Power," *Journal of Ritual Studies* 4:2 (1990) 299–313.

[36] Ibid., 309.

[37] Aylward Shorter, *Toward A Theology of Inculturation* (Maryknoll, N.Y.: Orbis Books, 1988) 11.

[38] Anscar J. Chupungco, O.S.B., *Liturgies of the Future: The Process and Methods of Inculturation* (Mahwah: Paulist Press, 1989) 29. See also Anscar J. Chupungco, O.S.B., *Liturgical Inculturation: Sacramentals, Religiosity, and Catechesis* (Collegeville: The Liturgical Press, 1992).

presented by the council, Joseph Komonchak has contrasted its recognition of local churches and cultural diversity with the Roman Catholicism which had been constructed in the course of several hundred years over against the challenges of the Reformation and modernity. He suggests that this Roman Catholicism constituted a culture and, in fact, embodied what Lonergan described as a classicist notion of culture. "It regarded the culture that Christendom had created as an unsurpassable ideal, which only needed minor adaptations to be relevant to new historical eras or to newly discovered societies."[39] Vatican II abandoned this ideal of a single normative culture and called, instead, for an incarnation of Catholic Christianity in diverse cultural contexts. Lonergan himself saw ecclesiological implications accompanying the shift from a classicist to an empirical notion of culture. Instead of thinking of the Church as "a perfect society endowed with all the powers necessary for its autonomy," one will have to think of the Church "as a *Selbstvollzug,* an ongoing process of self-realization, as an ongoing process in which the constitutive, the effective, and the cognitive meaning of Christianity is continuously realized in ever changing situations."[40]

The liturgy of the pre-Vatican II Church played a significant role in mediating the classicist culture of Roman Catholicism. Uniformity and the absence of change were held as significant values. Those old enough to remember that Church will recall hearing people say how wonderful it was to be able to travel anywhere in the world and attend Mass and find everything the same as it was back home. Those liturgical celebrations provided an occasion for enculturating persons into the culture of Roman Catholicism. What kind of environment was established for molding and shaping members of the ritual body? What were people being taught about their own bodies in relation to worship? Of course, it is impossible to state what people actually appropriated for their own self-understanding, but it is possible to articulate elements that were part of the public ritual field and therefore available for mediating the culture. I will touch briefly on two: bodily movement and the place of the female body in liturgical worship.

Persons being enculturated into the liturgical practices of Roman Catholicism were expected to learn when to use the ritual postures of kneeling, bowing, standing, and sitting during a Mass. They were also taught how to genuflect, how to sign themselves with the Sign of the Cross, and

[39] Joseph A. Komonchak, "The Local Realization of the Church," *The Reception of Vatican II,* eds. Giuseppe Alberigo, Jean-Pierre Jossua, and Joseph A. Komonchak trans. Matthew J. O'Connell (Washington, D.C.: The Catholic University of America Press, 1987) 80.

[40] Lonergan, "Revolution in Catholic Theology," 233–34.

how to hold their hands in prayer. Ritual actions of social decorum or face to face interaction were at a minimum and generally engaged the priest and congregation rather than members of the congregation with each other. An example would be the interaction that took place when a person received Holy Communion from the priest. Bodily movement in processions was usually restricted to walking, with the rest of the body held in a rather straight and stiff manner. Dancing was unheard of.

In the description presented earlier of part of a Mass celebrated in accord with the 1962 *Missale Romanum,* no women or girls participated in the procession or entered into the sanctuary area. This was typical of Roman Catholic liturgical practice in the pre-Vatican II era and continues in some places today. The classicist culture of Roman Catholicism offered women a place in the nave but clearly restricted them from the sanctuary during the ritual performance of the Mass. Female bodies were not seen in any visible liturgical ministerial role or position of liturgical leadership.[41] Were women participating in the spinning of this web of meaning about their place in the liturgical body or were they caught in a web spun by others? The fact that women had no role in the writing of liturgical texts or the composition of liturgical books as well as the androcentric bias of the liturgical tradition suggest there was more of a dynamic of being caught than of actual spinning.

The excerpt from the celebration of Mass in Malawi that was presented earlier provides an illustration of a local church engaged in negotiating its passage from the classicist culture of Roman Catholicism to an inculturated African Catholicism. The passage is being negotiated in ritual performance. The incorporation of dance, the rhythmic movement of bodies, the clapping of hands and swaying that have become part of this ritual performance are not insignificant. In his book *Worship as Body Language*

---

[41] Rules forbidding the presence of women in the sanctuary and keeping them from approaching the altar appeared many centuries before the construction of the culture of Roman Catholicism I have been discussing. For example, Joseph A. Jungmann, S.J., cited a canon from the Council of Laodicea in 571 which recognized a practice of allowing the faithful to ascend the steps to the altar when receiving Communion but rejected this practice for women. See *The Mass of the Roman Rite: Its Origins and Development,* vol. 2, trans. Francis A. Brunner, C.SS.R. (New York: Benziger Brothers, Inc., 1955; replica edition, Westminster, Md.: Christian Classics, Inc., 1986) 374, note 3. Teresa Berger suggests that in the Middle Ages women were on the whole virtually excluded from the sanctuary, but she is also careful to note the complexity of the story of the liturgical experience of women and the need for further research on the topic. See her essay "Women as Alien Bodies in the Body of Christ? The Place of Women in Worship," *Liturgy and the Body,* eds. Louis-Marie Chauvet and Francois Kabasele Lumbala (Maryknoll, N.Y.: Orbis Books, 1995) 114.

Elochukwu Uzukwu writes about the African experience of the body and notes the importance of bodily gestures for revealing persons in all their complex relationships, including relationship with the universe. Music and dance play a central role in allowing persons to connect with the rhythm of the universe and different social groups have unique patterns of experiencing and expressing the flow of the life force of the universe.[42] Elsewhere he connects the gestures of dance with the mediation of social memory and suggests that "by integrating hymns set to native tunes, the drum and the dance, hand-clapping or tapping to keep the beat, etc. into the Christian liturgy in Africa, one is integrating a whole local memory into Christianity to become carriers of the memory of Jesus."[43]

The video also revealed some negotiation regarding the place of female bodies in Roman Catholic liturgical worship. Women and young girls were very much present in the procession but only two women crossed the boundary into the sanctuary area. The woman who held the candle and stood next to the man who carried the book remained in the sanctuary all during the opening dance but only men danced around the altar. She and the other woman who somewhat playfully ran up the steps and joined the male dancers as they started to leave their place around the altar are among the many women throughout the world who are renegotiating their place in the ecclesial Body of Christ.

The Liturgical Body Is a Spiritual Body

The biological, social, cultural body which celebrates liturgy does so because it is a spiritual body, the body of Christ. In writing to the Corinthians Paul made it clear that the gift of the Spirit, given in baptism, is the source of life animating this corporate body (1 Cor 12:13). One can speak of this union as a communion in Christ's Spirit. The word "communion" has its roots in the Greek word *koinonia* which means to have a common share in something, to participate in something.[44] Paul used this word to describe the relationship of Christians with Christ and one another. In 1 Cor 1:9 he reminded the church of Corinth that it was God who called them to share in the life of Jesus Christ. To share in Christ's life, to have

---

[42] Elochukwu E. Uzukwu, C.S.Sp., *Worship as Body Language: Introduction to Christian Worship: An African Orientation* (Collegeville: The Liturgical Press, 1997) 1–14.

[43] Elochukwu E. Uzukwu, "Body and Memory in African Liturgy," *Liturgy and the Body*, 73.

[44] See Michael McDermott, "The Biblical Doctrine of *Koinonia*," *Biblische Zeitschrift* 19 (1975) 64–77; 219–33.

fellowship with him, is to share in his Spirit, which is God's Spirit. Therefore all who participate in Christ's life are related to God and one another. This is the relationship which is at the heart of the Church's identity and Paul made it clear in his writings that this was a gift which had to be continuously realized in the lives of those who had received it.

The bishops at Vatican II captured something of the complexity of the nature of the Church when they stated that "the society structured with hierarchical organs and the mystical body of Christ, the visible society and the spiritual community, the earthly church and the church endowed with heavenly riches, are not to be thought of as two realities. On the contrary, they form one complex reality which comes together from a human and divine element."[45] Joseph Komonchak has suggested that this statement identifies a significant task for ecclesiologists, that of trying to understand how it is "that the church is *both* God's gift—the mystery of his life communicated to us in word and grace—*and* our task—a human community constituted by the faith, hope and love of its members and by the social and interpersonal relationships those founding acts presuppose and engender."[46] To overlook either the divine or human element is to head in the direction of a reductionistic ecclesiology.

Using Bernard Lonergan's notion that the Church is the community which is the outcome of the gift of God's Spirit and the proclamation of Christ's message, Komonchak explores the dynamics of the historical and ongoing genesis of the Church. He notes the importance of both the Gospel proclaimed by Jesus Christ and the reception and appropriation of this Gospel by groups of men and women. The ongoing genesis of the church depends as much on the proclamation of the message as it does on the gift of the Spirit which enables people to receive and appropriate that message in their lives. "The church is born out of the communication and appropriation of the word of Christ and the grace of the Spirit" and this "always occurs locally."[47]

The message of Christ is proclaimed through symbols, language of various kinds, the arts, relationships, and the lives and deeds of those who make up the church. Liturgy, as the ritual performance of local assemblies, incorporates all of these and thus plays a significant role in the ongoing genesis of the Church. The liturgical worship of any local community discloses a vision of what it means to live as a Christian. It does this through

---

[45] *Lumen gentium* 8.

[46] Joseph A. Komonchak, "The Church: God's Gift and Our Task," *Origins* 16 (April 2, 1987) 739.

[47] Ibid., 740.

the symbols, language, actions, interactions, relationships that constitute the ritual performance. In other words, liturgy offers people a horizon, a world in which to live. Within this horizon certain beliefs, memories, values and hopes will be made available for the Christian imagination and for the personal appropriation of members of the assembly. Others will be kept out. Those that are admitted may be enhanced, impoverished, or modified in some way to fit the situation. Sometimes they may even be distorted. Imagination plays a significant role in the construction of personal and social identity. Liturgy acts as a censor for the Christian imagination and thus plays an important role in the construction of Christian identity.[48] For better or for worse, it expresses and gives shape to the gift of *koinonia* which gives life to the corporate body.

In Komonchak's words, the Church "is always and everywhere at once God's gift and our achievement . . . We are the body of Christ, incorporated into him by the Spirit of God; but we ourselves also build up the body of Christ."[49] This essay has attempted to demonstrate that liturgy is a significant source for exploring the building up of the ecclesial body of Christ and that the biological, social, cultural and spiritual aspects of that body all have to be given serious attention in such an exploration.

Suggestions for Further Reading

Bell, Catherine. *Ritual: Perspectives and Dimension.* New York: Oxford University Press, 1997.

Grimes, Ronald. *Beginnings in Ritual Studies.* Rev. ed. Columbia, S.C.: University of South Carolina Press, 1995.

Leonard, John K. and Nathan D. Mitchell. *The Postures of the Assembly During the Eucharistic Prayer.* Chicago: Liturgy Training Publications, 1994.

Turner, Victor. *From Ritual to Theatre: The Human Seriousness of Play.* New York: PAJ Publications, 1982.

Uzukwu, Elochukwu E. *Worship as Body Language. Introduction to Christian Worship: An African Orientation.* Collegeville: The Liturgical Press, 1997.

[48] See Margaret Mary Kelleher, "Liturgy and the Christian Imagination," *Worship* 66 (1992) 125–48.

[49] Komonchak, "The Church: God's Gift and Our Task," 740.

CHAPTER FOUR

Spirituality and the Body

 *Colleen M. Griffith*

The particular "liturgical body" addressed in this chapter is human physicality itself—flesh, bones, sinews, ligaments, tendons, a skeletal structure that bends and straightens, a heart which beats and contracts. "Oh, *that body*," the reader might respond with a twinge of discomfort, for we are not accustomed to focusing direct attention on our physical selves. Imagine raising this body up for theological consideration. Will reflection on it take us down an all too familiar and frequented road of individualism? Liturgy, after all, is a communal happening. Does turning to the physical body smack of a potential solipsism? And given present cultural obsession with body and body image, isn't discourse of this nature somewhat of a bourgeois fascination?

To these questions I respond with a resounding "no!" For I am convinced that honest reflection on human bodiliness, in all its vulnerability and limits, necessarily points us smack in the direction of other bodies. It moves us to reclaim the interdependence which is our hope, to recognize the ultimate Life through which we are created and sustained (however named), and to connect anew with the earth of which we are a part. Precisely this type of corporeal reflection is absent in the dominant strands of the historic Christian theological tradition.

The Missing Body: A Fable

It was there, buried in the deep recesses of Christian tradition. The mythic story of Creation affirmed its goodness. Incarnation gave it theological

67

significance. Resurrection deemed it integral to human fullness of life. But where did it go? How long has it been missing? Why has the body disappeared?

The theologians have claimed innocence. Engaged in worthy conceptual pursuits, they have concerned themselves with the accuracy and adequacy of theological claims and have not seen a trace of the body in a long while. Nor have educators seen it. In their commendable efforts to develop the rational capacities of the human, they too have emerged bodiless.

Who, then, filed the missing body report? I am told that many people did: the aged man who lives at the bottom of the hill—the one slowly losing his ambulatory power, the single mother with AIDS, the dancer who experiences integrated selfhood through movement, the family of color that frequents the shelter in the village for their meals, and the contemplative that lives in the hermitage in the woods. The fifty-four-year-old woman with cancer from my street knew it was missing, but she was too sick and too tired to file a report. There were others too, whose stories I know not.

One wonders why someone would want to take the body away in the first place. It was sacred space, storied place, ordinary enough all right, but with extraordinary capacity to access deeper levels of being. I know that several folks resented the limits that it imposed; some women and men from the village used to laugh at this, finding in these limits the basis for their bonding. Others looked upon the body with distrust and thought it best subjugated, dominated, controlled. Then there were those minimally acquainted with it who had little opinion one way or the other.

Admittedly, the body was a peculiar character, obvious but elusive, bound neither by mechanistic physics nor by metaphysics. Society and culture fashioned it; individuals and communities interpreted it. And the body retained organic functions and rhythms of its own.

Who could have committed the crime? For over a thousand years, dominant figures in Western Christian history strove to distinguish "body" sharply from the higher and more desirable "soul." Then, in the seventeenth century, René Descartes tried conceptually to separate the body completely from the soul. That makes him a suspect, but the man has been dead for years. More recently, twentieth-century-Pulitzer-prize-winner Ernst Becker lashed out at the body in print, calling it a material fleshy casing causing persons to be split tragically in two. Becker felt condemned by his finitude, but he does not seem like an abductor; like many, he was only looking for heroic transcendence in some immortality-ideology. Some women from town came to resent the way in which persons overly associated them with the body, but this was not a motive for kidnapping. Finally one has to wonder about church authorities; they were always so suspicious of the body.

The search for the missing body has become more urgent. In the absence of clear and certain evidence, high-tech rationality has begun telling people that they do not need to worry about the body anymore; it can be transcended by technology. At the same time, consumerism is promoting an alternative body that it has produced, one that can be sold ever better looks, more vivaciousness, increased appeal and freshness.

Time is running short. People of diverse physicalities with clues to uncovering the missing body must step forward. No insight born of carnal remnants is too small or insignificant to matter. Meanwhile, the search continues.

A Possible "Clue"

This introductory fable serves to focus attention on the human body as a neglected area of theological reflection. Bodies, with their instincts, dispositions, proclivities and perceptions, are the most obvious and unavoidable fact of our human existence. How we reckon with them, how we come to view their nature and function influences our daily choices, our attitudes, lifestyles, relations with others, and our experiences of God. Yet the matter of our matter continues to be undervalued in religious thought and practice.

Bodiliness is an overlooked component in descriptions of spirituality as well. One seldom finds specific reference to the fleshliness of our engagement with the world and our fleshly positioning within God. There is little mention of the body as the place where desire for God manifests itself, the body as the standpoint of relational exchange between the human, the world and God, and the place where we come to know and receive the abundant giving of Godself. Though we proclaim that God has opted "to pitch God's tent" (Lev 26:11-12) in body, we forget that this "tent pitching," realized completely in the person of Jesus, continues to unfold in bodies throughout history, making the mystery of Incarnation an ongoing event.

A large clue to uncovering the "missing" body lies in our coming to a greater sense of *bodiliness as the location of our spirituality*. Such an acknowledgment could surely enrich our participation in liturgy, but it cannot be assumed. Rebecca Chopp explains: "Christian spirituality has often been understood to be at its highest point with various forms of detachment: from the body, from the earth, from the other."[1] A survey of historical Christian classics serves to substantiate Chopp's claim. While such forms of detachment are seldom advised today, they have had a long

[1] Rebecca S. Chopp, *Saving Work: Feminist Practices of Theological Education* (Louisville: Westminster John Knox Press, 1995) 69.

"effective history";[2] they continue to exert limited but real influence on patterns of thought and practice.

It takes more than a change in mindset to acknowledge bodiliness as the location of spirituality. It takes courage. There is, after all, a rawness to being bodily—a vulnerability, a finitude to be dealt with, a relationality and interdependence imposed that at times is frightening. And life in the body is never "tidy"; it is always changing. One has the distinct sense of being forever in process and behind in the process. There are challenges to bodily life that cannot be romanticized, making it less comforting to claim that the body is the location of spirituality.

Some of the biggest stumbling blocks of all in moving toward a spirituality of the body are the ghosts of our religious and philosophical traditions that continue to haunt us. Two of the most shadowy phantoms and persistent ways of presenting bodiliness in the historic Christian West have been the hierarchical ordering of body and soul, and the dualistic rendering of them. The umbras from these notions of body present irrectibible obstacles to a full embrace of bodiliness as the place of spirituality.

Two Historical Portrayals of the Body

The history of Western Christian thought on the body is remarkably complex. Throughout the tradition, diverse judgments have existed concerning the meaning of the body and its function. Bodies have been revered and held suspect, problematized and anathematized. The wide range of motivations, procedures and goals present in historical Christian asceticism attest to this type of fluctuation in thought.[3]

Discrepancies exist often between the theoretical reflections of historic Christian authors regarding bodiliness and the pastoral practices advised by these same authors. One finds metaphysical affirmation of the body in texts coupled with denigration of it in practical guidelines for Christian life, especially in matters of sex and sexuality.[4] In general, historic Christian treatment of the body has been at best ambiguous.

---

[2] "Effective history" is Hans-Georg Gadamer's term for the history of the influence of an idea. Persons inherit not only models but their effects. See *Truth and Method* (New York: Seabury Press, 1975) 267.

[3] See Margaret Miles, *Practicing Christianity: Critical Perspectives for an Embodied Spirituality* (New York: Crossroads, 1988) ch. 5.

[4] There is a tendency in dominant historic Christianity to associate body and its functions with evil. Bryan Turner comments: "The frailty and eventual decay of the human body and the inevitable physical finitude of human beings provided an obvious metaphor for original sin and natural depravity." Turner, *The Body and Society* (Oxford: Basil Blackwell Publishers, 1984) 67.

The primary way that Christian religious and Western philosophical traditions have construed human bodily being has been in relation to a more desirable "soul." The hierarchical ordering of body and soul has been a consistent theme in dominant historical Christianity. The dualistic rendering of body and soul/mind emerges as a Western philosophical notion with strong Christian rootage. Both models continue to exert influence in stratas of contemporary culture.

Hierarchical Ordering

The hierarchical ordering of body and soul is an understanding of the human in which "body" and "soul" receive emphasis as constitutive dimensions of the person, but each element is given different rank. "Body" is perceived to be dependent upon the "soul" and is regarded, therefore, as inferior to the "soul." Examples of hierarchical ordering abound in the Christian tradition.

In the writings of Augustine (354–430), for example, one first notes a basic affirmation of the body as an essential aspect of personhood. Augustine writes: "A man's [sic] body is no mere adornment or external convenience; it belongs to his very nature as a man."[5] At the same time, body and soul do not receive the same valuation from Augustine. He continues: "the soul is not the whole man; it is the better part of the man, and the body is not the whole man; it is the lower part of the man."[6] Soul, according to Augustine and to many of the dominant figures of the historic Christian tradition is the body's greatest "good," because it is judged to have superior measure, form and order. Speaking about the soul, Augustine explains: "its nature is more excellent, and the blemishes of vice cannot make it inferior to the body—just as gold, even if dirty, is valued above silver and lead, however pure."[7]

In order for the two to be in right relationship according to the hierarchical ordering model, soul must rule the body. A relationship of domination

---

Common also is the association of body with woman and woman with evil. Rosemary Radford Ruether notes: "Femaleness is both the symbol and expression of the corruptible bodiliness that one must flee in order to purify the soul for eternal life. Female life processes—pregnancy, birth, suckling, indeed female flesh as such—become vile and impure and carry with them the taint of decay and death." Ruether, *Sexism and God-Talk: Towards a Feminist Theology* (Boston: Beacon Press, 1983) 245.

[5] Augustine, *City of God,* ed. David Knowles, trans. Harry Bettenson (New York: Penguin Books, 1972) I. 13: 22.

[6] Ibid., XII. 24: 541.

[7] Ibid., XIV, 9: 354.

ensues. At the end of Part One of Catherine of Genoa's (1447–1510) *Spiritual Dialogue,* in which "Body" and "Soul" journey together in dialogue form, Soul addresses Body: "Now I will once more be in charge. If you wish to serve me, I will take care of all your needs; if not, I will still be mistress and be served. If need be, I will compel you to be my servant— and that will put an end to our arguments."[8] Soul obtains greater valuation than body in the dominant strands of historic Christian tradition because it is assumed that its perception far transcends that of the body. It is the soul, for example, that gets credited as the "placedness" which "receives" God, and it is the soul that then serves as the animating source of the body. Soul is described as having distinctly finer faculties. Thomas Aquinas (1225–1274), writing in the thirteenth century, writes: "The human soul, by reason of its perfection, is not a form merged in matter or entirely embraced by matter."[9] For Thomas, it is specifically the intellective power of the soul that stretches beyond the body organism.[10]

The Christian tradition affirms the body insofar as it is related to the soul, and hierarchically orders it, thereby assigning less value to it. The existential unity of body and soul described by key figures in the tradition never overpowers the essential separation through ranking established by these same authors. Far too often, the hierarchy endorsed in the tradition gets extended outward to the social order where male and female bodies get differentiated by means of a parallel association with soul and body and spiritual/intellectual nature is made to stand over and against corporeal nature. A whole division of creatures ensues. Thomas, for example, writes: ". . . God rules corporeal creatures through spiritual creatures. Hence it is fitting that the spiritual nature should be established over the entire corporeal nature, as presiding over it."[11] Right ordering appears to reign supreme and it depends upon an unequal ranking in the possession of being. The hierarchical viewpoint in the historic Christian tradition overshadows a less dominant incarnational one. This has led to a very ambiguous and problematic valuation of human bodiliness.

---

[8] Catherine of Genoa, "The Spiritual Dialogue: Part One," *Catherine of Genoa: Purgatory and Purgation; The Spiritual Dialogue,* trans. Serge Hughes (New York: Paulist Press, 1979) 114.

[9] Thomas Aquinas, *Summa Theologica,* vol. I, trans. Fathers of the English Dominican Province (Westminster, Md.: Benziger Bros., Inc., 1948) q. 76, a. 1: 372.

[10] For Thomas, intelligence and will are faculties of the intellective part of the soul. About them he writes: "The powers of these operations are in the *soul* as their subject." Thomas Aquinas, *Summa Theologica,* vol. I, q. 77, a. 5: 387. By contrast, Thomas claims that operations of the soul that rely on corporeal organs, operations such as sight and hearing, find their subject in the human composite, rather than the soul alone.

[11] Ibid., q. 102, a. 2: 501.

Vestiges of the hierarchical ordering model remain today in Christian practices which ignore or negate the body, "spiritualities" which focus on transcending physicality, traditions that suggest that a celibate lifestyle is "higher" than the married state, and wherever relations of domination exist on the basis of particular physicalities. The hierarchical ordering model certainly deserves analysis from an historical perspective, but it also ought to be evaluated from a contemporary standpoint. A helpful guideline for doing this comes from theologian Francis Schüssler Fiorenza who writes:

> The justification and confirmation of a theory proceeds retroductively from a theory's fertility, that is, from its explanatory and pragmatic success. . . . It has a present ability to illumine and it has a potential for further developments. Moreover, a theory is more warranted to the degree that it can guide praxis.[12]

Cognizant of the context in which this historical formulation of bodiliness arose, one must inquire into its validity for our time by considering its present warrants.

The key, it seems, is to bring the criteria of conceptual and moral adequacy to the task of evaluating its present warrants. Is the hierarchical ordering model conceptually adequate for understanding the body, given the consciousness of our time? Is it morally adequate considering the ethical responsibilities of this era? Does this way of construing bodiliness as inferior to soul have the potential to encourage and stimulate humanizing practices in people's lives? Is it in keeping with twentieth-century socio-ethical concerns? To these questions, we must respond negatively.

Dualism

In the seventeenth century, with the work of Christian philosopher Descartes (1596–1650), another historical portrayal of the body arises: the dualistic rendering of it in relation to soul/mind. The dualism of Descartes depended upon an initial hierarchicalization of body and soul, but it carried a further intention that distinguished it from hierarchical ordering strictly understood. In Cartesian dualism, the subjective "I" becomes associated with one part of the hierarchy, namely the soul/mind.

Descartes set out to establish a qualitative difference between body and soul/mind and to identify the essence of the human as soul/mind alone. His famous *cogito,* "I think, therefore I am" (thinking here being any mental

[12] Francis Schüssler Fiorenza, *Foundational Theology: Jesus and the Church* (New York: Crossroad, 1984) 307.

activity of which one is consciously aware) serves as the cornerstone of his system. He establishes the consciously knowing subject as a first truth and then turns to the "I," the one doing the thinking, to examine it more closely. Believing that thought is the attribute for positing existence, Descartes jumps to the conclusion that the mind is essential to human identity in a way that the body is not. In *Meditation on First Philosophy,* Descartes writes: ". . . this single 'I,' the soul by which I am what I am—is entirely distinct from the body, and indeed it is easier to know than the body, and would not fail to be whatever it is, even if the body did not exist."[13] Being without a body in the strict sense in what Descartes believes to be his core essence, he seemingly has no need of "place." Feminist philosopher Susan Bordo comments: ". . . [Descartes] can relate with absolute neutrality to the object he surveys unfettered by the perspectival nature of embodied vision. He has become quite literally 'objective.'"[14] Descartes presumes a false objectivity, one that purports to transcend bodiliness.

Descartes takes flight into a realm of "pure" knowing, inviting others to aspire to a place of bodiless truth that is detached, impersonal, and notably above critique. Sadly for Descartes, and fortunately for us, truth of this sort does not exist. Limit and perspective are endemic to human thinking precisely because of the distinctive bodily experiences that serve as the condition of thought.

Like the hierarchical ordering model, the dualistic rendering of body in relation to soul/mind has had a life span well beyond Descartes, its primary architect. Contemporary philosopher Paul Churchland, author of *Matter and Consciousness,* writes:

> Dualism is not the most widely held view in the current philosophical and scientific community, but it is the most common theory of mind in the public at large. It is deeply entrenched in most of the world's popular religions and it has been the dominant theory of mind in most of Western history.[15]

Philosophers and psychologists frown upon dualism, yet it continues to persist in the popular mind.

---

[13] René Descartes, *Discourse on the Method* in *The Philosophical Writings of Descartes,* vol. I, trans. John Cottingham, Robert Stoothoff, and Dugald Murdoch (Cambridge: Cambridge University Press, 1984) 127.

[14] Susan R. Bordo, *The Flight to Objectivity: Essays on Cartesianism and Culture* (Albany, N.Y.: State University of New York Press, 1987) 95.

[15] Paul M. Churchland, *Matter and Consciousness* (Cambridge, Mass.: The MIT Press, 1984) 7.

Dualism remains alive also in the very subsoil of our cultural terrain. We continue to educate minds while largely ignoring bodies. Our consumerist mentality encourages a separation of body from self, treating the body as a thing with use-value and exchange value to be improved upon with the help of products. Mechanistic treatment of body parts separated from the whole self ensures the success of impersonalistic medicine. The contemporary postmodernist body is frequently disembodied; what remains is socially constructed physicality only, a privileging of culture over nature yet one more time. Finally, though the body is seemingly flaunted everywhere in image and discourse today, it is fading from view on the cybernet.

Hierarchical ordering and dualism construe bodiliness in ways that are inadequate for our time. The understanding of the body inherent in these models is neither credible enough or substantive enough to stand as the location point for spirituality. The body that serves as this location point must be more than an appendage to something else or an afterthought. It is imperative for lived faith and for our participation in liturgy that we rethink the human body today in broader and more comprehensive terms than the dominant Christian West has envisioned it.

When we claim that bodiliness is the location of our spirituality, and that this is what is to be engaged liturgically, what do we mean by bodiliness?

Bodiliness: A Proposal

The understanding of bodiliness I propose here is a three-fold notion of the body as *vital organism,* as *socio-cultural site,* and as *product of consciousness and will.* This three-fold description corresponds with what is biologically given about the body, what is socially constructed, and what is personally chosen about human bodiliness. These interrelated facets of being bodily must be held together as a whole, as strands of a braid, in order to reflect adequately the contemporary experience of being bodily. While there is necessary overlap between the three dimensions, each highlights a significant aspect of the body that cannot be ignored if we are to live our corporeality with awareness and intentionality as the location of our spirituality.

The Body as Vital Organism

The body as *vital organism* refers to the many physiological aspects of the body that enable it to act at once as environment for and vehicle of representation of the self. There is an existential content to being bodily, a givenness to it. As living matter, the body has a particular physical and historical situatedness that is pre-conceptual. Human bodies actualize themselves in specific space and time according to inherent developmental principles of maturation. Undoubtedly this actualization is socio-culturally influenced as well, and shaped by personal choice, but the basic biological ontogeny of the organism unfolds, resulting in an emanation of life stages, biological rhythms and cycles: as body selves we are born, we grow to maturity and persist for a time, we age and die.

The spatiality that the body as vital organism assumes becomes the elemental raw material of a *presence,* one that the French phenomenologist Maurice Merleau-Ponty referred to as "our general medium for having a world"[16] and "our point of view on the world."[17] This presence, the situatedness of the body, becomes a perspective and a living context for a self growing toward maturity. The vital organism suggests a self in process that is always in dynamic relation with the world.

At a most fundamental physiological level of existence, one not dependent upon our conscious knowing or naming of it, human beings are profoundly *relational.* Live bodies depend upon a dialectical exchange with the world that is ongoing. To breathe, for example, we must draw in oxygen from outside ourselves and push out carbon dioxide. In accordance with our metabolic system then, we look to the world outside ourselves for raw materials we don't have, and we excrete the waste products. Respiration and metabolism highlight our interdependence with the created order.

Further examples of the basic "givenness" of the vital organism include bodies having weight, color, texture, symmetry, interior ecologies, and exterior surfaces. There are also the dynamic strivings of the organism which are richly suggestive for a spirituality of the body. These include the body's consistent *favoring of wholeness* in its operations, and its *efforts to maintain balance*.

Every aspect of the body's framework, each tissue and organ, is made up of microscopically small units, the cells. The body is a giant community of cells, hundreds of billions of them, each with a specific way of developing and life of its own. The high level of cooperation between cells and the manner in which they cluster together, working for the body as a whole, point to a unity and soundness, a fundamental integrity to the vital organism. Cells act for the integrity of the tissue; tissues seek the integrity of the organs, and the organs work for the basic integrity of the whole organism suggesting an accord between parts.

---

[16] Maurice Merleau-Ponty, *Phenomenology of Perception,* trans. Colin Smith (London: Routledge and Kegan Paul, 1962) 146.

[17] Maurice Merleau-Ponty, *The Primacy of Perception,* ed. James M. Edie (Evanston, Ill.: Northwestern University Press, 1964) 5.

The *conatus*[18] or leaning of the body then is toward lifefulness and maintenance of that life. The organism strives for *homeostasis,* a balancing of the body's inner workings that keeps its physiology intact. When that balance is disrupted the body begins at once the job of repairing itself. It is as though the body as vital organism recognizes the inner upkeeping required for a balanced physiology and is forever checking and adjusting its operations to keep close to this state.[19]

To pause before the body as vital organism is to join with the psalmist's praise recognizing that we are indeed "fearfully, wonderfully made" (Ps 139:14). The body as vital organism points to the wisdom of God as creator. And it underscores our particular connection with each other and with the earth.

The Body as Socio-Cultural Site

In addition to the physical givenness of the body, society and culture exert formative and transformative influence on it. The surface of the flesh is porous; bodies soak in distinct socio-historical contexts. The cultural soul of a people and a time spreads over a body's parts, inscribing and shaping them.

The vital organism assumes its identity and lives in interaction with a social and cultural milieu. Society advises rituals, codes, and boundaries for persons' physical selves,[20] and human bodies become the carriers of society's mores. Society interprets the body and sustains itself by means of deliberate bodily investment.

Social theorist Michel Foucault has called attention to society's way of investing the body. He focuses on how the body functions as a material grounding for socio-cultural power. According to Foucault, ". . . nothing is more material, physical, corporeal than the exercise of power."[21] He turns to the body for its revelations regarding social discourses and cultural commitments.

Undoubtedly many "isms" that hold sway in our day look to the body as their playing field. Consumerism, sexism, and technocentrism, so rampant in contemporary North American culture, for example, target the body,

[18] For a detailed analysis of the origins and meaning of *conatus* and *conation,* see Thomas H. Groome, *Sharing Faith* (San Francisco: HarperCollins, 1991) 26–32.

[19] Examples of this include the body's efforts to maintain its temperature, to keep blood pressure stable, and to continue the process of cell replacement.

[20] See Mary Douglas, *Purity and Danger: An Analysis of Concepts of Pollution and Taboo* (Harmondsworth, N.Y.: Penguin Books, 1973).

[21] Michel Foucault, *Power/Knowledge: Selected Interviews and Other Writings,* trans. and ed. Colin Gordon (New York: Pantheon Books, 1980) 57–58.

fastening themselves in seductive ways to flesh, influencing the desires of persons and causing them, through deliberate investment of their bodies, to support socio-cultural positions. Consumerism, by means of strategic commercial intervention, successfully guides persons to long for alterations of their physical selves in accord with a body image presented by the media, which can be attained by means of products that promise to move one closer to this attainment. Sexism inscribes a "feminine ideal" for the postures, gaits, gestures, and bodily ways of women. Technocentrism leads people to suspend critical review of carcinogens, radiation, ozone depletion and toxic chemical release for the sake of a reified technological advance, giving technology permission to enter persons' bodies at will. In all of this, the human body is more than a point of application. It becomes a participant in the ongoing perpetuation of socio-cultural stances.

Bodies also serve as the vehicles/carriers of powerfully positive social discourses and cherished cultural commitments. They can be the producers and sustainers of life-generating religious values and traditions through community-influenced modes of bodily being. In his book *Landscapes of the Sacred*, Belden Lane recounts a story about Rabbi Schneur Zalman, founder of Lubavitcher Hasidim. Rabbi Zalman was reported to be a mystic and a person of intellect who could argue Talmud in unparalleled fashion. Once a man came from afar to learn from the tzaddik. The proud villagers of Ladi, realizing the visitor's desire, asked if he intended to listen to the great rabbi read Talmud first or hear him pray. "Neither," said the man. He wanted only "to watch him cut bread and tie his shoes." The villagers were mesmerized as the visitor simply observed the rabbi sitting and moving round in the light of the noon sun, and then went away inspired.[22] He had come to learn from the rabbi's bodily way. He left taught by the power of a rich spiritual tradition and the wisdom of a faith community that had been inscribed in this rabbi's body. It had lodged itself so deeply there that the rabbi's bodily presence was itself one of blessing, peace and truth.

To pause before the body as socio-cultural site is to recognize that social and religious practices, discourses, and traditions all sculpt the body. When, for example, persons assemble for liturgy as communities of faith, the symbols and practices they gather around have enormous power to grip people in body, to attach themselves to bodies in effective and transformative ways. Initiation into and participation in a community of faith helps cultivate this kind of *bodily knowing*. Louis-Marie Chauvet writes,

---

[22] See Belden Lane, *Landscapes of the Sacred: Geography and Narrative in American Spirituality* (New York: Paulist Press, 1988) 40.

"To be initiated is not to have learned 'truths to believe' but to have received a tradition, in a way through all the pores of one's skin."[23] Liturgical theologian Bruce Morrill notes that tradition is not to be located exclusively "in the forms of the liturgy itself,"[24] as people sometimes suppose, but rather in the very bodies and bodily practices of the participants. Herein lies "living" tradition.

Not all religious or socio-cultural constructions, of course, are equal. There have been negative and positive ways in which bodies have been inscribed. What seems imperative is that a community's spiritual practice of discernment be an ongoing reading of what has been written on the body, a conscious decision to resist ways that bodies have been invested for evil, and a choice for a fashioning of our bodies in a way of life that is respectful and caring of self and others.

The Body as Product of Consciousness and Will

What one thinks about the body, how one reflects upon it, integrates it, adjudicates amongst body concepts, and uses the body in tasks of everyday living are matters of conscious choice and will. To some extent, persons choose what bodies they will become, what incarnate identities they will assume, and how they will interpret their bodiliness in relation to self and world. Freedom, agency and choice safeguard against biological or socio-cultural determinism. It does ultimately matter whether or not we attend to the body, and whether or not we meaningfully interpret and creatively engage it. These factors influence our experience of bodiliness.

Persons cultivate body consciousness by: (1) deliberately attending to the body, (2) meaningfully interpreting it, and (3) creatively engaging it.

Attending to the Body: Bodiliness is an inescapable fact of human existence. One can attempt to ignore this multivalent space or consider it. Attending to the body involves focusing on it, listening, sensing the workings of the vital organism, and feeling one's body from within.

Proprioception is an umbrella term for persons' sense of their physical selves, something innate that can be finely tuned and developed. Proprioception enables people to feel the rightness of good physical functioning in bodily activity. It provides a sense of equilibrium and imbalance, alignment and misalignment. Proprioception makes it possible to connect with

---

[23] Louis-Marie Chauvet, "The Liturgy in its Symbolic Space," in *Liturgy and the Body: Concilium* 1995/3, eds. Louis-Marie Chauvet and Francois Kabasele Lumbala (Maryknoll, N.Y.: Orbis Books, 1995) 31.

[24] Bruce T. Morrill, "The Struggle for Tradition," in *Liturgy and the Moral Self*, eds. E. Byron Anderson and Bruce T. Morrill (Collegeville: The Liturgical Press, 1998) 68.

limbs and with breath, to experience movement and stillness, expansion and contraction.

Attending to the body means developing our sense of our physical selves. It implies having basic familiarity with "bodily felt sense,"[25] that excess of meaning and feeling carried in the body. And it urges that we incline our ear toward stress signals like back pain, neck pain, sweaty palms and physical tension in order to free up emotions trapped in armored muscles and skin, and experience the energy release elicited in the process.

Interpreting the Body: Attending to the body leads to interpretations of it. The experience of bodiliness cannot be severed from the interpretive meanings with which persons appliqué it. There are determining dimensions to being bodily, but individuals and communities retain the freedom to ground these symbolically.

Interpretation highlights aspects of a body's significance. It is a conscious process that enables us to enter into the subjective formation of our physical selves. Frequently, the activity of interpreting includes envisioning an optimal mode of being for the body, one that provides direction and offers hope.

Persons depend upon symbolic, interpretive frameworks as they live their bodiliness, negotiating physical challenges, experiencing bodily limits and changes. A meaningful and evocative interpretation of the body encourages persons to tend to the body with dignity. It is an integral component of identity formation and self-esteem.

Engaging the Body: Interpretation influences actions. A rich understanding of and vision for the body stimulates praxis, which in turn helps persons locate and ground further meanings in the body. Activities in which we consciously engage serve to fashion our bodiliness.

We engage the body as women, men, Chinese, French, Africans, Jews, Muslims, pre-schoolers, seniors, Olympians, cancer patients, musicians, worshippers, students, paraplegics, and so on. Regardless of our specific bodily context, ways of engagement for all of us include acts of bodily maintenance and acts of bodily enhancement.

The first involves the upkeep and management of one's body. Corporeal life carries with it definite and uncompromising demands: persons must eat and sleep, wash and groom themselves, drink fluids and excrete waste, give and receive physical affection in order to avoid disease and disorder. How one specifically addresses these existentials of corporeal life, how-

---

[25] See Eugene Gendlin, "The Wider Role of Bodily Sense in Thought and Language," in *Giving the Body Its Due*. Ed. Maxine Sheets-Johnstone (Albany, N.Y.: State University of New York Press, 1992) 192–207.

ever, remains a matter of choice, except in situations of oppression where this basic right is wrongfully denied. Bodily maintenance is a universal imperative, but persons have their own distinctive styles and set of governing principles with respect to this.

The second way we engage the body is through acts of enhancement. Deliberate use of the body in acquiring a skill or sustaining an acquired skill is a prime example of an enhancement. Intentional participation in sensual or aesthetic experiences is yet another. By exposing ourselves to sensual and aesthetic experiences, it is possible to come to a way of knowing that is profoundly somatic, one closely affiliated with religious awareness.[26]

To pause before the body as product of consciousness and will is to realize that how we live bodily is, in large part, a conscious decision. We have much freedom with respect to the bodies we fashion. Co-creating our bodily selves is intentional activity, and persons reserve the right to face this formidable task with a larger or lesser degree of consciousness and will.

Bodiliness as Location of Spirituality

The three-fold understanding of bodiliness as *vital organism, socio-cultural site,* and *product of consciousness and will,* is reflective of a large spectrum of contemporary discourse on the body. It stands in sharp contrast with the notion of body advanced by proponents of hierarchical ordering and dualism. This is an account of incarnate subjectivity that is not devoid of historical and sociological content, one that remains attentive to the biological givens of organic life as well. Most importantly, this description of bodiliness enables us to grasp some of the breadth and depth of human bodily being as the location of spirituality, something grasped not as isolated individuals but as people in relationship. Communities of faith are able to glimpse the breadth and depth of human bodily being in the practice of liturgy.

The spirituality alive in physicality gets highlighted in a unique and expansive way when we are joined with other bodies in conscious relationship with God. In his book *Worship as Theology,* Don Saliers describes liturgy as "a common art of the people of God in which the community brings the depths of emotion of our lives to the ethos of God."[27] Depth of emotion is always bodily lodged. It is when we bring the full gambit of

[26] See Margaret Miles, *Image as Insight: Visual Understandings in Western Christianity and Secular Culture* (Boston: Beacon Press, 1985) 3.

[27] Don E. Saliers, *Worship as Theology: Foretaste of Glory Divine* (Nashville: Abingdon Press, 1994) 27.

bodily emotions to the book, the font, the table that, in the words of Saliers, "the grace of God becomes audible, visible, palpable, kinetic."[28]

One can choose, of course, to leave real struggles in the body behind; countless folks attend liturgy this way. But to participate in liturgy without any sense of our bodies, without holding the challenges and graces of being bodily in two hands to be prayed, and without any attempt to integrate the bodily felt senses of longing, fear, or hope that we've known, is to deny ritual its power to attract and transform, and to remain indifferent to it. Truly participating in liturgy warrants our human bodiliness at full stretch.[29]

What is necessary is nothing less than the "full, conscious, and active participation" called for in paragraph 14 of the Constitution on the Sacred Liturgy. But it is a specific dimension of that participation addressed here, namely bodily conscious participation, leading to a fuller experience of *Liturgy, Incorporated.*

Liturgy, Inc.

Tracing back to the origins *incorporare, incorporatus,* "Liturgy, Incorporated" is liturgy that is embodied through and through. It means a communal glorifying of God from the standpoint of bodily selves in all their limits and neediness. It involves invoking the Spirit of God on the real struggles of aging, illness, disability and infertility and celebrating that same Spirit in the joys of relational sexuality, physical attributes discovered, the exhilaration of good health, and new births. Incorporated liturgy beseeches God from a bodily standpoint that knows both the felt sense of divine presence and the felt sense of absence as well. It includes an interceding that remembers the bodies of others in their struggle, that faces abuses rendered against the body, and recommits to a "heart of flesh." Most especially, "Liturgy, Inc." recognizes the creative and restorative activity of God pulsing in what is most fleshly, material and concrete. Liturgy must intentionally begin from a bodily standpoint and return to it anew.

In his axioms for the study of sacred place, Belden Lane states that sacred space is "ordinary place ritually made extraordinary."[30] On any given day, the *locus sacra* that is the human body may seem surprisingly unassuming. But when we bring that body consciously to our community worship and pause before it, we recognize the presence of God in this most relational and vulnerable aspect of ourselves.

[28] Ibid., 28.
[29] This is a nuancing of Don Saliers' reference to our "humanity at full stretch." See ibid., 28.
[30] Lane, *Landscapes of the Sacred,* 15.

Liturgy provides opportunities to delight in bodily lives as God's gift.

> *Blessed are you, Lord, God of all creation.*
> *Through your goodness we have these bodies to bring,*
> *which earth has nurtured and love has made.*

At the same time, liturgy gives us a context from which to speak the truth about being out of alignment with other bodies and in search of hope, forgiveness and healing.

> *Come, Holy Spirit. Make these bodies whole.*
> *Make these bodily lives holy.*

As we come face to face with our incompleteness, felt profoundly in body, the words, gestures, music and actions of liturgy speak to us of a God forever giving Godself, amazingly in and as body.

> *Take and eat.*
> *Lord, I am not worthy to receive you.*

In the receiving of Godself, mystery bears in on human bodies. We are drawn, repositioned, sent forth.

> *Filled with life and goodness, blessed and made holy,*
> *Go in peace to love, to serve.*

Thanks be to God.

Suggestions for Further Reading

Cooey, Paula. *Religious Imagination and the Body*. New York: Oxford University Press, 1994.

Dreyer, Elizabeth A. *Earth Crammed With Heaven: A Spirituality of Everyday Life*. New York: Paulist Press, 1994.

Levin, David Michael. *The Body's Recollection of Being*. London: Routledge and Kegan Paul, 1985.

Sheets-Johnstone, Maxine, ed. *Giving the Body Its Due*. New York: State University of New York Press, 1992.

Synnott, Anthony. *The Body Social: Symbolism, Self and Society*. New York: Routledge, 1993.

Wuellner, Flora Slossan. *Prayer and Our Bodies*. Nashville: Upper Room, 1987.

CHAPTER FIVE

The Cultural Bodies of Worship

——————— *James L. Empereur, S.J.* ———————

There are so many definitions of culture, and there is such an immense literature on the topic that any attempt at summarization becomes ludicrous. We are all part of a culture. It is as difficult to point to our culture as it is to show the fish the ocean. Like the joke about the weather forecaster who is made to say' "Tomorrow we shall have weather and the day after tomorrow we shall have more weather," we shall always have culture. Whatever we might think or like, culture there is, and our disbelief cannot make it go away. Nor do we create culture on the spot. It is there. The issue for the cultural embodiment of worship is at what level are culture and liturgy connected.[1]

Edward T. Hall in his book *The Dance of Life: The Other Dimension of Time*[2] refers to a primary level of culture which we need to be particularly aware of in locating the cultural body of liturgy. He says:

> There is an underlying, hidden level of culture that is highly patterned— a set of unspoken, implicit rules of behavior and thought that controls everything we do. This hidden cultural grammar defines the way in which people view the world, determines their values, and establishes the basic tempo and rhythms of life. Most of us are either totally unaware or else

---

[1] For a discussion of some of the issues involved in liturgical inculturation, see *Liturgical Ministry* 6 (Summer 1997).

[2] Edward T. Hall, *The Dance of Life: The Other Dimension of Time* (New York: Doubleday, 1983).

only peripherally aware of this. I call these hidden paradigms primary level culture. Primary level culture, core culture, or basic level culture . . . is somewhat analogous to the hardware of a computer. Conscious, explicit, manifest culture, the part that people talk about and can describe, is analogous to the software—the computer programs.[3]

As we move through life and through other cultures, whether as participants, participant-observers or simply as tourists, we too often view cultural differences as slight differences in the software and none at all in the hardware. Most changes are seen as surface and relatively superficial ones, although we acknowledge that they are very different from our own and we sometimes find them to be exotic. The core culture is understood to be similar since we are all human beings. Apart from the often unintended condescension toward other cultures which is implied in this presupposition, it is a fact that we miss opportunities to engage other cultures effectively.

Primary level culture operates according to its own rules and changes according to its own dynamic. If the one who is assisting in the process of inculturation or as a pastoral minister makes changes, that level of culture remains in place and resists any outside pressure. Thus, Hall distinguishes among the levels of cultures. There is the conscious level where specific symbols are most prominent. There is a private level which is a kind of gnostic restriction to the initiated. And there is the primary level of which we are usually unaware. This is probably a less verbal level, a less articulate level. Although we may describe the cultural bodies of worship more along the lines of the first two levels, the core level is ever present, though it might be unperceived.[4] It is at this primary level where authentic inculturation takes place.

In the past when our living under the imperialism of one culture was less challenged, we may have paid little attention to the levels of culture. Postmodern Christians must attend to the diversity of cultures, and one of the most effective ways to become sensitive both to being acculturated and to cultural diversity is to study contrasting cultures. We might think that we are being culturally sensitive and then find out that we are not because we have acclimatized ourselves to only the conscious levels of culture. The primary level still escapes us. A fuller understanding of ourselves depends on our being more aware of the deeper levels of others cultures.[5] For instance, there is much about the Latino cultures that I appreciate. There are aspects with which I am uncomfortable or unsympathetic. When I ex-

---

[3] Ibid., 6.
[4] See ibid., 7.
[5] See ibid., 8.

perience the latter I try to look more deeply to find the underlying principles at work, and this gives me a new way to enter that cultural world.

To illustrate this point Hall draws a contrast between the American-European experience and that of the Japanese. He uses art to show how different Japanese and Americans are: "Art in Japan encompasses all the Zen disciplines, including flower arraignment, archery, and swordsmanship. As a result, much of art is highly contexted. . . . Nature is not something that is outside and separate which he [the Japanese artist] is trying to reproduce."[6]

According to Hall Western artists are more aware of following certain aesthetic trends or artistic styles. Such conventions and not nature make up the context of their work. Western artists direct their work toward an end in a way unfamiliar to the Japanese artists who are led by the artistic media, by the brush, because they paint with their whole selves. They become one with the object they are painting. To become better artists they must be more enlightened, less ego-centered, more contemplative. Western artists, given the commercial artistic world, must have strong egos to survive. They tend to concentrate on the aesthetic context or the object or both, rather "than to use arts as a way of gaining insight into the workings of their own psyches."[7] While Hall would not be so unreflective as to say that Western artists never learn anything about themselves in their art making, he does see their works as more outward moving, whether to express an experience of the external world or as way of comprehending it. The point is that art in Japan is less separated from the rest of life. It is more engaged with the interior of the artist. Perhaps it is summed up best when Hall says, "Silences in Japan shout the deepest feelings. With us, the silences stand for embarrassment, 'dead air,' a time when nothing is going on."[8]

For many the matter of the cultural bodies of worship leads to a dead end because cultures have swallowed up liturgy, have co-opted worship. Ritual is quickly evanescing. Nathan Mitchell argues persuasively against that position as he examines emerging rituals in contemporary culture. He refers to those who, like the late Mark Searle, see Catholics as more American than Catholic, and so "in the liturgies of typical American parishes, pragmatism triumphs over symbolism; individualism prevails over a ritually mediated sense of communal identity; and personal autonomy

---

[6] Ibid., 98–99.

[7] Ibid., 100.

[8] Ibid., 99. For another example of this cultural difference, see Jyoti Sahi, "The Body in Search of Interiority," *Liturgy and the Body,* eds. Louis-Marie Chauvet and Francis Kabasele Lumbala, *Concilium* 1995/3 (London/Maryknoll, N.Y.: SCM Press/Orbis Books, 1995) 87–95.

(rather than tradition, authority and the public interest) determines ethical value."[9]

Mitchell disagrees with that assessment pointing out areas of ritualizing which are taking place. For instance, high school and college graduation ceremonies can be significant moments for young people who have no other reference points to mark a change in their status. Now that family members no longer live in the same neighborhood, the commercial, religious holidays from Thanksgiving to New Years have become a time for re-establishing connections. Witness the crowded airports at these times. Anniversaries, baptisms, weddings offer ritual moments for people to reaffirm their identity. And these connections are not necessarily based on blood relationship. Mitchell notes that "Participation in these rites embodies and objectifies one's relation to a particular family group. Ironically, in a supposedly 'ritual-less' contemporary American society, ritual ties have become stronger than blood."[10]

For those willing to extend the definition of ritual beyond its usual characteristics "as tradition-bound, repetitive, formal, resistant to change, precritical, unself-conscious, collective and referential,"[11] there are emerging rituals all over. We find them especially in therapeutic support groups such as men's and women's groups, gay pride parades, and the various million men marches. That liturgy needs a cultural body can be demonstrated by considering rituals in the following groups: Southwest Hispanics, African-Americans, Feminists, and gays and lesbians.[12]

The Hispanic Body of Worship

The particular cultural body that Hispanic worship bears is that of popular religion. Most people who are not part of the Hispanic world would understand popular religion through its various rites and practices. These rituals constitute a parallel experience of worship alongside the official liturgy. For example, popular religion has its own liturgical year.[13] Probably the two best known of such rituals are the celebrations which surround

---

[9] Mark Searle, "Emerging Rituals in Contemporary Culture," *Liturgy and the Body* (see reference in previous note), 122.

[10] Ibid., 123–24.

[11] Ibid., 124.

[12] For a brief and persuasive statement on the need for the inculturation of the liturgy, see David N. Power, O.M.I., "Inculturation, the Roman Rite, and Plurality of Liturgies," *Pastoral Music* 22:5 (June–July 1998) 26–29.

[13] See Mark R. Francis, "The Hispanic Liturgical Year: The People's Calendar," *Liturgical Ministry* 7, (Summer 1998) 129–35.

the feast of Our Lady of Guadalupe on December 12 and the passion play performed on Good Friday. But there are many other customs such as the posada around Christmas time, when people march through the streets of neighborhoods with a couple dressed as Mary and Joseph looking for a place to stay. They are rejected at many places until they are received in one of the homes. Also at this time of year we can experience the "acostada" or the placing of the baby Jesus in the crib and the "levantada" around the feast of the Presentation (February 2). In the latter custom, Jesus is taken out of the crib, dressed as a boy and placed in a chair to reign over the household.

These various practices of popular religion testify to how the Hispanic cultural body is dependent on the families in a community, often with the women playing a central role. The most important thing to note about Hispanic popular religious practices, whether they be the many ways of doing the *Quinceanera,* the debut of the young woman at her fifteenth birthday, or the presentation of the child at the age of three, is that they are not identical to the religious devotions which in the nineteenth century were transported from Europe to North America. These latter devotions are more Tridentine in spirit, more under the control of the clergy, and more individualistic in piety. Popular religion, on the other hand, is more medieval in spirituality, very much under the control of the people, and definitely more communitarian. The fact that popular religion escaped the influences of the Protestant Reformation and the Enlightenment is of major importance in understanding this difference.[14]

A number of Hispanic theologians have been writing about the importance of popular religion and have been clarifying its place in Hispanic spirituality.[15] In giving a definition of popular religion one of these theologians, Orlando Espín, limiting himself to popular Catholicism, says:

> By "Popular" I do not mean "widespread," although popular Catholicism certainly is. "Popular," rather, is the adjective to the noun, "people." Thus popular Catholicism is "popular" because it is the people's own. Although it is evident that not every single Latino Catholic person shares in this tradition within Catholicism, most Latinos do, and all of our cultures are clearly grounded in it.[16]

---

[14] For an extended treatment of these dimensions of popular religion, see Orlando Espín, *The Faith of the People: Theological Reflections on Popular Catholicism* (Maryknoll, N.Y.: Orbis Books, 1997).

[15] For an extended bibliography on this matter, see Robert E. Wright, "Popular Religiosity: Review of Literature," *Liturgical Ministry* 7 (Summer 1998) 141–46.

[16] Espín, *The Faith of the People,* 3.

Hispanic popular religion was begun by the people, was sustained by them, often with great opposition from the church, and is continued by them, as a form of resistance to the larger American culture. Another theologian, Virgil Elizondo, sees popular religion as intrinsic to the very identity of Hispanics and has developed this in conjunction with his understanding of *mestizaje,* the coming together of the Spanish and Indigenous cultures to create the Mexican one.[17]

A third Hispanic theologian, Roberto Goizueta, sees popular religion in the larger context of sacramental theology. For him the popular rites and practices are not inimical to or in competition with the liturgy itself. Both are ways of expressing the basic sacramentality of creation and our humanity.[18] For this reason he sees Hispanic anthropology to be the opposite of liberal individualism. It is communal, that is, relational, reflecting the community that exists not only among human beings, but with creation itself. He sees the objects of popular religion such as statues, crosses, and images as symbols of the presence of Christ in a way that is similar to how the bread and wine in the Eucharist are symbols.[19]

Goizueta sees these same customs and practices of popular religion conveying an aesthetic quality to the liturgy. They help to embody worship by bringing a deeper symbolic dimension, by providing a world where beauty and justice meet, and by being concrete experiences of the analogical imagination at work.[20] Goizueta sees both the liturgy and popular religion as aesthetic performances. This does not mean that they must rank with one of the fine arts. Rather, it means that they are ends in themselves.

[17] Elizondo in many ways began what can be called Hispanic theology. Among his many writings, see in particular "Popular Religion as the Core of Cultural Identity Based on the Mexican American Experience in the United States," *An Enduring Flame,* eds. Stevens-Arroyo and Dias-Stevens (New York: Bildner Center for Western Hemisphere Studies, 1994) 113–32. There are those who believe that a new *mestizaje* is taking place between the Hispanic and North American cultures. See also, Virgil Elizondo and Timothy Matovina, *Mestizo Worship: A Pastoral Approach to Liturgical Ministry* (Collegeville: The Liturgical Press, 1998).

[18] See his very fine work, *Caminemos Con Jesus: Toward a Hispanic/Latino Theology of Accompaniment* (Maryknoll, N.Y.: Orbis Books, 1995).

[19] As an example, see Goizueta, *Caminemos,* 65. Obviously, Goizueta would make the necessary distinctions between the eucharistic elements and statues and the like. The point is what is going on here sacramentally.

[20] For further discussion, see Allan Deck, S.J., "Hispanic Catholic Prayer and Worship," *¡Alabadle! Hispanic Christian Worship,* ed. Justo L. González (Nashville: Abingdon Press, 1996) 34–35; and Alex García-Rivera, "Religious Imagination," *Perspectivas: Hispanic Ministry,* eds. Allan Figueroa Deck, Yolanda Tarango, Timothy M. Matovina (Kansas City, Mo.: Sheed and Ward, 1995) 97.

The people do not engage in them in order to get something done but for the joy of doing them, for the love that they have for them.[21] As I have noted elsewhere,

> [T]he purpose is not to achieve some result but rather to take part in a sacramental event. Because the persons enter into the life of Jesus with their total bodies they are sacramental, and so are intrinsically related to their communities where they find their identities and self-worth, and are empowered 'to resist the dominant culture's attempts to destroy that identity through assimilation.'[22]

An example of putting the flesh, blood, and bones of popular religion on the liturgy is *Primero Dios* by Arturo Perez-Rodriguez and Mark Francis.[23] Perez and Francis have long been involved in the specific relationship of popular religion and the liturgy. Perez, as other Hispanic scholars, identifies certain characteristics as specifically Hispanic, qualities found in popular religion which can enrich the official liturgy of the church. Hispanic worship is family-centered, with family here including the extended family such as cousins, aunts and uncles, and grandchildren. Women play a central role since they are the caretakers of the domestic church where popular religion resides. Mary plays an indispensable role in Hispanic religion. For Mexico and much of the Southwest, Our Lady of Guadalupe is the primary icon of the people's identity. It is sensual worship with all the senses engaged in the process. These are descriptions of the Hispanic cultural body.

For Perez, Hispanic worship is held together by a basic harmony which flows from the indigenous perspective of the intellect, the body, sexuality, and nature, as connected by the spirit of life. He says, "Humanity, and all that makes up a person, is part of creation. The sensual nature of our body is the bridge of connection with nature. Sensuality forms the language of prayer."[24] The sensual nature of Hispanic worship shows itself in the way the liturgy is celebrated. For example, one can see it at the beginning of the liturgy as Hispanics gather for worship. Some are praying the Rosary. Others are lighting candles, while others are touching statues. Some kiss the hands of the priests. Some are talking with animation. Many treat the

---

[21] Goizueta, *Caminemos,* 101–05.

[22] James L. Empereur, S.J., "Popular Religion and the Liturgy: The State of the Question," *Liturgical Ministry* 7 (Summer 1998) 110; also, Goizueta, *Caminemos,* 105.

[23] Arturo Perez-Rodriguez and Mark Francis, *Primero Dios* (Chicago: Liturgy Training Publications, 1997). See also, Arturo Perez Rodriguez, "Mestizo Liturgy: A Mestizaje of the Roman and Hispanic Rites of Worship," *Liturgical Ministry* 6 (Summer 1997) 141–47.

[24] Taken from an essay soon to be published, "Sensual Liturgy as Hispanic Worship."

church building as they treat their home. This at times makes for a certain amount of informality—some would say messiness. The words of the liturgy themselves are sensual because they are communicated more metaphorically and imaginatively than conceptually. As Perez puts it, "The word does not have to bear the full burden of the message . . . Our starting point in the liturgy is the body and everything that the body has to offer."[25] Truly, Hispanic worship wears a body that is very sensual and permeates all levels of culture.

The African-American Body of Worship

African-American Catholics have found that if they wish to make their worship respond more to their culture, they must do more than borrow elements from Protestant black worship. While there are connections between the two in terms of black culture itself, black Catholics are dealing with a fully developed liturgy of word and sacrament that is often not found in Protestant churches. There is a different rhythm and ethos between Roman Catholic and Evangelical worship. This is not to deny the great commonalities among all forms of black worship. But there are also specific contributions made by Roman Catholic theology and ritual. The black body of worship takes different forms.

Black Roman Catholic theologians will readily claim that any Black worship must begin with black spirituality. "It is a spirituality that is born of moments of the African-American sense of 'conversion.'"[26] African-American bishops have delineated some of the characteristics of black spirituality: contemplative, holistic, joyful, communitarian. It is contemplative because it is aware of the transcendence of God. God is very near and very intimate. It is holistic in so far as it treats the person as a whole without bifurcations into heart and head, feelings and intellect, individual and community, and sacred and secular. Emotions play a significant role in black worship. Liturgy as a joyful experience is something that is passed from generation to generation. What gets African-Americans through their times of trouble is that their spirituality "explodes in the joy of the movement, song, rhythm, feeling, color, and sensation."[27] To say African-American spirituality is to say a spirituality of community. There is in the

---

[25] Ibid.

[26] Secretariat for the Liturgy and Secretariat for Black Catholics, *Plenty Good Room: The Spirit and Truth of African American Catholic Worship* (Washington D.C.: United States Catholic Conference, 1990) 48.

[27] Ibid., 49.

community a concern for the struggles and sufferings of others. Individual members derive their identity from the larger community.[28]

Perhaps that which we most associate with black worship is its emotive and intuitive spirit. This is its most obvious quality as embodied worship. This is not the mere expression of emotion. It is a way of knowing the world around us. Traditions whose origins are based in orality tend to have a stronger historical and poetic character. It is now twenty years ago that Clarence Rivers told us about this kind of knowing where "there is a natural tendency for interpenetration and interplay, creating a concert or orchestration in which the ear sees, the eye hears, and where one both smells and tastes color; wherein all the senses, unmuted, engage in every experience."[29] This is not some kind of mindless knowing. It is simply a primary way of communicating the faith. It is not mind versus feeling, but mind and feeling together, although mind feels and feelings think.

African-American worship must be African and American. Helpful hints are gained from a study of liturgical inculturation in Africa.[30] But that does not mean that we can import the Zairean (Congolese) rite into Alabama.[31] Black praise and adoration must take place in American churches, but ones where all the senses are not only welcomed but demanded. The liturgical spaces of the worshippers must become homes where they deal with their present struggles, not the actual slavery that kept the economy of the plantations alive, but the new slavery of gangs, drugs, and fatherless families. The liturgical spaces must be "places that give full sway to the rich array of the auditory, tactile, visual, and olfactory senses."[32] The challenge for African-American liturgies is to be both African, black, and denominational at the same time.[33] In Hispanic theology we describe this mingling of cultures to produce something new as *mestizaje*. There is a kind of mestizaje going on for African-Americans.

When those of us who are not African-American find their liturgies rather lengthy, we need to remember that going to church for them is spending time with God. "Praise the Lord" comes easily to the lips because

---

[28] See ibid., 49.

[29] Ibid., 45.

[30] For a discussion of African worship, see Elochukwu E. Uzukwu's *Worship as Body Language: Introduction to Christian Worship: An African Orientation* (Collegeville: The Liturgical Press, 1997).

[31] We can learn much about ritualizing by studying the ways other cultures ritualize. See Malidoma Patrice Some, *Ritual: Power, Healing, and Community* (New York: Penguin Putnam, Inc., 1993).

[32] *Plenty Good Room,* 51.

[33] See ibid., 52.

they enjoy the Spirit breathing through their assembly. Such sacred time cannot and should not be measured chronologically.

The breath of the Spirit can take on rather dramatic expression, especially in black Pentecostal churches, where people swoon and faint or engage in dramatic gesticulation. Some of these antics are more Pentecostal than black, but even for African-Americans who are Roman Catholics, there must be place for gesture. Apart from the traditional gestures in the church, black Roman Catholic worship must allow for gestures that reveal "inner feelings, hopes, fears, dreams and longing for freedom."[34] Touch will play a more significant role and not be limited to the kiss of peace. This worship is embodied because posture says so much about the prayer. One could say that what one does with one's body becomes the very structure of the prayer. The singing, the confessing, the waving of hands all respond to a need to give praise. There is no need to justify gestures in Roman Catholic liturgy. The question is: What further gestures are needed to make this a truly African-American liturgy?

Black liturgies make use of the poetic aspect of liturgical language. In general, liturgy's language is metaphorical. It is narrative in style and African American liturgy is more so. The narrative is tied to their former condition as a people who hoped for their freedom. Their soulful prayers, their proclamatory witnessing, their personal but non-excluding language, their songs fixed in this world but directed to another world make for a language which calls for that full active participation that liturgical scholars have continued to hold up as an ideal.[35] It is the same attitude and atmosphere that one finds in the novels of Toni Morrison or, perhaps, a movie like *Amistad*.

Those who have participated in black worship know that the preaching is dialogic. One can hear the congregations muttering, humming, shouting "Amen," "Yes, Lord," and "Thank You, Jesus." This preaching is often accompanied by gesture, on the part of the preacher certainly, but also on the part of the members of the congregation—even to the point of hysteria. Although this kind of spontaneity is beyond rubrical control, it does not mean that it is totally spontaneous. Visitors, especially non African-Americans, cannot simply shout out "Amen" at their pleasure because it would create a sense of something out of place. There are no rubrics, but there is procedure.

Because of the importance of the narrative in the black experience, the liturgy of the word should take on that character even more strongly than it

---

[34] Ibid.
[35] See ibid., 54.

usually does. This may require more than a good storyteller. It may be necessary to redo the format so as to allow for a better flow of narrative. One thinks immediately of fewer and longer readings. But most of all, black preaching must become a folk art.[36]

In no place do we find African-American creativity as much as in the music. Even when the music is prepared the congregation frees it from any possible rigidity through their acclamations and words of encouragement. Singing is the concrete sign of the presence of the Spirit. We have to note that

> African-Americans are heirs to the West African musical aesthetic of the call-and-response structure, extensive melodic ornamentation (e.g. slurs, slides, bends, moans, shouts, wails, and so forth), complex rhythmic structures and the integration of song and dance. . . . African American Catholic worship may be greatly enhanced by spirituals and gospel music, both of which are representations of this aesthetic. But classical music, anthems, African Christian hymns, jazz, South American, African-Caribbean, and Haitian music may also be used where appropriate. It is not just the style of music that makes it African American, but the African American assembly that sings it and the people who spirits are uplifted by it.[37]

There are variations in any cultural group, African Americans being no exception. For example, let us consider briefly black feminists. They may be worshipping in women's groups, black groups or any other mix. Their participation in the liturgy will be expressed in areas of struggle in regard to race, sex, or class, as well as issues which are specifically women's issues for the most part, such as domestic abuse, rape, and health care. They will also be praying about the racism they find in the white women's movement. They will want their stories included in feminist liturgies so that white women's liturgy does more than superficially pay attention to their black history and culture. They will try to bring about this fuller level of consciousness raising through a collective presence. This is one example of how black worship bears the body of a struggling community moving toward liberation. The cultural body of all black worship at the primary level of culture is deeply emotional and intuitive in its telling of its story of moving toward redemption. This is not a hidden body of worship, but manifests itself through the other levels of culture.

---

[36] See ibid., 55.
[37] Ibid., 56.

The Womanist/Feminist Body of Worship

Women have always worshiped in groups. There have been women's societies in the pre-Christian era, and in the lifetime of Christianity the most obvious example of women worshipping without the presence of men are the religious orders. The feminist movement in its more contemporary form has provoked considerable historical research in women's ritual. Interest in witchcraft and pagan practices have further encouraged the study of this area which was overlooked by male researchers in the past. Changing views about women's place in society and the achieving of considerable autonomy on the part of women play an important role here. The awareness of feminist spirituality has logically called for women's rituals. In her wonderfully insightful book, *Ritualizing Women,* Lesley A. Northup[38] notes that

> In the West, many Jewish and Christian women, finding a lack of wide-spread support for even such conservative goals as integrating women into existing liturgies through ordination, imaginative biblical interpretation, and the use of expansive language in ritual texts, have formed themselves into ritualizing groups—Christian, Jewish, pagan, feminist, and/or non-theistic—that seek a unique women's spirituality.[39]

As with any form of categorization, we must be cautious about any kind of generalizations here. This is especially true when dealing with half of the human race. It may have been presumed several years ago that there is such a thing as "woman's experience." Clearly, feminists themselves have moved from this kind of generalization to make more nuanced and even more modest claims. The challenge for the researcher here is to draw conclusions which avoid absolute claims on the one hand, and avoid a kind of solipsism where every woman is so unique that you cannot say anything at all. While still considering "women's experience" as a helpful category, many prefer to speak of feminist rituals rather than women's rituals.[40]

Since women are part of every human culture, they manifest the cultural body of worship in an equally varied number of ways. This makes generalizations even more difficult, although this problem is alleviated by the specific intentionality of many women's groups. In these groups certain concerns such as those involving relationships transcend cultural differences.

---

[38] Lesley A. Northup, *Ritualizing Women* (Cleveland: The Pilgrim Press, 1997).
[39] Ibid., 2–3.
[40] For a more extended discussion, see ibid., 3ff.

Northup has very articulately listed three major hurdles for any one doing research on women's ritualizing. First, what is it exactly that we are researching? So many of the present studies are dominated by a feminist perspective. Second, since most of these liturgies are episodic and particular to the times and circumstances, there is little consistent textual evidence. And third, as she puts it, "the movement toward women's worship has no central trunk; rather it has evolved as random branches, with no coordination, from the discontents and yearnings of women, in one small group after another."[41]

Despite the difficulties of generalization already indicated, it seems possible to discover areas of similarities in the present process of women creating rituals. When women do ritual, what is it that they do that is similar? Northup describes three kinds of features of these rituals. Her classification is helpful, so I will follow it. They are: ritual images, ritual elements, and ritual characteristics. Of the over dozen images she describes I focus on only a few.

If we examine women's rituals either through participation or through report, we find the circle universally present. The circle represents nature as in the earth and the moon, human experiences as in the womb and spiral dance, and religious symbolism as in the mandala and font.[42] The circle is present in the cyclical rather than the linear approach to time. It is obvious that the menstrual cycle will resonate through women's rituals. This ties them closely to the seasons of the year, the recurrence of the moon, and the cycle of life found in nature. Such earthiness in ritual images is in contrast to the vertical symbols of a more masculine and hierarchical centered liturgy. Rather, it allows the participants to celebrate the connections created by human relationships, the fecundity of their bodies and the appreciation of their sexuality. Such appreciation is not limited to individual embodiment but redounds back to the earth in environmental sensitivity. Of the many forms nature images take, the concern is the same—to locate divinity here.[43]

Basic to women's ritual is the body as a place of the holy, a primary symbol which underlies all further ritualization. The body is affirmed in celebrations of life in community as well as in healing services dealing with violence and abuse. Specific rituals deal with areas of healing such as abortion or rape as well as those which honor women, such as when they are wisdom figures.

[41] Ibid., 7.
[42] Ibid., 24.
[43] See ibid. This is a summary of Northup's thought from pages 28–52.

Sacramental theologian Susan Ross makes a persuasive case that there is much in feminist theology which can enrich sacramental theology today, especially in terms of embodiment and connection.

> What unites the sacramental tradition and the feminist movement is a concern for the integrity of the body and nature. What divides them is the way the body has been understood. . . . A feminist sacramental theology would be concerned to integrate the spiritual and the physical: the spiritual should be seen as a dimension of the physical, not opposed to it. . . . By enabling both women and men to administer the sacraments, we would break down the division between male and female, between church and the world, between spiritual and physical and we would understand our sacramental life not in a dualistic way, but in an integrated and differentiated way.[44]

Of the several ritual actions noted by Northup, what she calls reflexivity seems to be the most universal. Unlike traditional rituals women's, especially feminists', rituals have discussions of the ritual as part of the service. Some would see this as gender specific, that women want to reflect on their experiences with others. What is not clear is how essential this reflection is to the ritual when the ritual itself is no longer emerging, but enjoys a greater acceptance. Some would claim that such reflexivity is necessary in an approach that is egalitarian and that the process itself is to be valued.[45] However, it is still not clear that this reflexivity will feature so strongly in women's rituals in the future.

Narrative is a significant part of most traditional liturgies. It is found in black worship, and it plays an especially central role in women's worship. It is not simply that women are telling stories that were once suppressed, although they are doing that. The storytelling is different. Once again it is oral. The stories are informal recollections of their predecessors. They are anecdotal, autobiographical. They are meant to elicit a response from the hearers and they stand in contrast to the written narratives of the official dominant liturgies.[46]

Of the ritual characteristics Northup lists, a universal one is the de-emphasis on formal leadership. Despite the difficulties in preparing such liturgies and the sometime attendant lack of focus, women find that rotating leadership is a principle they wish to continue. Although feminist

---

[44] Susan Ross, "Women, Body and Sacrament: Toward a Renewed Sacramental Theology," *Miriam's Song II Patriarchy: A Feminist Critique* (West Hyattsville, Md.: Priests for Equality, P. O. Box 5243, n.d.) 21.

[45] See Northup, *Ritualizing Women*, 38.

[46] See ibid., 41–42.

Christian and Jewish women groups deny any form of hidden and implicit leadership in their liturgies, there is a growing number of feminist ritualists who are emerging.[47]

Such lack of single leadership means that the texts of the ritual are not determinative in the way they are in the official church liturgies. Rites are passing in character.

> Each rite is understood to be rooted in the particularities of the occasion it observes, the group that enacts it, and the process that creates it; not only is the ritualization of a given place and time perceived as unavailable for repetition, but it also raises questions of appropriation and attribution.[48]

To summarize the principles of this sometimes complex phenomenon of feminist liturgies, I refer to the results of the discussion of the feminist liturgy group of the North American Academy of Liturgy[49] which took place in January, 1990. Although the group was referring to feminist ritual in particular, I believe that their conclusions would be applicable to all forms of women's ritualizing. Among the many qualities of feminist liturgies they mentioned I note the following which constitute the feminist body of worship at all levels of culture:

1. It is embodied action, that is, it is not primarily verbal, but rather speaks through color, gesture, touch, sound and all the senses. The creative imagination is prominent in ensuring that the liturgies are engaging.
2. The leadership is reciprocal and the participation is interactive. That means that the creation of these liturgies is a collaborative effort. The worship is not passive but encourages self-generated response, especially in promoting sisterhood and in supporting action on behalf of the poor and oppressed.
3. Although they give priority to women's experience, they honor all experience, the subjective as well as the objective. This is important for having positive images and stories about women in the liturgy. The experience, stories, images of women from the world religious traditions are welcomed.

---

[47] See ibid., 46–47. One of the better known of these ritualists is Diann Neu, a former student of mine. Her rituals often appear in *Waterwheel,* which is a quarterly newsletter of Women's Alliance for Theology, Ethics and Ritual, (8035 13th St., Silver Spring, Md. 20910-4803).

[48] See Northup, *Ritualizing Women,* 48.

[49] NAAL is an ecumenical group of professional liturgists which is divided into study groups, allowing the members to pursue their interests with colleagues.

4. They are both experimental and self-critical. They call into question the traditional rites while recognizing that mistakes are made in these liturgies too.

The Gay/Lesbian Body of Worship

Rituals which are generated by gays and lesbians have a strong emphasis on the affirmation of their personhood. In these liturgies, as well as those rites of the Christian churches which they may regularly or sporadically be part of, gays and lesbians look to their liturgies to validate their experiences. It is often their way of going public with their identity. Worshipping in an assembly of gay Christians carries with it an affirming quality that few private coming-out moments can have. As in the case of feminist-womanist liturgies, the new rites by gays and lesbians stand over against the official rituals of the churches which they so frequently find oppressive. They often find these liturgies of the church very ambiguous about their sexuality. "Worship has become all too often an occasion of sin rather than redemption, a place from which lesbians and gays come away angry and frustrated rather than enlighten and healed."[50] In my own book *Spiritual Direction and the Gay Person*,[51] I have tried to show that there are ways in which gays and lesbians can find Christian worship affirming of their lives and of their homosexuality as a gift. However, many will remain unconvinced by my argument.

Although homosexuality is present in all cultures, it takes on a different character when we are dealing with a Latino gay man or an Asian lesbian. Moreover, there is a kind of analogous culture of the gay/lesbian community emerging which is not to be equated with the gay subculture of the bars, bathhouses, male prostitution or sado-masochistic practices. The word "queer" has been rehabilitated to mean "Queer Nation," with its own symbols, values, and vocabulary.[52] How can the Gospel be heard in this culture?

Language issues may arise in some gay/lesbian worship situations. As in the case of many women, gays and lesbians are sensitive about inclusive language, although in a different way. The concern is whether gay and lesbian liturgies are inclusive enough, not only in terms of the language used

---

[50] Kittredge Cherry and Zalmon Sherwood, eds., *Equal Rites: Lesbian and Gay Worship, Ceremonies, and Celebration* (Louisville: Westminster John Knox Press, 1995) xv.

[51] James L. Empereur, *Spiritual Direction and the Gay Person* (New York/London: Continuum/Cassell, 1998).

[52] See *Equal Rites*, xv.

but in regard to the very presence of gays and lesbians. Is this liturgy truly hospitable? Can homosexuals be mentioned in homilies or the intercessory prayers? Or are they still kept in a limbo of silence?[53]

Perhaps, the greatest challenge in gay and lesbian ritual making is that they have a special need to live symbolically because they do not have "the benefit of inspiring myths and rituals that are attuned to the unique needs of sexual minorities."[54] An assembly of gays and lesbians is made of people who have had their self-images diminished because most will have had painful experiences in a heterosexual dominant society. Many have never had the opportunity or even the possibility of developing a positive self-image. So, gay/lesbian rites are justified for no other reason than that they can offer gays and lesbians images and symbols that affirm their experience.

Gay/lesbian worship may be symbol specific. Apart from the full repertoire of traditional symbols, we might expect to see pictures of modern day defenders of gay rights, the rainbow which represents diversity, and the pink triangle, the sign that gay prisoners in Nazi concentration camps had to wear. The Greek letter, lambda, is a symbol of gay/lesbian liberation. In addition there is a kind of calendar of feasts developing such as those connected with the Stonewall rebellion. On June 29, 1969, gays and lesbians fought back against the harassment of the police. This beginning of the gay rights movement is often now commemorated by gay pride parades. The repertory of gay symbols is increasing: the red lapel ribbon "to show solidarity with and compassion for those living with AIDS,"[55] the AIDS quilt, and the double-head ax as a lesbian symbol.

Just as the tradition has assigned names to God based on our ordinary relationships such as mother or father, gays may well address God with the term, lover. Often they feel free to see God as someone with a sexual orientation like their own, e.g., "The Great Gay Spirit." The theological difficulties in emphasizing this should be obvious. Often the structure of gay/lesbian liturgies resembles that of the mainline churches, but it is the image which makes the difference. Images of God which see God as present with us in our human struggles, our God as vulnerable, or God as healer, Comforter, Companion and so forth make for a less offensive and oppressive experience. Because gays have often experienced their parents or the Church in a judging role, that image (e.g., father) would be counterproductive. The

---

[53] An example of the gay/lesbian desire for more inclusivity in language would be the many who want to use the word, queer, so as to include bisexuality, transvestitism. And how are we to call heterosexual supporters of gays? "Family and friends"? "Allies"? "Supporters"? See ibid., xv.

[54] Ibid.

[55] Ibid., xvi.

image of Justice-seeker might well be substituted with any image which contributes to their liberation, helps them deal with their marginality and their feelings of diminishment.

A large and challenging task in emerging gay liturgies is to make the Christian scriptures still work for them. Publicly, they have so often heard their condemners quote Scripture, or at least refer to the Bible in a general and usually uncritical way, that one wonders how the biblical readings can be retrieved for them. Elsewhere I have pointed out the need to understand properly the few passages in the Bible which refer to homosexuality as well as not to let a fundamentalistic and unnuanced reading of them poison the whole body of the Scriptures.[56] We need more artists and writers to portray some of the gay heroes and heroines of the past as the saints to be remembered today.

The position of the Churches regarding homosexuality and certain forms of gay worship has been ambiguous. It is getting less so. The Metropolitan Church has been the most welcoming. There are other gay/lesbian church groups: Dignity and Courage (Roman Catholic), Integrity (Episcopal), Axios (Orthodox), American Baptists Concerned, and Affirmation (United Methodists). A great deal of networking is going on among congregations more open to gays. And despite harsh statements from church authorities, others are taking a more humane approach.

Many gays and lesbians who belong to explicitly Christian groups like Dignity tend to celebrate according to the official rites of the Churches. Other claim that it will not do to stay with heterosexual models of worship.[57] However, my impression is that many of the published models of new gay liturgies resemble some version of an old Protestant service, as evidenced by those found in *Equal Rites*. The important thing is that authentic worship will give voice and tongue to people who have been closeted from the rest of us. If there is a liturgy that does justice[58] then surely gay/lesbian worship is called to do that.

Just as feminist theology has stressed the importance of creating new rituals which deal with their various struggles, the same is true for gays and lesbians, especially as they deal with AIDS and homophobia. These matters are not mere psychological life crises but also turning points which provoke basic religious questions. Part of this process is to recognize the symbols that have already developed among gays and lesbians. There are several

---

[56] See Empereur, *Spiritual Direction and the Gay Person,* ch. 5.

[57] See *Equal Rites,* xviii.

[58] That is the title of my book, co-authored with Christopher Kiesling, O.P., *The Liturgy That Does Justice,* (Collegeville: The Liturgical Press, 1990).

situations where rituals have emerged. There is the gay bar subculture with its ritualized patterns for meeting and engaging a sexual partner, previously unknown. But there are such fundamental problems with the subculture's presuppositions about religion and even about what makes for a good human being that these experiences may be of little value.

An area of ritualizing which provides us with experiences of repetitive gay ritual would include AIDS support liturgies, memorial services, services of healing as well as the celebration of holidays and anniversaries. A more specific, but very controversial, example of the cultural body of gay worship would be the celebrations of same sex unions, and any rituals of love and commitment.[59]

There are also other new intentional rituals, the most significant of which are those of coming out. Many of these coming out celebrations carry implicit or explicit overtones of baptism. They are a form of rebirthing, a rite of passage, and entrance into a new found community. Apart from rituals of holy union for the couple, other liturgies are developing: to bless a couple's first home, to celebrate a longstanding relationship or the dissolution of one, to celebrate the development of the children involved (e.g., bar/bat mitzvah celebrations).[60] Here we should note how gay men and women have claimed certain festivals, e.g., Halloween, New Year's Eve, Mardi Gras, and given them their own interpretation. Many Jewish gays are appropriating the passover. Passover recalls God's liberation of marginalized people. Its power as a symbol goes beyond this historical event and celebrates God's being with any marginalized group. Michael Clark wrote:

> So understood, Passover celebrates not only God's liberating power in history, but God's liberating empowerment on behalf of all people still on the margin. It also symbolically signifies God as the grounding and source of empowerment for any people to actively seek their own liberation. Furthermore, by its customary celebration in a familiar and/or communal context, Passover underscores our need as gay men and lesbians to celebrate and sanctify our couplings and our surrogate families.[61]

In these situations just as God was understood to be one of the powerless at Auschwitz so God suffers with the victims of homophobia and those living with AIDS.

---

[59] J. Michael Clark, *A Place to Start* (Dallas: The Monument Press, 1989) 176.

[60] For more gay/lesbian rituals see Elizabeth Stuart, ed., *Daring to Speak Love's Name: A Gay and Lesbian Prayer Book* (London: Hamish Hamilton, 1992). *White Crane: A Journal Exploring Gay Men's Spirituality* often contains articles on prayer and ritual. It is published at this address: P.O. Box 1018, Conifer, Co. 80433-1018.

[61] Clark, *A Place to Start,* 178.

The gay/lesbian body of worship will sometimes takes its own unique form, but often it will be indistinguishable from the official worship of the Churches. In either case, on the primary cultural level something very profound is happening. The images of God are changing in such a powerfully self-affirming way that the experience of God itself is different from that which heterosexuals have. Gay/lesbian theology and liturgy has yet to catch up with the restructuring of theology which the feminist critique has done. But this work of gay/lesbian theology and spirituality has begun.

Conclusion

We are left with this question: What is happening when the liturgy takes on these different cultural bodies? The integration of popular religion, the incorporation of the black religious experience, the challenging of male dominated and hierarchical forms of worship, and the creation of new rituals by gays and lesbians are a monumental reframing of the experience of God in public worship.[62] This recasting of symbols is in fact a recasting of the images of God. This can only change our very religious experience in the future, and in ways we cannot predict. It is a dynamic process in its earliest stages.

Suggestions for Further Reading

Francis, Mark R. and Arturo Perez-Rodriguez. *Primero Dios: Hispanic Liturgical Resource*. Chicago: Liturgy Training Publications, 1997.

Keleman, Stanley. *Somatic Reality: Bodily Experience and Emotional Truth*. Berkeley: Center Press, 1997.

Law, Jane Marie, ed. *Religious Reflections on the Human Body*. Bloomington, Ind.: Indiana University Press, 1995.

Mollenkott, Virginia Ramey. *Sensuous Spirituality: Out From Fundamentalism*. New York: Crossroad Publishing, 1993.

Spencer, Daniel T. *Gay and Gaia: Ethics, Ecology, and the Erotic*. Cleveland: Pilgrim Press, 1996.

---

[62] An omission here is a treatment of the Asian cultural body of worship. For those wishing to pursue that study I suggest beginning with the work of Aloysius Pieris. See in particular his article "Christianity and Buddhism in Core-to-Core Dialogue" *Cross Currents* vol. xxxvii, no 1 (Spring 1987) 47–75.

PART TWO

Pastoral Practice: Bodies at Worship

CHAPTER SIX

Christian Marriage:
Sacramentality and Ritual Forms

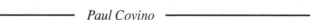

Paul Covino

Beginning with the book of Genesis, the body has been a characteristic referent for marriage in the Judeo-Christian tradition: "Therefore a man leaves his father and his mother and cleaves to his wife, and they become one flesh" (2:24). At times, the bodiliness of marriage has been only reluctantly accepted, as in Saint Paul's advice that the unmarried and widows who "are not practicing self-control . . . should marry. For it is better to marry than to be aflame with passion" (1 Cor 7:9). Contemporary writings on Christian marriage generally take a more wholistic approach: "Conjugal love involves a totality, in which all the elements of the person enter—appeal of the body and instinct, power of feeling and affectivity, aspiration of the spirit and of will. It aims at a deeply personal unity, a unity that, beyond union in one flesh, leads to forming one heart and soul."[1]

Most wedding receptions are unabashedly bodily celebrations with "food from the earth and wine to gladden the human heart" (Ps 104:14-15) and dancing that lures even the most inhibited and rhythmically challenged of guests. The costuming of bodies for a wedding runs the gamut from turquoise bridesmaids' dresses that will never be worn again to the brown suit that Uncle Harry has worn to every wedding and funeral for the last thirty years. Receiving lines and reception seating plans are carefully

---

[1] Pope John Paul II, *Familiaris consortio* (1981).

designed to introduce those who do not know one another and facilitate the formation of a corporate body that can celebrate together.

For all this attention to the bodily aspects of marriage and weddings, there is surprisingly little attention given to the role of the body in the celebration of wedding liturgies. The wedding planning guides available in most bookstores seem primarily concerned with making the wedding day "picture perfect."[2] The little that is said about religious ceremonies is usually too generic for any religious tradition, yet these books and magazines often have a profound influence on popular assumptions concerning the priorities in a wedding liturgy. Even some of the resources designed specifically for Catholic weddings seem to imply that preparation for the wedding liturgy is limited to choosing scripture readings, prayer texts and musical pieces.

This lack of attention to the role of the body should be disconcerting for pastoral ministers as well as sacramental theologians. As a *sacramental* religion, Catholicism embodies its faith in liturgical words *and* actions. In the words of the Second Vatican Council, sacraments "not only presuppose faith, but by words and objects they also nourish, strengthen, and express it."[3] Explaining the ancient maxim of Prosper of Aquitaine *(lex orandi, lex credendi)*, the *Catechism of the Catholic Church* says: "The law of prayer is the law of faith: the Church believes as she prays. Liturgy is a constitutive element of the holy and living Tradition."[4] Referring more specifically to the body, Lawrence Cunningham states the issue this way: "Gestures are a complex form of body language that express serious theological truth . . . If one desires to learn, say, about Catholicism, it would be far better to go to Mass in a typical parish and ask 'What is going on?' than simply to read books on what Catholicism teaches and believes."[5]

Catechisms, church documents and theological writings certainly contribute to the understanding of marriage in the Catholic tradition. For most people, though, the most frequent encounter with the Catholic faith concerning marriage is in the celebration of the wedding liturgy and, hopefully, in the marriage covenants lived out by Catholic couples. The latter would take a lifetime to discuss. The former will be the focus of these next pages.

---

[2] For a discussion of the danger inherent in this approach, see Herbert Anderson and Edward Foley, *Mighty Stories, Dangerous Rituals* (San Francisco: Jossey-Bass Publishers, 1998) 86–90.

[3] *Sacrosanctum concilium*, 59.

[4] *Catechism of the Catholic Church*, 1124.

[5] Lawrence Cunningham, "As Silence Is to Music," *Notre Dame Magazine* (Spring 1998) 31.

The Church as Body in the Wedding Liturgy

In chapter two of this volume, Bernard Cooke has explored the reality of *communio* and the notion of the Church as "body of Christ." Ancient Christian texts applied this image to the Church at worship: "Let no one deprive the church by staying away; if they do, they deprive the body of Christ of one of its members . . . Do not then make light of your own selves, do not deprive our Saviour of his members, do not rend, do not scatter his Body."[6] This same understanding was expressed by Vatican II: "Liturgical services are not private functions, but are celebrations of the Church, which is the 'sacrament of unity,' namely, the holy people united and ordered under their bishops. Therefore liturgical services pertain to the whole body of the Church; they manifest it and have effects upon it."[7]

This corporate dimension of liturgy has, by and large, remained an elusive goal in the celebration of marriage. While the communal character of the Eucharist, Christian initiation and even penance has been stressed in the postconciliar reforms, marriage has continued to be seen by many as a family celebration that takes place in a church. Vatican II's strong preference for "communal celebration involving the presence and active participation of the faithful . . . to a celebration that is individual and quasi-private"[8] was not explicitly reiterated in the 1969 *Rite of Marriage*. Catholics who actively participate in Sunday Mass succumb to the social custom of attending weddings as polite, but passive, observers. Encounters with couples who seem uninterested in or even resistant to promoting communal participation in the wedding liturgy have led some clergy and pastoral musicians to declare: "I'll take ten funerals to a wedding anyday!"

So, how does the body of the Church celebrate the matrimonial covenant in which two members of this body become one flesh? How can pastoral ministers help engaged couples to prepare the wedding liturgy so that it is truly a corporate act of worship? The first, and probably most fundamental, step is one that does not involve the engaged couple at all. Instead, it involves the various people who minister in the name of the Church to the engaged: diocesan and parish family life ministers, parish priests and deacons, pastoral musicians, wedding coordinators, and liturgists. In one way or another, all of these people are involved in the Church's pastoral care of the engaged. To be most effective, their pastoral care must have a common vision, and this includes a shared understanding of the communal

---

[6] *The Didascalia of the Apostles,* ch. 13, from Lucien Deiss, *Early Sources of the Liturgy* (Staten Island, N.Y.: Alba House, 1967) 91–92.

[7] *Sacrosanctum concilium,* 26.

[8] Ibid., 27.

character of the wedding liturgy. Just as liturgists and pastoral musicians need to be interested in the unique journey that has brought each engaged couple to the point of marriage, so family life ministers need to see the wedding liturgy as more than the couple's special moment. Without such a shared vision, pastoral ministers will be operating from different assumptions about the priorities in the wedding liturgy, and they will be sending mixed, or even conflicting, messages to the engaged couples with whom they work.[9]

Ritual Considerations

In 1990, the Vatican's Congregation for Divine Worship and the Discipline of the Sacraments published a second edition of the postconciliar marriage rites. In 1996, the U.S. Bishops' Committee on the Liturgy established a task group on adaptations for the U.S. version of this second edition which has been titled *The Order of Celebrating Marriage*. Unlike the current *Rite of Marriage,* this second edition of the marriage rite does refer explicitly to the communal character of the wedding liturgy and presents a couple of options that will come as a surprise to many:

> Marriage is meant to increase and sanctify the people of God and therefore its celebration has a communal character that calls for the participation even of the parish community, at least in the person of some of its members. With due regard for local custom and as occasion suggests, several marriages may be celebrated at the same time or the celebration of the sacrament may take place during the Sunday assembly.[10]

Celebrating several marriages at the same time and celebrating marriage during Sunday Mass are options that are only comprehensible if one understands the wedding liturgy as an action of the whole body of the Church. To those who see marriage primarily or exclusively as "the couple's special day," these options will seem preposterous. It remains to be seen whether these options will appear in the U.S. version of the *Order*

---

[9] An excellent resource to help parish staffs enunciate a common understanding of weddings is Austin Fleming, *Parish Weddings* (Chicago: Liturgy Training Publications, 1987).

[10] *Order of Celebrating Marriage* 28 (Washington, D.C.: International Commission on English in the Liturgy, 1996). The second *editio typica* of the marriage rite was issued by the Apostolic See on March 19, 1990 under the Latin title *Ordo celebrandi Matrimonium.* ICEL issued a draft English translation of this rite in 1996. That same year, the bishops of the United States established a task group on adaptations for the U.S. version of the rite.

of Celebrating Marriage, and, if they do, to what extent they will find acceptance among couples and parish staffs.

Even apart from these options, though, there are practices that enhance the communal character and sacramental significance of the wedding liturgy, just as there are customs that obscure them. What follows is equally pertinent to the current *Rite of Marriage* as it is to the revised *Order of Celebrating Marriage.*

Gathering Rites: Americans, for the most part, are culturally conditioned to approach wedding liturgies as observers. Typically, any attempts to foster a corporate body that will celebrate together are reserved to the reception after the liturgy. If a wedding is going to call on the active participation of all present, then efforts need to be made before the entrance procession even comes down the aisle. The stony silence that often follows the presider's opening greeting, "The Lord be with you," is ample evidence of this. Several practices seem to help, and, in each, bodily presence is more important than words. Together, these practices have helped to overcome the cultural tendency toward passivity at weddings, and create an assembly that is ready to celebrate the wedding liturgy as a corporate body.

(1) Arriving guests are met at the church doors by the bride, the groom and their parents. The hospitality that Abraham and Sarah offered to the three men who came to their tent (Gen 18:1-8) is a wonderful model of the care for others that couples are called to in the prayers of the wedding liturgy.[11] There is perhaps no better way to begin incorporating this virtuous practice in married life than for the couple to offer hospitality to those who have come from near and far to join in the celebration of their marriage. By their personal presence and words of welcome, the bride and groom let arriving guests know how important their presence and participation are. The parents join in this welcome and introduce themselves to guests whom they may not know. Human instinct tells us that such greetings and introductions are important; that's why most wedding receptions begin with a receiving line. This suggestion simply moves the practice to the beginning of the wedding liturgy where it can replace such unhealthy customs as drinking champagne in the limousine before the wedding, pacing nervously in the sacristy, and not allowing the groom to see the bride because of a superstition that, honestly, has no place in a Christian marriage.

---

[11] The *Order of Celebrating Marriage* provides five additional Scripture readings for weddings. One of them, Heb 13:1-4a, 5-6b, alludes to the hospitality of Abraham and Sarah: "Do not neglect to show hospitality to strangers, for by doing that some have entertained angels without knowing it."

(2) Members of the wedding party seat guests together and toward the front of the church. One of the social customs that can be used to great advantage is the expectation that wedding guests are shown to their seats. Male *and* female members of the wedding party (i.e., ushers and bridesmaids) can join in escorting guests to seats toward the front of the church. Saving the first one or two rows for immediate family, subsequent rows are filled on both sides of the aisle as guests arrive. There is no reason to designate a "bride's side" and "groom's side," just as there is no reason to leave rows half empty. Those who escort guests to their seats could introduce them to the people with whom they will be sitting. The aim of seating is to encourage people to form a cohesive assembly, not to separate them into different contingents.

(3) Music prior to the entrance procession serves the action of gathering the assembly. Pastoral musicians have emphasized in recent years the importance of "ritual music" for liturgy. Simply put, "ritual music" is music that serves as a constitutive element of a ritual, as opposed to music that is played at a particular time during the ritual but that has no essential relation to that part of the ritual. Applied to the time before the entrance procession at a wedding liturgy, appropriate "ritual music" would be music that serves the action of gathering the assembly. It is not music that calls attention to itself or that demands attentive listening. It does not overpower the greeting of guests at the church door or the introduction of guests to those with whom they will be sitting.

(4) A cantor leads a brief rehearsal of the music that will be sung by the entire assembly. Participation by the gathered body of the Church at weddings is usually at its lowest when it comes to music. This is partly an expression of the spectator attitude with which many approach weddings; it is also partly a result of the diversity present in most wedding assemblies. At any given wedding, there are some who do not sing because they are not Christian. To sing words of faith without believing them would be hypocrisy. Many others are Christians, but from various faith traditions. Among the Catholics present, different parishes are represented. To promote communal participation, familiarity should be a criterion in the selection of music. A wedding is not the time to debut the parish music minister's latest composition. There are appropriate hymns for weddings that enjoy broad recognition among Christian churches, just as there are settings of responsorial psalms and Mass parts that are well known among Catholics across the United States.

The choice of relatively familiar music is the first step. The second, and just as important, step is a brief rehearsal with the assembly before the entrance procession. Even when they know the music, many Americans are timid about singing in public in the presence of strangers. The greetings and introductions described above can put people more at ease, but a welcoming invitation to sing is usually necessary. The rehearsal need not cover every piece of music in the wedding. As the first words that are addressed to the entire assembly, the rehearsal is primarily a public statement that this wedding is going to be something that this group does *together* as a corporate act of worship.

Entrance Procession: Processions within liturgy, like all liturgical actions, express and form faith. They are not simply a fancy way to get from one place to another. Processions are also one of the more obviously bodily activities of liturgy. Much planning often goes into the exact timing and order of the entrance procession at weddings. For all of that planning, though, few wedding entrance processions in the United States even come close to the procession envisioned by the *Rite of Marriage:* "If there is a procession to the altar, the ministers go first, followed by the priest, and then the bride and the bridegroom. According to local custom, they may be escorted by at least their parents and the two witnesses."[12]

If our actions speak louder than our words, then what does it mean when a bride is escorted down the aisle by her father who then hands her over to her groom? Most women today would resent the implication that they are being "given away" by one man to another man, yet there is still strong emotional attachment to this form of the wedding entrance procession. "Tradition," a wise person once said, "is the living faith of the dead. Traditionalism is the dead faith of the living." The customary American form of the wedding entrance procession seems no longer to reflect what we actually believe about marriage, as Americans and as Catholics. It would be safe to say that this is a case of traditionalism, not tradition.

The *Rite of Marriage* presents bride *and* groom as well as *all* of their parents as essential members of the wedding entrance procession. Members of the wedding party other than the two witnesses (i.e., best man and maid of honor) are not explicitly included, although the rubrics do not specifically exclude them either. This arrangement of the entrance procession was not inserted because of a "feminist agenda" or a bias against fathers of brides. In fact, it represents the usual and traditional form of the wedding entrance processions in many countries. It is, more importantly, a better enfleshment of the Catholic faith concerning marriage. By including both bride and groom, this form of the entrance procession gives bodily expression to the understanding of marriage as a sacrament undertaken by two equal and complementary people. The inclusion of all the parents honors the role of fathers *and* mothers in bringing daughters *and* sons to this

---

[12] *Rite of Marriage,* 20.

point in their lives.[13] Such a wedding entrance procession not only expresses the Catholic faith concerning marriage, it also faithfully shapes the understanding of this sacrament among those who participate in the liturgy.

Positioning of the Ministers: "In the Latin Church, it is ordinarily understood that the spouses, as ministers of Christ's grace, mutually confer upon each other the sacrament of Matrimony by expressing their consent before the Church."[14] While a priest or deacon presides at the wedding liturgy, the couple serves as the minister of the sacrament of marriage. This aspect of Catholic faith is often obscured by the way the couple is positioned during the liturgy. It is almost unheard of that the minister in any other sacramental liturgy would have his or her back to the rest of the assembly during the entire liturgy, yet that practice is still common at weddings. Even when it comes to the exchange of consent that establishes the marital covenant, it is not unusual for the couple to kneel with their backs toward the assembly or for the priest or deacon to visibly obscure the couple by standing directly in front of them.

A few simple changes in the positioning of the couple and the presiding priest or deacon gives more faithful bodily expression to the sacramental reality. If the couple is to be seated in the sanctuary, their seats could be turned to face the assembly, but at a slight diagonal so that they can easily see the lectern and the altar as well. For the exchange of consent, they could remain at these places or come to the front of the altar. The couple may just as easily be seated in the first row with the rest of the assembly and come to the front of the altar after the homily for the marriage rite. During the marriage rite (i.e., introduction, questions, consent, blessing and exchange of rings), the couple faces the assembly so that all may see and hear. The priest or deacon's role as presider and chief witness for the Church may be best served by his standing forward and to the side of the couple or even at the head of the aisle. This suggestion is consistent with the recent notes on the wedding liturgy from the Pontifical Council for the Family: "It will be the duty of whoever presides to make use of the possibilities which the ritual itself offers . . . so as to highlight the role of the ministers of the sacrament who for Christians of the Latin rite are the spouses themselves."[15]

---

[13] Family life ministers have emphasized in recent years the importance of one's "family of origin" in marriage preparation and enrichment. See, for example, Kenneth Mitchell and Herbert Anderson, "You Must Leave Before You Can Cleave: A Family Systems Approach to Premarital Pastoral Work," *Pastoral Psychology* 30 (Winter 1981) 71–88.

[14] *Catechism of the Catholic Church,* 1623.

[15] Pontifical Council for the Family, *Preparation for the Sacrament of Marriage* (1996) 63.

Gathering Song: The *Rite of Marriage* assumes that an entrance song is sung during the entrance procession.[16] While this has worked in some places, instrumental music seems to be the most common accompaniment for the entrance procession. This is probably a result of people's natural desire to watch the entrance procession. In this situation, the use of a "gathering song" is emerging as a way to involve the entire assembly in corporate singing at the beginning of the liturgy. Following the Sign of the Cross and greeting, the presider introduces the gathering song in words such as these: "Gathered to witness the marriage of John and Susan, let us praise the God who has brought them together and who blesses their love by singing 'All Creatures of Our God and King.'" Without an entrance song or a gathering song, the body of the Church will not join in singing until the responsorial psalm. The gathering song is yet another opportunity early in the wedding liturgy to foster "the active participation of those present (which) is to be favored in every way."[17]

Proclamation of Scripture: Postconciliar liturgical documents from the Constitution on the Sacred Liturgy through the Introduction to the second U.S. edition of the *Lectionary for Mass* have consistently affirmed Christ's presence in his word proclaimed at liturgy.[18] Commenting on the ministry of lectors, Aelred Rosser, O.S.B., adds that "the proclamation of the word . . . is far more than a telling, a relating, a recounting; it is God's Word becoming flesh in our midst in order to achieve the purpose for which it was sent—to redeem us in love."[19] Like their counterparts at Sunday Eucharist, lectors at weddings are involved in nothing less than the enfleshment, or embodiment, of God's Word. The selection of lectors for a wedding, then, is more a matter of discernment of gifts than a simple filling of slots on a planning sheet with the names of people who need to be somehow honored or recognized during the marriage festivities. From the list of those who will be at their wedding, couples could be invited to look first for anyone who is a lector at his or her parish, then for individuals who exhibit some of the skills required of lectors: e.g., ease with public speaking, willingness to prepare, sensitivity to the different kinds of biblical literature.

Gifts for the Poor: The *General Instruction of the Roman Missal* speaks of the Preparation of the Gifts during Mass as "the time to receive money or other gifts for the church or the poor."[20] At Sunday Eucharist, the collection

---

[16] *Rite of Marriage,* 20.

[17] Pontifical Council for the Family, *Preparation for the Sacrament of Marriage,* 61.

[18] *Lectionary for Mass: Introduction,* 4.

[19] Aelred Rosser, O.S.B., *Guide for Lectors* (Chicago: Liturgy Training Publications, 1998) 3.

[20] *General Instruction of the Roman Missal,* 49.

of money is standard and the presentation of food or other gifts for the poor is gradually becoming more common. The action of presenting such gifts embodies the gospel value of sharing what God has given us with those who are in need.

At perhaps no other time in life are people as overwhelmed with gifts as couples are at their wedding. Whether it's the duplicate toasters or more placemats than any family could possibly use, many couples receive more gifts than they need. From this bounty, a practice is slowly emerging in which couples share their excess with those in need. In one example, the newly married couple brings forward a basket of food and a box containing the extra toaster or set of placemats for the parish outreach committee or a local shelter during the Preparation of Gifts. In another, cited by Paul Turner, the wedding invitation includes a request that guests bring canned goods for the parish food pantry. "For once," Turner comments, "a couple had it figured out. Marriage implies service to others. Eucharist, even a wedding eucharist, implies gifts for the poor."[21]

Blessing the Couple: The revised *Order of Celebrating Marriage* stresses the importance of the Nuptial Blessing, stating that it "is never omitted."[22] During this "ancient prayer by which the blessing of God is invoked upon the bride and groom,"[23] the priest or deacon extends his hands over the couple. While this gesture is officially reserved to an ordained minister— and, in fact, a lay presider at a wedding is directed to keep hands joined while praying the Nuptial Blessing[24]—some presiders invite members of the assembly to extend their hands toward the couple during the Nuptial Blessing. This allows the assembly to give bodily expression to its prayerful hopes for God's blessing on the couple. The U.S. Bishops' Committee on the Liturgy recommends this communal gesture of blessing for domestic rituals in *Catholic Household Blessings and Prayers*.[25] To avoid any resemblance to a Nazi salute, the gesture should involve *both* hands. Otherwise, this beautiful gesture "could be read improperly, especially if Jews are present (as might be the case at initiation or marriage) or if Eastern European immigrants or people who have had brushes with neo-Nazi racist groups are in the assembly."[26]

---

[21] Paul Turner, "Gifts for the Poor," *Assembly* (September 1998) 34.
[22] *Order of Celebrating Marriage,* 68.
[23] Ibid., 35.
[24] Ibid., 153.
[25] Bishops' Committee on the Liturgy, *Catholic Household Blessings and Prayers* (Washington, D.C.: United States Catholic Conference, 1989). See, for example, the blessings at 221 and 279.
[26] "No Seig Heil," *Liturgy 90* (November/December 1996) 2.

Additional Customs: Throughout the centuries, Christian marriage rites have been influenced by social and cultural customs surrounding marriage. The Constitution on the Sacred Liturgy reiterated the Council of Trent's desire that "praiseworthy customs and ceremonies" in different regions be retained in the celebration of marriage, and went on to state that a local conference of bishops "is free to draw up . . . its own rite, suited to the usages of place and people."[27] Anscar Chupungco, O.S.B., notes that this text "reiterates a long-standing practice of the Roman church to make allowances for the development of local marriage rites," making marriage "for now the only sacramental rite that enjoys such a wide range of options for its *aggiornamento.*"[28] The words and actions of such additional customs and alternative rites provide another layer of meaning for those participating in the wedding liturgy.

Among Hispanics, there is a richly developed set of wedding rituals that complement the basic liturgical structure of the *Rite of Marriage.* One such ritual involves the *arras* which literally means pledge. Originally exchanged by the spouses as a token of their marriage contract, the *arras* eventually "came to symbolize the husband's promise to provide what would be necessary for the sustenance of the home as well as the wife's promise to make sure that what was provided would be used to maximum benefit in the home."[29] Today, the *arras,* which is usually a small cask containing thirteen coins, is being adapted to reflect the reality that many wives, as well as husbands, work outside the home, and that household responsibilities are more and more often shared by husband and wife. Other Hispanic rituals include placing a *lazo* or yoke (often a double-looped rosary) across the shoulders of the couple as a symbol of the marriage union, and placing a portion of the bride's veil on the groom's shoulders to signify the couple's commitment to a chaste and pure marriage. Each of these customs involves a ritual action that embodies and amplifies the sacramental faith enunciated in the liturgical texts.

A popular custom that seems to transcend ethnic boundaries is the lighting of a wedding, or unity, candle. A recent adaptation that some say is of Eastern European origin[30] and that is understandably well promoted by ecclesiastical candle manufacturers, this custom involves the lighting of a

---

[27] Constitution on the Sacred Liturgy, 77.

[28] Anscar Chupungco, O.S.B., *Liturgies of the Future: The Process and Methods of Inculturation* (New York: Paulist Press, 1989) 105.

[29] Instituto de Liturgia Hispana, *Gift and Promise: Customs and Traditions in Hispanic Rites of Marriage* (Portland, Or.: Oregon Catholic Press, 1997) 12.

[30] "The Use of the 'Unity Candle' at Weddings," *Bishops' Committee on the Liturgy Newsletter* (July/August 1991) 26.

single central candle from two smaller side candles representing the bride and groom. Like the *lazo,* this custom usually follows the consent and exchange of rings, and affirms the unity of the bride and groom in marriage. In 1991, the U.S. Bishops' Committee on the Liturgy issued a statement questioning the symbolism of the unity candle and its integration into the liturgy. Responses to a survey by the Bishops' Committee on the Liturgy task group for adaptations to the revised marriage rite indicated strong interest in this practice, with responses evenly divided between those who favor inclusion of the unity candle as an option and those who oppose the practice.[31]

The difference of opinion regarding the unity candle illustrates the various issues that are at stake in a discussion of the body and the wedding liturgy. People who differ about the unity candle nevertheless agree that its popularity is an indication that the Roman marriage rite would benefit from additional ritualization. Part of the problem, as was discussed earlier in this chapter, is a lack of attention to the bodily considerations already present in the *Rite of Marriage.* Beyond that, though, the very structure of the wedding liturgy seems ritually impoverished, especially when viewed against Christian marriage rites throughout the centuries.[32]

On the one hand, the unity candle is an existing, popular practice that could ritually enrich the wedding liturgy by giving expression to the joining of husband and wife. On the other hand, the custom is so often accompanied in practice by excessive explanations that the action is overshadowed by the words. Additionally, there are questions about what is actually embodied in this custom: Does the central candle represent the couple or Christ? Candles in the Roman rite are most commonly used as a symbol of Christ, but if the central candle represents Christ, is it appropriate to light it from the bride and groom's individual candles, or should it rather be burning from the very beginning of the liturgy? If the central candle represents the married couple, then the custom "seems to be at variance with liturgical tradition."[33] If the two individual candles are extinguished after lighting the central candle, does that mean that the bride and groom's indi-

---

[31] "Consultation on *The Order for Celebrating Marriage,*" *Bishops' Committee on the Liturgy Newsletter* (September 1997) 40, and "*Order for Celebrating Marriage* Task Group Survey," *Bishops' Committee on the Liturgy Newsletter* (December 1997) 49–50.

[32] Good historical overviews may be found in Kenneth W. Stevenson, *To Join Together: The Rite of Marriage* (New York: Pueblo Publishing Company, 1987) and German Martinez, *Worship: Wedding to Marriage* (Washington, D.C.: Pastoral Press, 1993).

[33] "The Use of the 'Unity Candles' at Weddings," 26.

vidual lives are "snuffed out" when they marry? These are questions that will need to be resolved if the unity candle is to become an officially recognized option in the revised *Order of Celebrating Marriage*. The issue is not whether the marriage rites of the Roman Catholic Church can admit of additional bodily actions; they can and probably need to. The issue is whether such additional rites "nourish, strengthen, and express"[34] the faith of the body of the Church regarding marriage.

Suggestions for Further Reading

Cooke, Bernard, ed. *Alternative Futures for Worship, Volume 5: Christian Marriage*. Collegeville: The Liturgical Press, 1987.

Covino, Paul, ed. *Celebrating Marriage: Preparing the Wedding Liturgy*. Portland, Or.: Pastoral Press, 1994.

Fleming, Austin, *Parish Weddings*. Chicago: Liturgy Training Publications, 1987.

Instituto de Liturgia Hispana, *Gift and Promise: Customs and Traditions in Hispanic Rites of Marriage*. Portland, Or.: Oregon Catholic Press, 1997.

Martinez, German, *Worship: Wedding to Marriage*. Washington, D.C.: The Pastoral Press, 1993.

Stevenson, Kenneth W., *To Join Together: The Rite of Marriage*. New York: Pueblo Publishing Company, 1987.

[34] *Sacrosanctum concilium*, 59.

From Lauren Artress, *Walking a Sacred Path* (New York: Riverhead Books, 1995) xv.

CHAPTER SEVEN

Walking the Labyrinth:
Recovering a Sacred Tradition

Bruce T. Morrill, S.J., with Leo Keegan

One of the ritual opportunities during the "Liturgy and the Body" conference week at the Institute of Religious Education and Pastoral Ministry[1] was a guided walking of the labyrinth, an intricate geometric art form that was common to the floors of numerous medieval cathedrals and has undergone a fascinating revival over this last decade of the twentieth century in the United States. Leo Keegan, liturgical director for the summer sessions of the Institute, obtained on loan a large canvas labyrinth from an Episcopal church in Illinois, and scores of people walked it during one of the Institute's customary noon hours for worship. On the following day Leo offered a workshop on the labyrinth experience to conference participants. This chapter introduces readers to the history and contemporary practice of the labyrinth by means of an interview format, with Bruce Morrill engaging Leo Keegan in conversation.

Morrill: You were anxious to make the experience of walking the labyrinth available as part of a theological conference on the relationship between liturgy and the body. Why the eagerness and enthusiasm?

Keegan: I first heard of the labyrinth in the 1980s when Sr. Joan Macmillan was taking a labyrinth around the Bay Area, offering prayer experiences and composing music in relation to it. During that time also

---

[1] See Preface.

choreographer Carla DeSola created a dance based on the labyrinth. The big step in its emerging as a contemporary form of spirituality came in the early 1990s at Grace Episcopal Cathedral in San Francisco, where Canon Lauren Artress first made a canvas labyrinth available and then, within next couple of years, oversaw the permanent installation of a wool carpet labyrinth in the cathedral's nave and one of terrazzo stone outside in the courtyard. Artress has created a network that is realizing a rapid spread of labyrinths across the United States, and her beautifully written book, *Walking a Sacred Path: Rediscovering the Labyrinth as a Spiritual Tool* is widely read.[2] The book has been a key source for my own research on the labyrinth, along with the work of Max Oppenheimer and Sig Lonegren.[3]

The pastoral experience that personally convinced me of what a powerful means of transformation and healing the labyrinth can be happened last year when in my capacity as liturgical coordinator for the National Catholic AIDS Conference I used the labyrinth as the ritual form for the memorial service on Saturday evening of the annual meeting. The meeting's theme was "Companions on the Journey," building on the gospel story of the road to Emmaus, and it dawned on me that the labyrinth would be a wonderful form of prayer for the service. I spread a canvas labyrinth on the floor of the Madonna della Strada Chapel at Loyola University of Chicago, and guided the 300 participants into the labyrinth, handing each a lighted candle to walk with the intention of remembering somebody who had died of the disease. More than three hours later, these hundreds of caregivers, ministers and people with HIV or AIDS had completed the circuitous walk, placing their still-burning candles in sandboxes around the perimeter of the labyrinth. The light created a powerful sight, as did the faces, tears, gestures and movement of the people. The connection of the contemporary memorial of the dead and the blight of disease with the ancient ritual form was profoundly significant for these people.

It is that experience that convinced me that I wanted to share this embodied way of prayer and spirituality, of encountering God, of being pilgrims on the way in the company of others, with participants in this conference. When considering the body in relation to liturgy, the labyrinth has proven to be a non-threatening, ancient, cross-cultural form that has a history spanning religious traditions and is so inclusive that it clearly is an archetype.

---

[2] Lauren Artress, *Walking a Sacred Path: Rediscovering the Labyrinth as a Spiritual Tool* (New York: Riverhead Books, 1995).

[3] Sig Lonegren, *Labyrinths: Ancient Myths and Modern Uses,* 2d ed. (Somerset, Great Britain: Gothic Image Publications, 1996).

Morrill: Perhaps this would be the point, then, for you to describe what a labyrinth is.

Keegan: Basically, a labyrinth is a long, meandering path that continuously turns back into and around itself in a circular pattern until it reaches a center, from which the path can be followed back out again. The most ancient and widespread pattern is called a seven-circuit labyrinth, since the turns in its path create seven concentric rings around the center. The Middle Ages, however, saw the development of church labyrinths with eleven circuits circling from the entrance at the perimeter to a rosette-shaped center. In either case, the key distinction generally made between a labyrinth and a maze is that a labyrinth is unicursal, that is, it has only one path from the entry to the center and back. A maze, in contrast, is multicursal, presenting those who enter it with numerous junctures and paths that they must choose among, analyze and solve.[4]

Morrill: So, is it this unicursal, circuiting quality that contributes to the labyrinth being an archetype?

Keegan: Yes, that starts to get at it. What is most important is the design or pattern of the labyrinth overall, the way in which its circular or contained shape represents or elicits a sense of unity and wholeness and, thus, the sacred. But furthermore, the intricate lines of the path, which include the pattern of a cross, convey the sense of journeying, inviting the imagination to reflect on the journey of life as a whole, between birth and death, or on some particular life passage, which often moves through danger to deliverance. In any case, much of the power of the labyrinth lies in its container-like quality, the safety and completeness its perimeter establishes, while nonetheless enchanting the eyes as they survey its pattern. This sense of wholeness and yet journeying or searching is especially pronounced when one approaches a large, walkable labyrinth—at first, just looking at it. I found this to be the case with the canvas labyrinth, based on the pattern of the eleven circuit labyrinth on the cathedral floor in Chartres, which we used both in Chicago and Boston. Even though in the latter case we had to spread it (some thirty feet in diameter) in a very institutional, multi-purpose meeting room, I could recognize that it had an impact on people as they first saw it and then sat around it waiting to begin the walk. The bodily and spiritual impact intensify as you walk on it. You concentrate on the path's turns, and yet you are also often aware of the broader expanse of

---

[4] For an illustrated historical discussion of the multicursal and unicursal paradigms of the labyrinth, see Penelope Reed Doob, *The Idea of the Labyrinth from Classical Antiquity through the Middle Ages* (Ithaca, N.Y.: Cornell University Press, 1990) 39–60.

the labyrinth, of the attraction yet elusiveness of the center, of the distance back to the mouth or entry.

Morrill: Before we consider further the elements of design, as well as the approaches and stages to walking that Chartres-style labyrinth, can you give a brief history of labyrinths, including some places they've been found and their apparent significance?

Keegan: Labyrinths are found in cultures and religious traditions all around the world and have a wide variety of myths, beliefs, and practices associated with them.[5] Egyptians in 2000 B.C.E. built an immense labyrinth as a burial crypt, and centuries later Herodotus gave an enthusiastic written report of it. Other ancient writings mention labyrinths in Crete, Lemnos, and Etruria.[6] In Greek mythology the labyrinth is an inescapable jail; it is the entrance to the underworld in the *Aeneid.*[7] The classical and widespread Cretan labyrinth, with its seven circuits, dates from some four thousand years ago. In Europe, renditions of this pattern carved in rock, inscribed in clay tablets, etched in walls, and cast on coins have been found in various parts of Greece, Crete, Sardinia, Spain, England, and Ireland. In North America, the Hopi people in the Grand Canyon have petroglyphs of the seven-circuit labyrinth, up to eight hundred years old, symbolizing the paths of the heavenly bodies, the womb of Mother Earth, and the passage between lives. Today the Hopi feature the pattern on pottery, jewelry and weavings with the figure of "the Man in the Maze" or "Elder Brother," whose legendary journey to the center procured eternal life. Among island peoples off New Zealand and Australia the labyrinth is a map of the underworld, the soul's way to the afterlife. In China the labyrinth was a time-telling device. For the Celts, knot labyrinths represented life and fate. The largest concentration of classical labyrinths is located along the coasts of Scandinavian countries, where until recent times fishermen would run the circuits symbolically to escape storm winds and evil spirits, ensuring a bountiful catch.

The earliest known Christian labyrinth is on the floor of the fourth-century basilica of Reparatus, Orleansville, Algeria. The ninth-century cathedral of St. Lucca, Italy, has the earliest Christian wall labyrinth, about eighteen inches square, which the visitor entering the cathedral

---

[5] In addition to the works already cited, see Scott Campbell, *Mazes and Labyrinths: The Search for the Center,* 30 min., A Cyclone Production, 1996, videocassette.

[6] See Doob, *The Idea of the Labyrinth,* 18–25.

[7] For a treatment of the labyrinth as a crucial "narrative image" in Virgil's *Aeneid,* wherein conversion from Labyrinthine confusion to comprehension is a central issue, see ibid., 227–53.

could trace with a finger—an exercise for calming the mind.[8] The High Middle Ages, however, was the prosperous European period that witnessed the installation of labyrinths in cathedrals and churches throughout Italy and France. They tended to be located near the threshold so that as the faithful entered the nave, the devil got trapped in the labyrinth, allowing the worshiper to proceed in peace.

Of greater significance during the twelfth and thirteenth centuries, however, was the emergence of the eleven circuit pattern, which achieved a less linear path moving throughout the circle, meandering far less predictably than the classical style, which moves from quadrant to quadrant. As the Holy Land became too dangerous for Christian pilgrims, this new style of labyrinth became a substitute for those vowed to make pilgrimage. Thus it was called the *chemin de Jerusalem*.[9] As a greater act of devotion, some monks would do the labyrinth on their knees. In any event, the one in the cathedral of Chartres (circa 1220) has endured as the most stunningly beautiful example, some forty-two feet in diameter with hundreds of lunar cusps and foils adorning its perimeter. Its serene majesty is enhanced by its relationship to the great rose window that towers behind it on the west wall. The two share the same diameter, as well as a similar rosette pattern for their centers. The labyrinth is situated at a certain distance into the nave such that if you could collapse the west wall onto the nave's floor, the window would almost perfectly align over the labyrinth.[10]

Morrill: Ah, yes. Now we are touching on the remarkable "sacred geometry," to use the phrase Richard Lawlor has promoted in his scholarship,[11] which the medieval architects and master craftsmen employed in designing the Gothic cathedrals. Drawing on some of Plato's philosophical principles and the mathematics of Pythagoras, the medieval builders developed a system of complementary numbers and angles as well as an artful proportionality and placement of various materials and colors (stone, wood, glass) that all together created in the cathedral a uniquely balanced space, a serene environment for body, mind, and soul.

In her book, Artress is particularly helpful in explaining how the lost art of sacred geometry functions within the design of the Chartres labyrinth itself, enabling it to convey a sense of the whole cosmos. In her attempts to

---

[8] See Helmut Jaskolski, *The Labyrinth: Symbol of Fear, Rebirth, and Liberation,* trans. Michael H. Kohn (Boston: Shambhala, 1997) 53–54.

[9] See ibid., 69, 73.

[10] See Doob, *The Idea of the Labyrinth,* 131.

[11] Richard Lawlor, *Sacred Geometry: Philosophy and Practice* (London: Thames and Hudson Ltd., 1982, 1989) 4–25.

replicate the Chartres pattern, Artress learned that one can only situate the center properly, and then all the other elements in relation to it, by first drawing an "invisible" thirteen-point star within the circumference of the entire circle. This star seems to come from the Pythagorean geometry that informs the entire cathedral's design. Artress is convinced that this invisible star—whose number of points harmonizes with a number symbolic both of Christ (twelve plus one) and the annual number of full moons, as well as with the thirteen turns in the labyrinth that point the walker to the center—is crucial to keeping the flow of energy within the labyrinth centered and powerful, affording an integrative experience for those who enter and walk it.[12]

All of which leads us to consider the visible design of the labyrinth and how this promotes through the bodily senses and imagination an experience of deep, clear, intuitive thought and reflection.

Keegan: The Chartres-style labyrinth has eleven circuits or concentric circles leading in to a twelfth circle in the center. This number twelve helps the labyrinth to symbolize the entire cosmos, being the product of three, a number representative of heaven, and four, which represents earth. The opening in the perimeter where one begins the walk is called the *mouth* or *entrance*. When a large group is walking the labyrinth together, I have found that it is important to have a couple of people standing at the mouth, holding the gate, as it were, so that those entering and exiting have some human contact in what can be a powerful liminal moment.

The surface walked on is called the *path* or *circuit*. On the way into the center it takes thirty-four turns, six of which are semi-right angle turns, with the other twenty-eight being 180 degree or "U" turns. The dividers running along and separating the path are called *walls*. Unlike the walls of mazes (think of British hedge mazes, for example), which are too high to see over, causing left-brain confusion, the walls of the labyrinth are low, allowing a contemplative gaze over the expanse of the circuits, the ornamented perimeter, and the center. The walls between the 180 degree turns form *labyrs,* which take the shape of a double-headed ax and seem to be the root of the labyrinth's name.

The *center* or *goal* of the Chartres labyrinth has six petals that comprise a rose, a symbol of the Blessed Virgin Mary, the medieval Rose of Sharon. The rosette, however, can also symbolize the Holy Spirit in the mystical tradition, as well as the six days of creation. The goal or center is really only the mid-point of the labyrinth experience, since one walks back along the same path to exit again at the mouth. The mouth itself breaks an other-

---

[12] See Artress, *Walking a Sacred Path,* 64.

wise continuous border pattern that runs all around the perimeter. This feature, unique to the labyrinth at Chartres, is a series of two-thirds circles called *foils,* 112 in all, divided by a total of 113 points, called *cusps.* The circles are also named *lunations,* for when divided into the four quadrants of the outer circle (representing the seasons of the year), they number twenty-eight and one-half, with twenty-eight cusps. Artress reports that these numbers have led some to conclude that this labyrinth functioned as a calendar, providing a method for tracking the (twenty-eight day) lunar cycles, as well as for determining the date of Easter, a lunar feast.

Morrill: This starts to become a rather complex, heady business!

Keegan: But to allow that to happen is to begin straying from the gift that the labyrinth is for us. While it is fascinating to learn about the visible and invisible features of the medieval eleven circuit labyrinth, or the Chartres one we are using in particular, it is important to realize that this is a situation in which the whole is clearly something more than a summation of all its parts. Attention to the latter, rather, can provide delightful, even profound, insights for people when they reflect on their experiences of meditation on the labyrinth, as well as a consoling connection to earlier religious traditions, for which so many of us modern people are hungering at this point. In the end, however, we do not have definitive historical knowledge of the origins and development of labyrinths, nor precise scientific explanations for how they provide the sense of sacred space that affords the sort of intuitive thought and personal insight, the flow of imagination, and the healing integration of memory, body, and spirit that characterize people's experiences of walking labyrinths today. Hearing about those experiences is really valuable to me.

Morrill: You have touched on a key interest in my own theological work, namely, the function (and for many people, the recovery) of tradition as an essential resource in our lives at this late stage of modernity.[13] While this is anything but a call for a return of blind submission to hegemonic authority (which characterizes the modern distrust of religion), I am convinced of the human value in giving oneself over to the practical wisdom in a tradition. I realize that this is a complex topic, if for no other reason than there

---

[13] For a discussion of the imperiled state of tradition in modernity, see Johann Baptist Metz, *Faith in History and Society: Toward a Practical Fundamental Theology,* trans. David Smith (New York: Crossroad, 1980) 32–48. See also Bruce T. Morrill, "The Struggle for Tradition," *Liturgy and the Moral Self: Humanity at Full Stretch Before God,* eds. E. Byron Anderson and Bruce T. Morrill (Collegeville: The Liturgical Press, 1998) 55–65.

being no one simple, abstract thing called "tradition," let alone the fact that traditions are always developing in contexts. My point here, nonetheless, is to note (and affirm) your own openness to the recovery of this labyrinth tradition as it is coming about today.

Keegan: Walking the Chartres-style labyrinth is the recovery of a mystical tradition. But it also provides people a safe place in a larger tradition, that is, the tradition of walking.

Morrill: Yes, as we're entertaining the notion of tradition, it might be helpful to consider more broadly the role of walking in religious traditions, especially since it is such a stellar example of the interrelatedness of body and spirit in religious practice.

Obviously notable is the role of meditative walking within the various Buddhist traditions that are attracting large numbers of people in Western societies today. Authors in the Theravada tradition of Buddhism describe the value of walking meditation in terms of the way it grounds awareness of the self in the present moment through paying attention to one's breath, the movement of one's legs and feet, and the feeling of their impact with the ground. This fosters wakeful presence in daily life.[14] Vietnamese Zen master Thich Nhat Hanh affirms similar benefits in the monk's practice of "contemplating the body in the body."[15] He encourages walking meditation as an enjoyable exercise meant for finding life in the present moment, and for freeing oneself from getting caught up in one's thought and, thus, the past and the future. Hanh also extols walking meditation in terms of its impact on the planet, arguing that peaceful footprints provide healing to the damage we have inflicted on the earth, as well as contributing to peace and harmony among humanity.[16]

Given our earlier attention to the sacred geometry of the medieval cathedrals and labyrinths, we might also acknowledge the tradition of creating a meditative environment in Japanese gardens. The crafters of such gardens pay careful attention to the terrain to discern the flow of paths that will foster meditative walking, along with purposeful choices in the types of plants and their placement, the course of running water, and the location of

[14] See Joseph Goldstein, *Insight Meditation: The Practice of Freedom* (Boston: Shambhala Publications, 1993) 139; and Jack Kornfield, *A Path With Heart: A Guide Through the Perils and Promises of Spiritual Life* (New York: Bantam Books, 1993) 66–67.

[15] Thich Nhat Hanh, *The Miracle of Mindfulness: A Manual on Meditation,* trans. Mobi Ho, rev. ed. (Boston: Beacon Press, 1975, 1987) 111–14.

[16] Thich Nhat Hahn, *Peace in Every Step: The Path of Mindfulness in Everyday Life,* ed. Arnold Kotler (New York: Bantam Books, 1991) 28–29.

benches. The overall effect of the garden invites those walking it into a space and time set apart for calming the body, clearing and refreshing the mind, and meditatively reflecting. Such a general description can lead our own thought back in the direction of the West, where monastic cloisters are centuries old spaces for walking in meditation and prayer. Placing a rosary in the hands of our imagined monks adds to the affinity of theirs with other traditions of prayerful walking that encourage the mantra-like repetition of prayers, phrases or songs to calm and focus mind, soul, and body.

A final tradition of walking to consider as we return to our contemporary revival of the medieval labyrinth is that of the pilgrimage. Pilgrims consecrate the time of their journey to their relationship with God, expecting to encounter the divine not only at the holy site that is their path's goal or destination, but also along the way of that path, coming and going, leaving something behind or anticipating a new beginning, meeting others or being absorbed in contemplation. As Victor Tuner has so famously demonstrated, the pilgrimage is a liminal experience, affording experiences of wholeness, encounters with the sacred, special interpersonal presence among community members *(communitas),* new intuitions and degrees of self-knowledge, and much more.[17] The walk or journey, nonetheless, follows a path of pre-liminal, liminal, and post-liminal stages, with the first and last stages constituting periods of separation from and reintegration into the usual (profane) commerce of life in society.

Does any of this lend itself to the present way the medieval labyrinth is undergoing a revival as a mystical tradition?

Keegan: Yes, indeed, although you've given me a lot of information to assimilate! Perhaps the best thing to say at the start is that there is no single, prescribed way to walk the labyrinth. The intentions people bring to their particular walk, however, as well as the three-phased pattern the walk derives from the labyrinth's design itself, can have numerous affiliations with aspects of the larger "tradition" of walking you have described. Let me explain, then, the various intentional approaches people might adopt in walking the labyrinth on any given occasion. That can be followed by an exploration of the three phases of walking the labyrinth, which entails a significant form of spirituality.

As the Labyrinth Project has grown from Grace Cathedral across the country, brief introductory literature (usually a single photocopied sheet) with guidelines for walking the labyrinth has developed. The suggested

---

[17] See Victor Turner, *Dramas, Fields, and Metaphors: Symbolic Action in Human Society* (Ithaca, N.Y.: Cornell University Press, 1974) 166–230; *The Ritual Process: Structure and Anti-Structure* (Ithaca, N.Y.: Cornell University Press, 1969) 94–165.

process entails a person's first quieting the mind through breathing and then considering whether one of several approaches or "paths" to the labyrinth seems inviting or right at this moment. "The Path of Image" invites the mind to become aware of and follow an image, memories, or dreams that present themselves in one's imagination. Those attracted to "The Path of Silence" empty their minds of the thoughts, details and distractions of life in the world, in a manner akin to some of the Eastern practices of meditation, in order to open the mind and "heart" and enhance awareness in the moment. In contrast to this, one might desire to walk a "Path of Questioning," seeking the answer to a question. The purpose in this case is not to expect or force an answer but, rather, to explore possibilities or discover insights as one walks the turns and phases of the labyrinth. Finally, on "The Path of Prayer" a person repeatedly recites a traditional prayer, mantra, phrase, line of poetry, biblical verse, or some prayer of one's own making. Lest one reduce these four to prescribed formulas or mutually exclusive methods, it is important to recognize that they are indeed *approaches* to the walk. Much of the beauty and power of the experience lies in the way that the labyrinth's design creates a space that fosters creative imagination, quiets judgmental thinking, and leads one to intuition. So, as the process unfolds for people, they often find themselves moving among various aspects of the various approaches. In fact, this seems to be one of the qualities of the labyrinth as a form of meditation.

Having said this much about the role of intentionality, and thus of the mind, in approaching the labyrinth walk, I want to note a few elements that directly concern the body. The custom is to ask people to remove their shoes before walking, unless that would prove uncomfortable for a given individual. The reason for this is not just to help keep the path, which on the canvas labyrinth is white, clean. Removing shoes connects a person more directly with a sense of the earth, or perhaps a sense of vulnerability in relation to the path, and enables a feeling of groundedness not only in the feet but up through the entire body. As we noted from the Buddhist traditions, this enhances awareness, clears thought, and can give a sense of being firmly and peacefully situated on earth. When watching numerous people walk the labyrinth together I have also been moved by the sound of the feet on the canvas, as well as the footprints left on the surface. I should add that people in wheelchairs are welcomed on and can navigate the labyrinth.

Another piece of advise we give people before entering the labyrinth is that they allow their own bodies to tell them the pace and even the sort of gate that their walking should take. I have been fascinated by the changes that can happen to people's styles of walking in the course of the three phases (which I shall describe presently), as well as the ways at times people are arrested to a stop at some point or need to slow down or speed up. It is obvious that the turns and other features of the labyrinth free up these moments of bodily awareness. Then there is the factor of whether one is walking the labyrinth alone or with a group of people, which makes for different dynamics in bodily movement and thereby in feelings and thoughts. The presence of many people on the circuits requires individuals to decide whether and how they shall pass slower walkers, make eye contact with those they meet, or touch others. In this regard the labyrinth walk becomes metaphorical of people's life-patterns and habits, making people aware of their impatience or empathy, insecurity or anger or affection toward others. Insight, questions, memories, or prayer may ensue.

What makes the labyrinth a singular mystical plan—one that powerfully integrates body, mind, and spirit—is the three-staged meditative process inherent in its fundamental design. As one completes the entire route from the mouth into the center and back out to the mouth again, one passes through the three phases of purgation, illumination, and union. The first stage, walking toward the center, fosters a period of purgation, a process of release and letting go, shedding whatever thoughts or emotions might impede communication with the Holy Mystery. Arrival at the labyrinth's center, which often comes as a surprise due to the path's illogical meandering, begins the stage called illumination. The person rests in the rosette, assuming whatever posture proves comfortable, for as long as the Spirit moves. This is a time for meditation and prayer, for receiving divine wisdom in whatever way it is offered. As one makes the journey back over the same path returning to the mouth, one goes through a phase of union, a process of integrating what has occurred along the way, returning transformed by the experience.

Morrill: You have applied this notion of "transformation" to the labyrinth experience. What does that mean?

Keegan: Well, first, in my overall experience of watching people as they walk the labyrinth, which in itself can be a prayerful, meditative exercise, I have been able to recognize how people clearly experience changes in their self-awareness, in their thoughts and feelings, as they pass through the stages of the walk. I find that people are often more slow or seem ponderous on the way to the center, while they tend to move more quickly as they make their way back. I have even seen people begin to dance or skip along the way, while others, when reaching the mouth, are solemnly reverent. During one of my own walks on the labyrinth I became aware of a great sense of release as I made a certain turn. What a cathartic experience that was for me! It did not have a specific, significant meaning *per se,* but I appreciated the physical relief and release. Whatever intention a person brings to walking the labyrinth, something seems to happen for almost everyone who walks it. It is rare that a person relates having discovered no benefit in walking it.

Morrill: Perhaps we can get more specifically at this notion of transformation by following Artress, who summarizes her analysis of the labyrinth in terms of its being a tool that guides healing, deepens self-knowledge, and empowers creativity. I was interested to note that she identifies these same fruitful outcomes as characteristic of the practice of going on pilgrimage.[18]

Keegan: Yes. Given my work with the National Catholic AIDS Conference, the healing aspect is most prevalent for me. We used the labyrinth on that night of the annual meeting as a memorial tool, and it remains one of the most powerful ritual experiences I have had. We began the liturgy with a litany of saints, and then people were guided to enter the labyrinth in intervals, while the rest of community kept watch all around. We used Taize chanting and instrumental music at intervals, but there were also ample periods of silence, with just the sound of feet on the path. But there were also sobs and tears. The profound grief of this group came to symbolic expression, but in the process came healing and strength as well. People would hold each other as they walked along, or some embraced or held hands for intervals.

In walking there is a triggering of memories. Although this is true in general, we do not know exactly why. The experience of memories is certainly different for each person, but energy is certainly released or opened, often through tears. In this case of this particular service, we had constructed a communal ritual of memory which heightened the common experience of loss and grief. Afterwards people described their physical and emotional relief. I do not think that necessarily would have happened in a typical prayer service. The walking had everything to do with this corporate prayer experience.

Morrill: It strikes me that this was a different form of corporate or communal walking than the types that are generally known to us, such as protest marches or liturgical processions. Even while there would be a strong affinity with vigil marches done with candles, I think that the circular, self-contained space of the labyrinth, as well as all the "sacred geometry" in its design, provided a unique means for that community to share their memories and relate themselves as individuals and a corporate body to the journey of life across ages and generations.

---

[18] See Artress, *Walking a Sacred Path,* 20–21, 35.

Keegan: At Grace Cathedral every other week they hold a service called "Taize on the Labyrinth." Using the chants helps people to move out of their everyday experience and have an experience with God. Priests are available for private conversations or counseling, and various forms of healing take place in people's lives. We should keep in mind here the symbolic association and function of the circle in relation to rituals of healing across cultures.

Morrill: In that regard it is notable that hospitals and medical centers around the United States are beginning to install labyrinths, where they are walked not only by patients but also family members in waiting rooms.[19] For the latter, engaging in the walk provides a sort of mental relaxation that watching television or reading cannot.

Keegan: Walking the labyrinth is soothing and consoling and, therefore for many people, prayerful. I think that one of the key reasons for this is the medieval labyrinth's meandering design. A person must decide to let go of control for a while if he or she is going to walk the labyrinth. The fundamental decision is to enter onto the one path,[20] but once one is on it, one does not know exactly where it is going. It takes *you* for a walk. If you think about it, we live today in a society in which simply taking a meandering walk is unknown to the vast majority of people. People are always rushing by car to their next commitments or walking purposefully for shopping in malls and stores. I believe that part of the phenomenon of the labyrinth's rapid growth in popularity has to do with this need to meander. We need to meander in order to let our creative thoughts, imaginations, and intuitions flow. In the labyrinth's space, people's thought patterns can move between vacating and creating and remembering. It's a move out of the busy and linear time of *chronos* and into the generative or recreative moment of *kairos*.

Morrill: I am glad that you raise the issue of time because it has been tacitly pervading much of our discussion. We can recognize that walking the labyrinth creates a unique time unto itself, one in which we become more aware of ourselves, God, and others, not only in the present moment but through the exercise of memory. There is a kind of interplay between present, past and future that seems to be encouraged by the way in which the circuits within the circle as a whole create a metaphor of the journey in life. The participant brings his or her own intentionality or commitment to

---

[19] See Laurie Goodstein, "Reviving Labyrinths, Paths to Inner Peace," *The New York Times,* May 10, 1998, 1, 16.

[20] See Doob, *The Idea of the Labyrinth,* 50–51.

this sacred time, giving oneself over to this time for its own sake, much the way one does when going on retreat or—for the wider purpose of this present book—when entering into liturgy.

Keegan: I would add two points. First, I find that being aware of the ancient origins of the labyrinth gives me a profound sense of connection to the generations of women and men who have walked it over the centuries—an embodied practice of the communion of saints. Second, concerning the time on the labyrinth itself, I have found that whether one is walking it alone or amidst a group, the path has its own time. You cannot rush it, if you are being really present to it. People's experience of these aspects of walking the labyrinth, it seems to me, cannot help but contribute to their being more deeply engaged in the time created within the liturgical celebrations of the rites of the Church.

Morrill: The question of time is not unrelated to that of space. I think that the Chartres-style labyrinth, especially when we consider it in its original context of the entire sacred geometry of the medieval cathedral, also reminds us of the careful attention that needs to be paid to the architectural spaces we create for liturgy. We need spaces that welcome worshippers into an environment and time for intuitive thinking and creative engagement, with symbol, word and silence each contributing to people's encounter with God through their senses and spirits. Attention to liturgical environment can help current efforts to correct the excessively didactic quality that has developed in much of the liturgy in the United States over the past few decades.

Keegan: There certainly has developed over recent years a heightened desire among people to integrate body and soul in their spirituality, and for this reason the New Age communities have proven attractive to many. The church community has profound resources among its traditions but has been slower to answer to this due, it seems to me, to its history of ambivalence or even fear of embodiment or sexuality.[21] Yet we know that this challenge of integrating body and soul must be faced if we want to continue to engage people in liturgy and other practices of prayer. It is a further step for realizing the council's call for full, conscious, and active participation in the liturgy. A struggle and definite tension persists for the body, whether in the corporate, communal setting or within individuals, as believers seek to live the faith. It is precisely the tension that we who are

---

[21] For a concise history and analysis of the treatment of the body in Christian theology and practice, see Mary Timothy Prokes, *Toward a Theology of the Body* (Grand Rapids: William B. Eerdmans Publishing, 1996) 1–23.

ritual makers in the Church need to be attuned to if we wish to be of service in creating significant ritual experiences for people in community.

Suggestions for Further Reading

Artress, Lauren. *Walking a Sacred Path: Rediscovering the Labyrinth as a Spiritual Tool*. New York: Riverhead Books, 1995.

Doob, Penelope Reed. *The Idea of the Labyrinth from Classical Antiquity through the Middle Ages*. Ithaca, N.Y.: Cornell University Press, 1990.

Jaskolski, Helmut. *The Labyrinth: Symbol of Fear, Rebirth, and Liberation*. Trans. Michael H. Kohn. Boston: Shambhala Press, 1997.

Lonegren, Sig. *Labyrinths: Ancient Myths and Modern Uses*. 2nd. Ed. Somerset, Great Britain: Gothic Image Publications, 1996.

CHAPTER EIGHT

The Physicality of Worship

James L. Empereur, S.J.
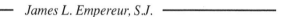

The Recovery of the Body in Spirituality

It is a truism to say that worship must be embodied. To deny such a principle would be tantamount to rendering an incarnational religion incredible. It would be to go against a universally accepted understanding of symbolism as something which cannot be replaced by words no matter how clear they are. It would be the equivalent to a kind of liturgical Cartesianism: I think, therefore, I worship. Almost every liturgical expert affirms the importance of embodied ritual as a balance to present rationalizing tendencies found in the revision of the official rites.

Such disembodying tendencies are understandable from several points of view, whether in reaction to excessive rubricism of the past, fear of subjective emotionalism, distortions on the level of popular piety, and most important of all, an abiding uncomfortableness with our own body.[1] John Baldovin argues, "What we do communally with our bodies at worship makes a great deal of difference when it comes to one of the main reasons for public worship in the first place—namely, to express who we are as community in the presence of the living God."[2]

---

[1] Michael Mansfield has created a body prayer called "Releasing Ritual Embarrassment," *Original Blessing: A Creation Spirituality Network Newsletter,* 1:1 (March–April 1998). The newsletter comes from CSN 2141 Broadway, Oakland, Calif. 94612.

[2] John Baldovin, "An Embodied Eucharistic Prayer," *The Posture of the Assembly During the Eucharistic Prayer,* eds. John K. Leonard and Nathan D. Mitchell (Chicago: Liturgy Training Publications, 1994) 3.

The very nature of liturgy as a ritual action has demanded and still demands bodily posture and movement. Certain gestures have been present in the liturgy throughout its history, some being more emphasized at times than others. We know that earlier Christians stood with their hands upraised (the "orans" position), that people knelt in adoration, and of course, people sat. There is an ongoing discussion about the appropriateness of gesture in the liturgy.[3] Our views about bodily gesture also reveal our theological slant. There is a growing consensus that there is a need to restore to the liturgy some of the choreography that it once possessed. Baldovin concludes his chapter with these words, "What we do with our bodies at worship has far more effect on our experience than we usually think. The question before the church today is not *whether* our liturgical prayer will be embodied but *how*."[4]

The question of the physicality of our worship is appropriately asked today as we are far more aware of the anthropology of the scriptures, namely, a non-dualistic one which does not see our "I," our psychological center, as having or possessing a body which can be used by the mind. Rather, our bodies are our whole selves in so far as they manifest our realities in this world of the senses. Bodily gestures and movements are necessary if our personal realities are not to remain hidden. Such gestures symbolize our interior reality. Unless we as individuals and the church as a local community make gestures we nor the church can exist in full. Something of transcendence will never reach visibility if our worshipping communities are not physical in their expression.[5]

Various church documents emphasize the importance of the nonverbal in the liturgy, *Environment and Art in Catholic Worship* being one of the most explicit. "It is critically important for the church to reemphasize a more total approach to the human person by opening up and developing the non-rational elements of the liturgical celebration: the concerns for feelings of conversion, support, joy, repentance, trust, love,

---

[3] See the various articles in the Leonard and Mitchell volume.

[4] Ibid., 11. A simple example of the "how" is found in Richard McCarron, "Gesture and the Eucharistic Prayer," *The Eucharistic Prayer at Sunday Mass* (Chicago: Liturgy Training Publications, 1997) 111.

[5] For an examination of the sociological and religious significance of standing and kneeling as well as the ritual postures in the context of meals and the meal ministry of Jesus and what this means for the postures during the Eucharistic Prayer, see *The Posture of the Assembly*. For the reasons why the present American practice of kneeling during the Eucharistic Prayer and during Communion is an anomaly and contradiction of both liturgical texts and official documentation, see Frank Quinn, O.P. "Posture and Prayer" *Worship* 72:1 (January 1998) 67–78.

memory, movement, gesture, wonder."[6] Number 56 of this same document says:

> The liturgy of the church has been rich in a tradition of ritual movement and gestures. These actions, subtly, yet really contribute to an environment which can foster prayer or which can distract from prayer. When the gestures are done in common, they contribute to the unity of the worshipping assembly. Gestures which are broad and full in both a visual and tactile sense, support the entire symbolic ritual. When the gesture is done by the presiding minster, they can either engage the entire assembly and bring them into an even greater unity, or if done poorly they can isolate.

Why is it that our liturgies lack vitality? We cannot blame, as we did in the past, excessive rubricism and an unintelligible language. The real reason is that *we* are without vitality. As living people our state of mind is to move, "to be on the move." We have lost touch with our own energies. If we are not in touch (often literally) with ourselves, we will have little contact with our fellow men and women. It is tragic that at a time when we are in such need of touch for our experiences being interrelated, touch itself has become so problematic. Still, in small ways, we are rediscovering the physicality of our relationships. There has been a reemphasis on the centrality of the laying on of hands in the liturgical rites. Although, gesture and movement are still only begrudgingly accepted, if at all. We need to explore the symbols of the tradition which call forth our bodiliness if the truth of our bodies is to emerge.[7] Joan Chodorow says, "In discussing ritual, Jung said that the gesture is the most archaic manifestation of culture and spiritual life. In the beginning was the symbolic gesture, not the word."[8]

E. Whitmont notes that "our emotions and problems are not merely in souls. They are also in our bodies."[9] And Jung says:

> If we can reconcile ourselves to the mysterious truth that the spirit is the life of the body seen from within, and the body is the outward manifestation of the life of the spirit—the two being really one—then we can

---

[6] *Environment and Art in Catholic Worship* (Chicago: Liturgy Training Publications, 1993) no. 35.

[7] *Liturgical Ministry* 6 (Spring 1997) is devoted to movement and gesture. Five authors involved in liturgical dance in some form have articles on different aspects of liturgical movement. They are Carla DeSola, Robert F. VerEecke, Gloria Weyman, Thomas A. Kane, and Patricia Curran.

[8] Joan Chodorow, "Dance/Movement and Body Experience in Analysis," *Jungian Analysis,* ed. by Murray Stein (Shambala 1984) 193.

[9] E. Whitmont, "Body Experience and Psychological Awareness," *Quadrant* 12 (1972) 5–16.

understand why the striving to transcend the present level of consciousness must give the body its due.[10]

Janet Barratt has developed a program of what she calls Christian exercise. These exercises are not simply calisthenics, that is, increasing our self-consciousness to strengthen muscle or lose weight, but rather, to enhance self-awareness so that wholeness may be achieved. "A true spirituality is where there is an integration . . . in our minds, bodies and spirits."[11] Her program is based on the presupposition that some of her exercises have symbolic meaning which facilitates meditation on certain Christian truths. Where such symbolism is lacking, specifically Christian music can supply the content and direction of the meditation. The idea is that exercise can lead to an integrated lifestyle based on Christ centeredness.[12]

Many books and manuals on spirituality and psychological growth are filled with myths, symbols and metaphors, but they ignore the sensory-motor experience. On the other hand, many spiritual exercises involve movement which is done in a ritualized way. As Steven Shafarman has demonstrated, however, there exist possibilities for a more integrated way. This begins with the recognition that regardless of one's beliefs or practices, each person is a bodily being; thus, the way one breathes or sits or walks is fundamental to one's way toward the infinite or eternal. "The word, *grace,* describes both spiritual attainment and aesthetically satisfying movement . . . awareness heals and reawakens one's sense of wholeness, of being fully alive, which is the essence of spiritual experience."[13]

The Wisdom of the Body

The reasons for the dualism in our culture which affects the way we try to divide our human experience into different categories has been rehearsed many times. That we divide ourselves in such a way so as to leave much of our physicality behind when we pray and worship has also been repeatedly pointed out. If we are to have embodied liturgical experiences we need to re-examine and re-affirm that physicality is basic. Such is the point of the writings of Phil Porter along with his dance colleague, Cyn-

[10] C. Jung, "The Spiritual Problem of Modern Man," *Collected Works* 10, 2nd ed. (Princeton: Princeton University Press, 1970) 93–94.

[11] Janet Barrett, *Glorify God in Your Body* (Cambridge: Grove Books Limited, 1989) no. 28, 20.

[12] Ibid., 21.

[13] Steven Shafarman, *Awareness Heals: The Feldenkrais Method for Dynamic Health,* (New York: Addison-Wesley Publishing Co., Inc., 1997) 184.

thia Winton-Henry: "We do not *have* bodies, we *are* bodies. All of our experience is physical. Feelings are physical, spirituality is physical, thinking is physical. How would we know that anything was going on if there weren't some sort of experience that was noticeable to us."[14]

One of the reasons for this continual split in our experience is that if we cannot describe nor understand our experience, we cannot really own it.[15] Despite the fact that we have many experiences which we cannot rationally explain, such as being in love or liking one food more than others, we rest uneasy with the more intuitive part of our lives.[16]

This means that we are often suspicious of the information coming through our bodies. The information or wisdom of the body is less articulate than that conveyed through academic means. This is one reason why so many people do not trust their own religious experiences. Since religious experience is not only physical but frequently mysterious, we need outside religious authorities to confirm it. As a result we become dependent on others for what is actually our own. "We are not taught to differentiate between information that is our own and that which has been drilled into us."[17]

The path to wholeness and integration begins by acknowledging the many splits in our lives. When we do not admit what is going on deep inside, when we hide that from others, we are creating a split in our experience. When we assume different roles, when we wear different masks and when we live according to false images, when we assume different personalities at home, at work, and at play, we create a split in our experience. There are seemingly endless ways in which our lives are split, such as between what we want and the wants of the groups to which we belong. There are racial and ethnic splits. There are religious and denominational splits. There are political and economic splits. There are societal and organizational splits. We have personal splits within ourselves such as the desire to be alone and the desire to be with others.[18]

By overcoming the splits in our lives we introduce the paradox that the spiritual is physical. There is much in our lives which cannot be described as purely materialistic, such as our concerns about our friendships, loyalties to families, the sanctity of life, our health care, the quality of life in our neighborhood. They are concerns and sources of information which

---

[14] Phil Porter and Cynthia Winton-Henry, *Having It All* (Oakland, Calif.: WING IT! Press, 1997) 17.

[15] See Phil Porter and Cynthia Winton-Henry, *Body and Soul: Excursions in the Realm of Physicality and Spirituality* (Oakland, Calif.: WING IT! Press, 1993).

[16] Porter and Winton-Henry, *Having It All,* 21.

[17] Ibid., 32.

[18] See ibid., 43–44.

belong to our spirit. But it is also true that these issues are woven into the very tissues of our bodies. And so they cannot be addressed in only spiritual ways.[19] In the words of Phil Porter:

> We believe that "spirit" is a physical experience. Even though it may seem to be larger than us, or outside of us, we would not be able to recognize or identify spiritual experience unless there were something going on in our bodies. This means that body and spirit are not separate at all, but are actually completely intertwined if not separable. We need our bodies to have spirit.[20]

To heal the splits in our lives we must recognize how physical experience creates spirit for us. For the Christian this would be a physical experience of grace leading to a fuller and more abundant life. Porter speaks of this grace in non-religious terms as the opposite of stress. When we recognize these healing moments we have body knowledge. When we enrich these lives through these experiences we have body wisdom. He is speaking of "graced" moments in human life where life becomes more expansive, communication with others is fuller, and the effects are long-term. He admits that this could be grace in the religious sense.[21]

Through body wisdom we can expand our experience of our physicality. Our bodies do not stop at our skin. We know that is the case when we experience someone standing too close to us, when we react to people moving around us, when we respond kinesthetically to dancers, swimmers, and runners, when we feel connected to people who are far away. Such a larger view is necessary for any integration of body and spirit to take place.[22]

Because of this larger physicality our special practices must be understood as physical. "They are about being in your body, not escaping it."[23] Sacramental worship will deepen if we are more into our bodies. To change our lives, to be more involved in sacramental living, means changing our physical activity. This enlarged experience of physicality means that the liturgy is not just a place that I visit from time to time. And growth in sacramental life requires practice. Thus the need to be physical. True conversion is a bodily experience. Because liturgical prayer is physical, it is also communal. An enlarged experience of physicality will help ground our own experiences in the experience of community. My larger world

---

[19] See ibid., 64–65.
[20] Ibid., 69–70.
[21] See ibid., 72–75.
[22] See ibid., 78–79.
[23] Ibid., 84.

connects with the larger world of the other worshippers.[24] As body speaks to body in worship, the liturgical assembly is born. This experiencing of life as a whole is the way in which we enter into the mystery of the liturgy. We need not understand everything conceptually when we have a more wholistic experience. The liturgical assembly is ideally where all are on the same journey to wholeness. Phil Porter puts it this way:

> The path toward claiming our own body wisdom is not just a journey deeper into individualism, it also leads us toward the wisdom of the corporate body. Each of us carries just a portion of the truth. It is also in the community that wisdom resides. We are inextricably linked to each other at the most basic physical level.[25]

He and Cynthia Winton-Henry then further note:

> What is currently referred to as being "in denial" may be this kind of split. There may be evidence in our experience of a certain reality that we aren't presently able to face. An admission to ourselves about this reality is a way of healing this kind of split, even if we are unable to express it to someone else.[26]

Several things go on in the body at the same time. We cannot focus on them all simultaneously. But because we receive this variety of information, we experience contradictory messages. Since the intellect is meant for analysis and division, we find ourselves split by such multiple experiences. To receive any experience as part of a whole, that is, to receive it physically, bodily, is to avoid such fragmentation. When we say "I am my body" we mean that even seemingly non-physical activities such as thinking and feeling are physical. Our very experience of God is physical. It is not correct to say that *I have feelings* because feelings as feelings are found in the tissues of the body. All of our body-based spiritual practices, such as breathing, chanting, and sitting, presuppose this unity of body and spirit. "To practice wholeness is to affirm the marvelous complexity of our physical experience: body, mind, and spirit are one, great complicated tapestry."[27] We need not categorize our experiences before we have them. We need not analyze love before being in love.

In therapeutic work it is helpful to distinguish thought from feeling and both of them from bodily sensations. In fact all are physical experiences

---

[24] See ibid., 118.

[25] Phil Porter with Cindy Winton-Henry, *The Wisdom of the Body: The Interplay Philosophy and Technique* (Oakland, Calif.: WING IT! Press, 1995) 7.

[26] Ibid., 20.

[27] Ibid., 28.

but we are so unused to claiming what is going on in our bodies that we need to separate what in fact is a whole experience. But once we know how to move from physical experience to our spiritual dimension, we are on our way to integration. Our sixth sense, our kinesthetic sense, makes it possible to gain body wisdom.[28]

The really significant thing we gain from our body wisdom is our authentic feelings, the information coming to me from the outside world and coming from within. We match our experiences with others because some are almost impossible to articulate. How does one describe "embarrassment" or "loneliness"? Yet these are experiences we share with others. Being in touch with our experiences we will not too readily presume that others are having identical experiences. During the liturgy there are manifold ways in which people are experiencing community. Does our experience of the body of Christ in assembly come from our body knowledge or from the internalized information of preachers and teachers? We are not taught to distinguish the two because we have not been taught to claim the authority of our own experiences. Some of our body information is buried so deep that we must do something to bring it to the surface through practices. A good liturgy so engages the body and the imagination that this happens. In that sense the liturgy becomes a form of spiritual discipline.

Sometimes the liturgy is described as a kind of play. Play as a form of our physicality is essential to our wholeness. Work has been raised to such an ideal that it is difficult to call people to a playful attitude. We are used to receiving data from the outside world. But when I play I change that direction. When I play I work with my own inner resources. Phil Porter says, "The 'stuff' of play is my own. It is not imposed from the outside. Play relies on, elicits, and processes my inner data. I bring my own resources to the task and in the process they are transformed, strengthened, and expanded."[29]

Liturgy as play means each person in the assembly is valued for who they are. Rigid conformity is not the value. Cooperation is meant to enhance celebration. Those who know how to play can live in the present, be lost in the celebration, and let themselves be caught up in the ritual. They can be more present to others in the liturgy.

Bodily Sacramental Awareness

In place of bodily sacramentality we could also speak of "physical sacramentality." As we have seen in the discussion thus far, a theology of the

---

[28] See ibid., 38.
[29] Ibid., 85.

body and an exploration of bodies at worship will only be credible to the degree that they integrate our physical realities. This means that in the liturgy the body of flesh, blood, and bones is less an object than it is an event. Bodily exercises release the many levels of energy which must be integrated into the person. With our attention directed outward in worship we often do not occupy our bodies. It is not enough to pay attention to our bodies. They must be avenues of exchange between the inner and the outer, the material and the spiritual, ourselves and humanity. The question is: What needs to take place in the body for it to become a liturgical event? This is done through bodily awareness, which heightens, enhances, and intensifies our sacramental awareness.

First, a word about the meaning of "awareness" as it is being used here. To be and act in an embodied way we must first be aware of our physical experience. We must pay attention to our physicality, to its uniqueness, its connection with other physical bodies, and the specific needs and requirements of each body. In that way we give voice and tongue to our bodies. It is our awareness of our bodies which will make them speak sacramentally. I especially appreciate what Steven Shafarman says about awareness:

> Awareness . . . involves consciousness plus knowledge. To know what we are doing and learn, we need to be aware. Awareness links self and environment, inner experience with outer world, enabling us to be here, now, whole. . . . When we clearly understand awareness as involving knowledge and relating oneself to one's environment, the term "self-awareness" becomes redundant. . . . Awareness . . . is like the light of the sun. You can see yourself and feel the warmth of the sun on your back while simultaneously looking out toward the horizon.[30]

What I do in the remainder of this chapter is to concentrate on various parts of the body and certain sacramental principles to show how awareness of the body assists in the awareness of our sacramentality. I make suggestions for some specific movement exercises for each section of the body. I rely on a number of approaches to body work. My practices are a combination of movements from t'ai chi,[31] Breema body method,[32] the

---

[30] Shafarman, *Awareness Heals,* 196, 199.

[31] I recommend these two books by Sophia Delza, *T'ai-Chi Ch'uan: Body and Mind in Harmony* (Albany, N.Y.: SUNY, 1985), and *The T'ai-Chi Chu'an Experience: Reflections and Perceptions on Body-Mind Harmony* (Albany, N.Y.: SUNY, 1996).

[32] John Schreiber, *Touching the Mountain* (Oakland, Calif.: California Health Publications, 1989).

Feldenkrais method,[33] and the chakra system.[34] None are followed slavishly or even consistently. Nor is it necessary for the practitioner to follow the exercises according to these various methods. They are provided merely as examples. Some one who has some depth of understanding about the relationship of the body and the liturgy, the body and the sacramentality of creation could well construct their own exercises.

Level One of Awareness

We begin with foundational sacramental awareness. Our very beings are based in the physical world. For this reason the various sacraments are also physical signs. Our humanity means that we are part of nature. It is no surprise, then, that so many of our signs are drawn from nature. We naturally seek to know the meaning of the world around us. Christian sacramentality presupposes the larger sacramentality of the world. Our basic sacramentality is so profound that it is deeper than gender differences, than being male or female. Liturgy transcends gender differences and barriers by reaching deeply into that world where we are all united. To belong to a sacramental world presupposes belonging to the natural world, for here our sense of purpose is based. Celebrating our sacramentality implies giving thanks for belonging to the physical world.

This sacramental awareness is connected to an awareness of our feet, legs, the base of the spine and the rectum.[35] The exercises I recommend for this section of the body are to help people pay attention to how they feel *in* their bodies and how they feel *about* their bodies. I suggest exercises which stress breathing especially in the pelvic area, those that have the spine make contact with the floor, those that stretch the legs, those that help reestablish our connectedness and rooting to the earth, especially balancing exercises.[36]

---

[33] In addition to Shafarman's *Awareness Heals,* I suggest Moshe Feldenkrais's own book, *Awareness Through Movement* (San Francisco: Harper, 1977).

[34] See the various exercises provided by Anodea Judith and Selene Vega, *The Sevenfold Journey: Reclaiming Mind, Body and Spirit Through the Chakras* (Freedom, Calif.: The Crossing Press, 1993) 46–65. See also Naomi Ozaniec, *The Elements of the Chakras* (Shaftesbury: Element Books Limited, 1996). I also make some reference to Caroline Myss, *Anatomy of the Spirit: The Seven Stages of Power and Healing* (New York: Three Rivers Press, 1996) 70–72, 79.

[35] The body parts referred to at each level of awareness are the usual ones connected with the seven chakras.

[36] An excellent exercise for working on balance is "Elegant Walking" in *Awareness Heals.*

The purpose of exercises on these parts of the body is to help us feel more rooted, more stable, and more securely grounded. But mere physical exercises are not enough. They must be accompanied by or supplemented with the use of the imagination. I recommend various visualization practices, whether already constructed or newly made.[37]

Many people are familiar with the Feldenkrais method, t'ai chi ch'uan, and the chakra system. Material on these three is easy to obtain. One other form of body work which may be less familiar is the already mentioned Breema method. It requires some introduction. The value of Breema practices is that they are easy to do and can be done alone. These ancient exercises are found in *Touching the Mountain: The Self-Breema Handbook: Ancient Exercises for the Modern World*. The author, John Schreiber, says this about the method:

> The most immediate aim and result of Self-Breema exercises is to support and balance the flow of energy in the body. This takes place, to a great extent, through what we know as the acupuncture meridians. These meridians are a set of 14 channels connecting the hundreds of acupuncture points identified by Oriental medicine with each other and the internal organs of the body. Blockage in the flow of energy along these meridians and imbalance between nurturing 'yin' energy and stimulating 'yang' energy are held by Oriental medicine to be the principal causes of tension, weakness, and other disease-precipitating conditions in the body.[38]

For this first level of sacramental awareness I would recommend three Breema exercises entitled: Circling the Knee, Tilling the Soil, and Giving to the Earth. Circling the Knee nurtures the knees and stretches the supporting muscles and ligaments. It involves placing one foot under the knee of the other leg, which is extended. Hands are place on top of and beneath the knee as the torso circles clockwise and counter clockwise.[39] The purpose of Tilling the Soil is to move excess energy from the upper part of our

---

[37] For a visualization which complements the exercises on these parts of the body, see Ozaniec, *The Elements of the Chakras,* 49–50.

[38] Schreiber, *Touching the Mountain,* 16. The name, Breema, comes from a Kurdish village in Breemava in the mountains that separate Iran from Afghanistan. This village of farmers and shepherds remained insulated from the history of the two countries on either side of it. As the people of this village struggled to exist in a hostile environment, they developed a form of body work based on their daily work and their closeness to nature. Although the Breema exercises are meant for health improvement and maintenance, I have found them very useful for becoming more aware of our bodies as a way of moving toward sacramental awareness. I was first taught this method by Dr. John Schreiber.

[39] For fuller details, see ibid., 77–81.

bodies towards the feet. This more equal distribution of energy aids the grounding process. This exercise involves a soft pounding on the heels.[40] Giving to the Earth which is similar to t'ai chi is "so named because it takes excess energy from the mind and brings it down to the Earth (body), and also because it increases one's connection with the Earth."[41] What effectively happens in the exercise is the lowering of one's center of gravity to the abdominal and pelvic area, which plants the feet firmly on the ground and gives strength and solidity to one's legs. This is a balancing, brushing, and bending exercise.[42]

Level Two of Awareness

At this level we become more aware of sexuality's connection to spirituality. The spirituality articulated by the sacraments is an embodied one, including the sexual dimension. Once we see how sexual union can be sacramental, we can grasp how the union with God expressed in the sacraments presupposes the union with each other in the assembly. Just as sexual energy can be transformed into other activity, so the energy released by the sacraments can be transformed into service in the Church and the world. Also, at this level we become more conscious of the life flowing beneath our external activities. The same is true of the sacraments. Sacramental life is more than ministerial practice. There is a deeper life.

To achieve this awareness we must focus in our practices on the genitals, hips, lower back, bladder, and large intestine. The human goal here is to promote a sense of well being, self-confidence, pleasure, relaxation, and fluidity.[43]

Exercises here would include opening the pelvic area through rocking back and forth and from side to side, as well as spreading the legs. There are a number of ways in which we tilt the pelvis forward and backward as well as from side to side. A good one is to move freely from side to side, circling and swaying with the hips.[44] Many of the Feldenkrais exercises which involve turning and twisting the pelvic area would be very useful for working at this level of awareness.[45] Self-Breema offers an exercise for breaking up the energy in the pelvis and making it available throughout

---

[40] Ibid., 148–51, give the full instructions.

[41] Ibid., 153.

[42] See ibid., 154–57.

[43] There are many excellent exercises for all the parts of the body in Ozaniec, *The Elements of Chakras.*

[44] For detailed instructions, see Judith and Vega, *The Sevenfold Journey,* 90–104.

[45] These exercises are scattered throughout Shafarman, *Awareness Heals.* See in particular chapter 5, "Effortless Sitting."

the body. It is called Grinding the Wheat. It involves rotating the hips and brushing with the hands down from the kidneys.[46] Another Breema exercise, Harvesting the Resin, involves leaning down into the legs, rhythmically bending forward and then straightening the torso. It increases flexibility in the lower back and hips.[47]

The Third Level of Awareness

The more we achieve a sense of strength regarding ourselves as persons, the more our sacramental identity will strengthen our own personhood in terms of others. Sacraments are public actions and if we wish for them to have apostolic implications, then we must be aware of our ability to project ordinary human energy into the world. Physical exercise helps us to accomplish this by creating a release of our feelings, energies, needs, and drives. In this way the ritual of the sacrament can become a free and neutral place for the expression of feelings. The ritual validates these feelings. With growing awareness at this level we awaken personally by seeing the body from within. Then our participation in the sacraments will become celebrations of personal integration, in particular, the overcoming of dualism, the splits in our lives. All ritual contains an ideal way of being and acting. Sacraments celebrate not only who we are but what we can become. This will not be if we do not have a sense of self-affirmation and self-esteem promoted through our physical movements.

The parts of the body where we bring our awareness at this level are the digestive system, liver, spleen, stomach, abdomen, small intestine, gall bladder, kidneys, pancreas, middle spine, and adrenal glands. The purpose of these exercises is to increase our personal vitality, strengthen our will, and deal with our feelings of joy and anger.

At this level of awareness we need movement that affects the whole body. The idea is to bring attention to the solar plexus and then move out from there to other areas of the body. These exercises affect the muscle groups which support this area of the body. One practice would be making gestures that move out from the solar plexus. Walking is one movement to help us recognize the way we move. The idea is to sense the different levels of energy as we walk and move.[48] Some of the turning, twisting exercises of Feldenkrais can be used.[49] They are designed so that we experience what is going on in the whole body as the back or pelvis rotates. The

---

[46] See Schreiber, *Touching the Mountain,* 71–75.

[47] See ibid., 97–101.

[48] See Judith and Vega, *The Sevenfold Journey,* 132–43.

[49] See Shafarman, *Awareness Heals,* 55 ff.

Breema exercise called Hulling the Walnut involves circling the hands on the hips from the sacrum and tailbone to the hip sockets. The body leans backwards and forwards while the hands move down the legs, the hands circle the knees, and then brush down from the kidneys.[50]

The Fourth Level of Awareness

The call to Christian love is basic. That is why unconditional and compassionate love is the goal of Christian liturgy. That is also why the nurturing, caring, supportive community plays a role in the spiritual life. The liturgical assembly is called to be the same. To be filled with the love of God leads to spiritual transformation. Sacramental transformation stresses the ability to give and receive, the power of mutuality and the love and care for another which presupposes a true love of the self. At this level we become aware of the healing power of touch. The sacraments use touch as part of the sacramental healing process. The most basic sacramental gesture is the imposition of hands. Such a gesture speaks of sacramental transformation. Our human transformation makes it possible for us to appreciate the symbolic nature of reality which moves us beyond the literal. Such an awareness is indispensable for understanding the metaphorical character of the liturgy.

Bodily awareness is achieved here primarily by attention to our breathing, both abdominal and thoracic. This automatically involves the lungs and diaphragm. Awareness here also extends to the heart, breast, arms, hands, and ribs. The hope is that such awareness will assist the person to achieve further balance and because the heart is involved, that compassion and acceptance of others will follow.

Much of the movement connected with this level of awareness is opening up the shoulders, opening up the heart, and stimulating the heart area. Various forms of stretches are helpful, as are different ways of opening and expanding the chest. Breathing techniques are central here. Not only is correct breathing more difficult than we think, but also the kind of breathing which brings awareness to this part of the body is very important. Some partner work here is recommended. For instance, as one person kneels, placing the hands on the floor, another person from behind applies pressure with the hands on the back of the kneeling person while directing the breath to that person. Any practices which expand the ribcage are recommended here.[51] Breathing is an essential part of Feldenkrais' approach to awareness.[52] Two appropriate Breema exercises are Gushing Spring and

[50] See Schreiber, *Touching the Mountain,* 108–11.
[51] See Judith and Vega, *The Sevenfold Journey,* 167–78.
[52] See Shafarman, *Awareness Heals,* especially "Lesson One: Bending and Breathing."

Touching the Mountain. In Gushing Spring the person alternately taps the sternum with the fingertips while hopping from foot to foot. In Touching the Mountain the person, while breathing, touches the abdomen and slides the hands over the heart and chest to the head and down again to the abdomen and sides.[53]

The Fifth Level of Awareness

At this level we become aware of the physicality of human actions which we do not always describe as physical, such as singing and reading. We need to realize the physical nature of our proclamation in the liturgy, that this call to decision to surrender oneself to God is not simply a spiritual reality.[54] The response to the word of God is the power of discrimination, that is, of discernment. To discern is to discover how to remove all negativity from our lives. We become more aware of the need to be fully honest in our human communication. Upon this is based the authenticity of our liturgical proclamation. We are aware of the power of silence. We know that the word of God cannot be effectively proclaimed and received without this prayerful silence. As we are increasingly aware of listening, speaking, and singing we also appreciate the mantra quality of words. There is a mantra feature to many of our liturgical words such as "amen," "alleluia," and "hosanna." Perhaps most important of all, we become attuned to our inner hearing, our inner listening. For the liturgy to be engaging there must be an inner proclamation correlative to the outer proclamation.

The parts of the body of which we must be more aware here are the neck, throat, trachea, mouth, teeth, gums, and esophagus. The purpose of these exercises is achieve greater clarity in our communication, more awareness of our bodily resonance, and a sense of our intuitive abilities.

At this level we are concerned with the rhythms in life. Such rhythms are necessary for communication. "All life is rhythmic, from the beating of one's heart, to the diurnal cycle of days and nights, to the vibration of the brain waves and nerve impulses. When these vibrations enter into a state of harmony among themselves, there is a profound sense of connectedness, deepening, and expansion that we can experience."[55] Physical exercises here would be such things as rolling the neck and shoulders, vocal

---

[53] See Schreiber, *Touching the Mountain,* 88–89 and 104–05.

[54] This point is explored further by Bruce Morrill and Andrea Goodrich in their chapter, "Liturgical Music: Bodies Proclaiming and Responding to the Word of God," below.

[55] See Judith and Vega, *The Sevenfold Journey,* 202.

warm-ups, moving to music, and improvised dance.[56] As already noted, many of the Feldenkrais exercises ask the person to experience what they are feeling in their neck and head and to compare that with what is going on in the rest of the body.[57]

Two Breema exercises I would recommend here are Creating Flow and Fire Posture. The first one, which involves movement of the neck and head, is meant to increase the blood flow and energy to the head. The second one, involving movement that resembles flames shooting up suddenly, is meant to create clarity in the person through attention and coordination.[58]

The Sixth Level of Awareness

At this level our attention moves to experiencing the sacred on our spiritual paths. And in our sacramental life we see the sacraments as the doors to the sacred. At this level we make more use of our imaginations in paying attention, in being more aware. The life and creativity of the liturgical experience dwells in the human imagination. Through the imaginative process we can experience the overcoming of the dualisms in our lives. Liturgy at its best is a holistic celebration of the union we find in our selves and our union with God. The imagination is also the place where the past, present, and future can be brought together. Only when we have such an experience can we truly understand the anamnestic quality of the liturgy. Awareness here gives us an experience of the deeper self. This, then, allows us to see into the depths of the sacramental experience.

Bodily awareness here is both direct, such as is the case with the eyes and ears and nose, while the experience of our brain and nervous system is more indirect. The goal here is familiarity with our imaginations and our ability not only to see with the eyes but also to see more than meets the eye.

At this level the practices may seem to be less obviously physical, although they are so. Meditation would be an important practice here. One of the purposes of meditation at this level would be to recognize patterns.

> Patterns reveal the underlying order of things. Through the understanding of a pattern we can predict what the next piece of the puzzle might be. Seeing is about recognition, or the process of re-cognizing or re-knowing. . . . To really "look" we need to let go of our preconceived patterns and see freshly, taking in new details and being open to the perception of new patterns. This requires practices that help clean the mind of old patterns and images, such as meditation.[59]

[56] For more detail, see ibid., 206–08.
[57] See Shafarman, *Awareness Heals,* chapter 3, "Leaning and Lifting."
[58] See Schreiber, *Touching the Mountain,* 135–45.
[59] See Judith and Vega, *The Sevenfold Journey,* 226.

Practices such as dream work, which allows us to get into our unconscious world, are appropriate at this a time. The task is to clear our minds of the images provided by the outside world, such as television, advertisements, and the movies, so that we can see ourselves more accurately.

Most of the Feldenkrais's practices include some movement of the eyes. A person who cannot do the movements can gain benefit by doing them in one's imagination. Two Breema exercises which are useful here are Erasing the Page and Palming the Eyes. The first is a series of simple movements of the hands over the face and the crown of the head, with the intention of releasing tension in the facial muscles and eyes. It also intends to break up mental tension. The second exercise involves rubbing the palms together until they are warm and then placing them over the eyes, with the purpose of releasing tension as is the case with the previous exercise.[60]

The Seventh Level of Awareness

This level deals holistically with reality. Awareness brings a sense of what is really real. The sacraments communicate a reality. But it is not this world only, but the world beyond which makes up reality. The liturgy itself speaks of being a reflection of the heavenly liturgy. When arriving at this point we see clearly the importance of wisdom and understanding in the spiritual life. Liturgy itself then becomes a form of spiritual direction and a place of insight. We become increasingly aware of our life in the present moment. Sacramental celebrations always celebrate the present faith of people. Finally, we reach the awareness that the purpose of life is union with God and the liturgy is there to accomplish that.

The areas of bodily awareness here are the skin and the skeletal system. In fact, the whole body is the object of our attention at this level. The goal of exercises at this level is to achieve real understanding, real spiritual wisdom.

We can make use of any of the forms of body exercise to achieve these goals. It could be t'ai chi or Sufi dancing. The authors of *Sevenfold Journey* see the purpose of movement at this level this way: "The fundamental premise is that our body is the most basic tool we have to work towards higher consciousness. It provides a means of practice that uses all our physical and mental resources towards the goal of transcendence. This does not mean that we leave the body behind, but rather that our consciousness can expand beyond the narrow confines of the body, that we are not limited to the body."[61] Some do this by practicing yoga. Others prefer something like movement meditation. The latter allows the body to dance

[60] Schreiber, *Touching the Mountain,* 124–27 and 172–73.
[61] Judith and Vega, *The Sevenfold Journey,* 262–63.

in whatever way it wants. The body itself determines the structure of the dance.

There is one Breema exercise which seems appropriate here. It is called Chasing the Arrow. One makes the movements of stringing a bow and then shooting an arrow. It involves jumping forward and backward and ends with laying the imaginary arrow at one's feet. It requires the full participation of the body and is meant to create vitality and joyful feelings.[62]

The Spirituality of the Body

All that I have written thus far can be summarized thus: The physicality of worship requires a spirituality of the body. The spirituality of the body is a spirituality of openness to life which is characterized by prayer, service and sharing with others. Spiritual body work, such as the exercises detailed above, is never a matter of mere maintenance. It is a journey toward completion. But we are so often subverted by our unconscious complexes which speak in the languages of fear, resentment, defeat, and failure. Doubt and self-depreciation slow the pilgrimage to wholeness. Often the experience of our bodies will resemble that of the disciples on the way to Emmaus. We do not recognize the stranger who is traveling with us on our painful and disappointing road. But as the disciples could say after the breaking of the bread, so often we can say after the breaking open of our personalities, both spiritual and physical: "Did we not feel our hearts on fire?"

The spirituality of the body requires the entry of the whole person into a way of life in which the seductions of the past are left behind in favor of service to others. Body work which is engaged in primarily for self-indulgence will leave us anchored in the past. Thus, the sacramentality of bodily movement is not something which is primarily good for the physical reality of the person, although it is that. It is a strengthening of the inner self whereby a person becomes responsive to serve God in their actions of service to others.

One of the fruits of a spiritual approach to the body is that it facilitates an unobstructed vision. We are often distracted, if not actually blinded, by the material and psychological debris which is around us. We will remain blind as long as we substitute selfish, individualistic endeavors for our true sight. Our view of reality is often distorted by the narrowness of our normal way of viewing reality. But narrowness of vision should not be confused with being single-minded. The latter is the quality of the person who

---

[62] See Schreiber, *Touching the Mountain,* 91–95.

is devoted completely to service of others and whose devotion springs from the totality of the person. This is the fully integrated person who can be defined as someone who when touched by another responds with full self and who in touching the other brings all the elements of the inner and physical life into play. This is the person of spiritual vision, made more glorious because it is accompanied by an enhanced psychic awareness brought about by greater contact with the physical body. This person challenges us all to the full realization of our personalities so that we can see (perhaps, for the first time) where we are going and can joyfully cooperate in the process. In other words, spiritual sight matches the gift of physical sight, and the whole body sees.

Suggestions for Further Reading

Delza, Sophia. *T'ai-chi Ch'uan: Body and Mind in Harmony*. New York: State University of New York Press, 1985.

Delza, Sophia. *The T'ai-Chi Chu'an Experience: Reflections and Perceptions on Body-Mind Harmony*. New York: State University of New York Press, 1996.

Judith, Anodea and Selene Vega. *The Sevenfold Journey: Reclaiming Mind, Body and Spirit Through the Chakras*. Freedom, Calif.: The Crossing Press, 1993.

Myss, Caroline. *Anatomy of the Spirit: The Seven Stages of Power and Healing*. New York: Three Rivers Press, 1996.

Ozaniec, Naomi. *The Elements of the Chakras*. Shaftesbury: Element Books, 1996.

Schreiber, John. *Touching the Mountain*. Oakland, Calif.: California Health Publications, 1989.

Shafarman, Steven. *Awareness Heals: The Feldenkrais Method for Dynamic Health*. New York: Addison-Wesley Publishing, 1997.

CHAPTER NINE

Liturgical Music: Bodies Proclaiming and Responding to the Word of God

Bruce T. Morrill, S.J., with Andrea Goodrich

Pastoral Prelude

The significance of music to the irreducibly bodily nature of Christian liturgy cannot be underestimated. The validity of this statement is readily evident in the practical, pastoral scene of the post-Vatican II Church in the United States. In Roman Catholic parishes that are sizable (and "clergy rich") enough to offer several masses on the Lord's Day, a common pastoral pattern has emerged whereby the presence or absence of music for each liturgy, as well as the "style" of music at each, is established. One still finds in some of these parishes that the earliest Mass on Sunday has no ritual music and that a number of those who attend that liturgy have made known their desire that there be none.

The decision to participate in a Lord's Day liturgy devoid of song is an intentional act concerning the "acoustical space"[1] of the worship being offered; it has no small impact upon the spatial, bodily, and temporal qualities of the liturgy—e.g., its pace and rhythm, the extent to which the participants do or do not share in the action together, and (often of no small concern) the overall length of the service. For these sorts of reasons many parishioners either seek out or avoid such an early morning Mass.

---

[1] For a treatment of this concept, based on the work of Walter Ong, see Edward Foley, "Toward a Sound Theology," *Studia Liturgica,* 23:2 (1993) 127–28.

They may well have several other options from which to choose, including a children's (or "family") Mass, liturgies exclusively featuring either "contemporary" or "traditional/classical" music (but both meeting the preferences of adults), or one engaging the musical tastes of teenagers and young adults. Ethnic identity, to which music provides an integral contribution, may also define one or more liturgies in today's parish, such that there is a Latino or Hispanic Mass, or one for Vietnamese or other communities from Southeast Asia or the Pacific.

The important point to note about these parochial situations is that people (lay and ordained alike) often express strong preferences for or against these musically varied liturgies. In their *Ten-Year Report,* The Milwaukee Symposia for Church Composers accurately signal a pastoral danger in this regard, observing that "the various forms of musical leadership that emerge during particular Sunday assemblies" can "express and create divisions within a community at the very heart of its identity."[2] The fact that people react strongly to various genres of music in liturgy, to the extent that some make it known that they would *never* attend a certain type of Mass, indicates that questions concerning the role of music in liturgy not only are matters of taste but also entail judgments touching on people's values. These judgments, far from being simply rational, that is, based on abstract conceptual ideas, entail our corporality, the traditional, social, and natural dimensions of our bodiliness.[3] Some people appreciate the use of the pipe organ, strophic hymns, or Gregorian chant because these provide them a sense of participating in tradition. Others might reject these musical forms for that very reason, while positively valuing ritual music that resonates with music in contemporary culture. People's natural bodies also respond to the rhythm, harmony, and tempo of a particular musical composition, as well as to the qualities of vibration, volume and tone produced by a specific instrument. At the extremes, some people cannot tolerate the sound of the pipe organ, just as others get a headache from hearing electric guitar and drums.

That pastoral staffs in many parishes have taken so seriously questions concerning whether and what kinds of music to incorporate into their Sunday liturgies indicates their engagement with the central but also most challenging mandate (both theoretically and practically) of Vatican II's Constitution on the Sacred Liturgy: "the restoration and promotion" of the

---

[2] *The Milwaukee Symposia for Church Composers: A Ten Year Report* (Chicago: Liturgy Training Publications, 1992) no. 22.

[3] Here we draw upon Louis-Marie Chauvet's theory of corporality, as rehearsed in the introductory chapter of this present book.

people's "full, conscious, and active participation in liturgical celebrations which is demanded by the very nature of the liturgy"—and this as the "right and obligation" of *all* believers "by reason of their baptism."[4] Among the various arts, the council placed "sacred music" in highest esteem, arguing that "it forms a necessary and integral part of the solemn liturgy" because of its ability to enhance both words and ritual actions, "whether making prayer more pleasing, promoting unity of minds, or conferring greater solemnity upon the sacred rites."[5]

Taken together, these assertions of the council provide ready analysis for why some people in American parishes resist the use of music while far more others have made the types and quality of liturgical music a major criterion in choosing among Sunday Masses. In all cases, what is at stake is people's understanding of and degree of commitment to the reform and renewal of the liturgy. Insofar as various polls and surveys continuously find the majority of Roman Catholics in the United States supportive of the liturgical reform, we should not be surprised to find the majority committed to participating in Sunday Masses robust with music, even if many critically desire an improvement in the quality thereof. On the other hand, the small minority who prefer the early morning "musicless" Mass would seem to be seeking a continuation of the pre-Vatican II "low Mass," attending the ritual performed by the priest, widely scattered throughout the pews, and largely silent or only muffled in their speaking of the prayers at varied paces.

Recent Scholarly Movement

If the close relationship between post-Vatican II developments in liturgical music and active involvement (or not) in the Mass of Paul VI has been evident in the practical field, the topic has been no less vital in theoretical circles as well. The rhetoric of official ecclesiastical statements concerning church music has set the agenda for inquiries of liturgical theologians into the nature and function of music in liturgy. In 1903, Pius X asserted music's "integral part" in the liturgy, a point made all the more provocative by Vatican II's wedding of the word "necessary" to "integral" when declaring music's liturgical function.[6] Subsequent documents by the U. S. Bishops

---

[4] *Sacrosanctum concilium,* no. 14. In *Vatican Council II: The Conciliar and Post Conciliar Documents,* vol. 1, rev. ed., ed. Austin Flannery (Grand Rapids: Eerdmans, 1992).

[5] *Sacrosanctum concilium,* no. 112.

[6] Ibid. For critical commentary on this point, see Foley, "Toward a Sound Theology," 121, 137.

Conference, published in 1972 and 1982, have taken as axiomatic the notion that music is integral to liturgy.[7] It is this repeated but unelaborated
insistence on the integral role of music in liturgy that has led certain theologians to inquire as to why and how this is the case. A necessarily brief review of recent contributors to this conversation will point toward the need
for closer consideration of the bodily nature of musical activity.

Edward Foley has sought to establish the integral role of music in Christian worship by moving from a sort of phenomenological analysis of the experience of sound, through an argument for not only the compatible but
enhancing relationship between music and ritual *("The 'Why' of Ritual
Music"*[8]*),* to a proposal that Christian ritual music is best understood as
sacramental in nature, insofar as the concept of sacrament has been broad-
ened since Vatican II to include all aspects of the Church's public acts of
worship. In the process, Foley concentrates on such experiential qualities of
sound as its impermanence, intangibility, and ability to engage people "personally." He finds these experiential categories eminently supportive of the
Judeo-Christian belief in a personal, relational God who communicates
through the historically perceivable but elusive sound-act of the word. Thus,
music uniquely contributes to the sacramental process of divine revelation.

Although he does not adopt the terminology of sacrament, Don Saliers
likewise draws on the depth and breadth of twentieth century philosophical reflection on signs and symbolic language in order to assert that "the
liturgy is intrinsically musical."[9] By "musical" here Saliers means the way
in which all human speech in the liturgy, even that which is spoken or
read, is extended through such musical qualities as rhythm, pitch, intensity
and tone to shape a unique acoustical milieu for those engaged in worship.
Saliers and Foley were both major contributors to the Milwaukee Symposia for Church Composers, whose 1992 report, not surprisingly, establishes music's integral role in liturgy in terms of its being a "unique
language of faith" and having "sacramental power . . . rooted in the nature of sound," its "raw material."[10] In a move that prevents misunder-
standing just what is being claimed when music is said to be integral to
liturgy, the document speaks of the "inherently lyrical" quality of Chris-

[7] See *Music in Catholic Worship* (Washington, D.C.: United States Catholic Conference, 1972; rev. 1983) no. 23; and *Liturgical Music Today* (Washington, D.C.:
United States Catholic Conference, 1982) no. 5.

[8] Foley, "Toward a Sound Theology," 130.

[9] Don E. Saliers, *Worship as Theology: Foretaste of Glory Divine* (Nashville:
Abingdon Press, 1994) 160–61. See also his earlier essay, "The Integrity of Sung
Prayer," *Worship* 55 (July 1981) 290–303.

[10] *The Milwaukee Symposia for Church Composers,* nos. 10, 13.

tian worship, which is to say that "the liturgy flourishes in a heightened auditory environment," that "blurs" the boundaries "between what we consider music and nonmusic" and provides beautiful and vital "sonic elements" that "inspire and engage believers in prayer."[11]

More recently, Judith Marie Kubicki,[12] while drawing on the work of Foley and Saliers (among others), has found that the questions of why and how music is integral to worship have still not been adequately addressed. Kubicki also turns to the symbolic nature of music, relying heavily on the thought of Louis-Marie Chauvet (among several other philosophers and theologians). What Kubicki notes in Chauvet is a more extensive theory of the bodily character of symbolism and symbolic exchange, which she finds pertinent "for a theory of music as ritual symbol since music-making, more than any other artistic enterprise, involves the body in an intimate and integral way."[13] Kubicki, however, still does not pursue *how* music does this in and among human bodies. She concentrates, rather, on the debate concerning whether music is expressive or evocative of emotion (the *cognitive* agenda set by Suzanne Langer[14]) and, like Foley, concludes with the promise of music's aptitude for serving the communicative process of divine revelation.

Helpful and learned as these attempts have been, we find that these liturgical theologians' theoretical efforts to support the practical implementation of the musical/lyrical dimension of Christian liturgy do indeed invite further efforts at exploration. Perhaps the good inclinations of Foley and Kubicki to focus upon the theoretical principles that might establish the integral role of music in Christian worship are nonetheless limited by an excessive isolation of this question of "why" from the more pragmatic issues of "how." The "how" at issue here, however, is not a question of the techniques of liturgical music *per se* but, far more fundamentally, the question of how we human beings breathe, sense vibrations as sounds (hear), and produce sounds of our own (including music). This is to return to Foley's first consideration, namely, the experience of sound, but from a different angle and, therefore, with recourse to different resources.

Our primary concern is with the physiological process of sensing and producing sound and music, as well as with the spiritual and mental role of *intention* in these bodily processes. We shall avail ourselves of research being done in the burgeoning field of sound healing and music therapy.

[11] Ibid., backnote 3.

[12] Judith Marie Kubicki, "The Role of Music as Ritual Symbol in Roman Catholic Liturgy," *Worship* 69:5 (September 1995) 427–46.

[13] Ibid., 431.

[14] See ibid., 436–40.

Our theoretical approach, then, shifts from language-based theories of symbol to work being done in the area of health and integrative healing of body, mind, and spirit. Lest one judge such an approach too quickly as following a latest fad or trend only tenuously related to Christian tradition, we remind the reader at the outset that the connection between Spirit (breath[15]) and Word not only pervades the Bible but also lies at the origins of trinitarian reflection.[16] In addition, we must remember that the discursive work of teaching was only one major characteristic of Jesus' ministry, one which functioned in a complementary fashion with his work as a healer.[17] Our own contribution to the questions of why and how music is so integral to Christian worship, therefore, presume this background of scripture and tradition, wherein are revealed divine plans of creation and redemption that fundamentally include designs for bodily wholeness and the integral healing of body, mind, and spirit.

Scientific and Therapeutic Research on
Sound and the Human Voice and Ear

The Church's recognition of the unique and privileged manner whereby the word of God in sacred Scripture comes to life in the liturgy through the pattern of proclamation and response, as well as the integral role of music in that process, can find its basis not only in the social-cultural and traditional dynamics of ritual performance but also in the physical or natural processes whereby human bodies produce, receive, and share sound. There is a difference in reading a text silently or even aloud to oneself and proclaiming it through speech and song in the social context (time and space) of a liturgical assembly. The difference lies most fundamentally in the body, in the production and reception of the vibrations within and among

[15] Systematic Theologian Donald Gelpi, in an effort to avoid the dichotomy of matter and spirit, refers to the third person of the Trinity as Holy Breath, arguing that "breath" more aptly translates the Hebrew *ruah*. See Donald L. Gelpi, *God Breathes: The Spirit in the World* (Wilmington, Del.: Michael Glazier, 1988).

[16] See George T. Montague, *The Holy Spirit: Growth of a Biblical Tradition* (New York: Paulist Press, 1976) 45–68; Bernard J. Lee, *Jesus and the Metaphors of God: The Christs of the New Testament* (New York: Paulist Press, 1993) 80–122; Yves Congar, *The Word and the Spirit,* trans. David Smith (London/San Francisco: Geoffrey Chapman/Harper & Row, 1986) 9–20; and Jürgen Moltmann, *The Spirit of Life: A Universal Affirmation* (Minneapolis: Fortress Press, 1992) 39–77.

[17] For an overview of the significance of teaching and healing in Jesus' mission, written with a view to sacramental liturgy, see Bernard Cooke, *Sacraments and Sacramentality,* rev. ed. (Mystic, Conn.: Twenty-Third Publications, 1994) 168–78.

the bodies of worship. The words of worship are not conveyed among the participants or, for that matter, offered to God by means of some sort of mental telepathy but, rather, through the soundings of bodies. The point here is to recognize that the transformative impact of proclamation and response upon the faithful occurs not only on the cognitive level of ideas conveyed but down to the very cellular level of vibrations in the body.[18] The pattern and quality of vibration is integral to the health and sense of well-being in persons, impacting moods, forming disposition, and fostering habits and memories that shape the outlook and ethical action of persons.

The physiological activity that provides the basis for human listening, as well as all forms of human vocalization, is vibration. Ongoing research in anatomy, neurophysiology, and therapeutic treatment has led to an increasing appreciation of the ear's vital role in the balanced, healthy integrated activity of the human brain with the entire body, as well as the special relationship between the ear and the voice. A pioneer in this field has been the French physician and auditory neurophysiologist Alfred A. Tomatis, whose unorthodox approaches to the structure and function of the human ear and its relationship to body, mind, and spirit have realized such theoretical and therapeutic breakthroughs as to garner him not only critical scientific acclaim but also several French cultural awards.[19] Most notable for our present study is Tomatis's demonstration that the ear and the human organs that produce vocalization comprise the same "neurological loop," whereby changes in the activity and receptivity of one directly appear in the functioning of the other.[20]

Over the course of some fifty years Tomatis has created what has been described as "a new paradigm of the ear's development" by taking into account not only the ear's auditory function but also its role in the vestibular system.[21] Thus, in addition to processing sound and integrating it in speech, the ear regulates the body's sense of the vertical and horizontal, contributing

---

[18] See Don G. Campbell, *The Mozart Effect: Tapping the Power of Music to Heal the Body, Strengthen the Mind, and Unlock the Creative Spirit* (New York: Avon Books, 1997) 158.

[19] See Bradford S. Weeks, M.D., "The Physician, the Ear and Sacred Music," *Music: Physician for Times to Come,* ed. Don Campbell (Wheaton, Ill.: Quest Books, 1991) 42.

[20] Tim Wilson, "Chant: The Healing Power of Voice and Ear," An interview with Alfred Tomatis, M.D. with commentary, *Music: Physician for Times to Come,* ed. Don Campbell (Wheaton, Ill.: Quest Books, 1991) 11. In his commentary, Wilson reports that The French Academies of Science and Medicine officially acknowledged Tomatis by naming this physiological phenomenon for him. The scope of Tomatis's therapeutic impact in the field of neurology is attested by the fact that there are over two hundred Tomatis Centers internationally. See Campbell, *The Mozart Effect,* 52.

[21] Campbell, *The Mozart Effect,* 52.

to motor coordination. Moreover, through the medulla (or brainstem) the auditory nerve connects the ear with all of the body's muscles, with the vagus nerve connecting the inner ear with all the major organs. The ear's vestibular function thereby influences ocular, labial, and other facial muscles, effecting such activities as seeing and eating. Research suggests that the interaction between auditory vibrations in the eardrum and parasympathetic nerves throughout the body result in the control and regulation of— to name just some of the major organs—the larynx, heart, lungs, bladder, kidneys, and stomach.[22] Tomatis has studied the evolution of the ear from the jellyfish through human beings, finding that the ear enables the entire body's receptivity to vibrations (from whatever source) and provides the key to the development of vertical posture in humans.

The theoretical force, as well as practical implications, of his work Tomatis encapsulates in a startling saying: "And so we've come to realize that the skin is only a piece of differentiated ear, and not the other way around!"[23] This reverses the conventional idea that ear tissue is derived from skin cells; on the contrary, the sensory cells throughout the body evolved from the tissue that produces the cortical cells of the ear. The ear functions, to speak metaphorically, as the gateway of stimulation or "charge" to the brain.[24] It is on this basis that Tomatis has been able to realize success in treating a wide range of human maladies through regulating the frequency, range, and rhythms of sound applied to the ear. Also crucial to the therapy, and thus to his theory, is the subject's posture, the proper form of which is a function of verticality: "What the ancients knew was that once one reaches perfect auditory posture, the body reaches out and literally incorporates all the sound that comes from outside . . . . It is impossible to arrive at good language without verticality, or to stimulate the brain to full consciousness."[25]

On the basis of his integrated theories of the cochlear and vestibular functions of the human ear Tomatis is credited with first recognizing the important distinction between hearing and listening.[26] In dealing with patients who have auditory problems, Tomatis tests not only the ear's physical

---

[22] See ibid., 53.

[23] Wilson, "Chant," 17. For the full reference for the main article in which Tomatis reports his research on this point, as well further bibliography of Tomatis's writings, see Weeks, "The Physician, the Ear and Sacred Music," 45, 54.

[24] Tomatis explains: "It is thanks to the ear that external stimuli are able to charge the cortical battery. I say electrical because the only way we know of measuring the brain's activity is through an electroencephalogram, which gives an electrical answer. But of course it's not electricity that's inside." Wilson, "Chant," 17.

[25] Ibid., 16.

[26] See Weeks, "The Physician, the Ear and Sacred Music," 44.

capabilities but also the extent to which the patient is utilizing their potential. Listening is an active exercise that includes the practice of one's will power, while hearing is the less rigorous process whereby the body and ear receive a panoply of vibrations, only some of which are distinguished as sounds. The human experience of sound is precisely a human production. While we conventionally consider sounds as existing outside of ourselves, strictly speaking, what exist are vibrations. It is our own bodies and minds which engage vibrations in such a way that we *listen* to them as sounds. This is why people who are deaf can listen to and produce music; they are able to sense reverberations in their bones, skin, and organs, picking up the rhythms and pulses and actively processing them as music.[27]

In the process of what sound researchers and therapists call "entrainment," the entire body engages in the process of listening. One's breathing and heartbeat enter into a synchrony with the more powerful pace, rhythm, and pulse of the vibrations in music, with the ear translating these impulses to the brain, thereby effecting one's consciousness as well.[28] As Don Campbell explains, the principle of entrainment is the key toward *some* understanding of why music helps with healing. In many indigenous cultures, entrainment by music sets the trance-like condition for healing to be practiced, and since ancient times music has been used in sacred ceremonies to transform people's consciousness.[29]

One further step in his research has been crucial to the theory and effective practices of Tomatis. This element of his work can lead us back to our

---

[27] See Campbell, *The Mozart Effect,* 40–41. Foley also discusses the distinction between "vibratory disturbances" and their actively being processed as human sound. See "Toward a Sound Theology," 123–24.

[28] See Jonathan Goldman. *Healing Sound: The Power of Harmonics* (Shaftesbury, Dorset/Rockport, Mass.: Element Books, 1992) 14–15; see also, Campbell, *The Mozart Effect,* 123. Don Campbell cites the significance of the work of Swiss engineer and doctor Hans Jenny for the experimental field of healing with sound and music: "[Jenny] showed that figures can be formed by vibrations, for instance by vibrating crystals with electric impulses and then transmitting the vibrations to a medium such as a plate, a diaphragm or a string. He also produced vibratory figures in liquids and gases. By changing the pitch, the harmonics of the tone and the material that is vibrating, a new form results. When harmonic ratios are added to the fundamental tone, the variants create either splendid beauty or chaotic stress." "Introduction: The Curative Potential of Sound," *Music: Physician for Times to Come,* ed. Don Campbell (Wheaton, Ill.: Quest Books, 1991) 4. See also, Campbell, *The Mozart Effect,* 33–34.

[29] See Campbell, *The Mozart Effect,* 136; and Goldman, *Healing Sounds,* 15. For an anthropologist's description and analysis of music, dance, and trance in rituals of healing, see Bruce Kapferer, *A Celebration of Demons: Exorcism and the Aesthetics of Healing in Sri Lanka,* 2nd ed. (Washington, D. C.: Berg/Smithsonian Institution Press, 1991) 245–84.

consideration of liturgical music: "We have largely overlooked . . . the sounds generated from inside the body, particularly the ear's relation to our own voice. This function I call self-listening or auditory-vocal control."[30] The production of rich overtones by a voice with good timbre supplies positive stimulation to the brain and charges the entire body. Tomatis came to appreciate the benefits of both producing and receiving sound for physical, mental, and spiritual well-being when he was called by the abbot of a Benedictine monastery where the monks had become chronically fatigued and listless. The abbot had convinced the community that in the reforming spirit of Vatican II (as he interpreted it) they should dispense with chanting the office and use the six to eight hours gained per day for more useful purposes. The directly opposite result, however, ensued. Whereas the monks, when chanting continually, had needed rather little sleep, they now were constantly tired. When Tomatis was summoned, he found more than three quarters of the monks listlessly slumping in their cells.[31] Their condition was further exacerbated by other doctors having prescribed that they abandon their simple vegetarian diet and eat meat to gain strength.

Tomatis treated the monks strictly by means of sound, returning them to their full schedule of chanting. The results were completely successful. He deduced that the monks needed the high cortical charge produced in their bodies through their singing. This led Tomatis to study extensively the quality of frequencies, pace, and rhythm in Gregorian chant. He finds that persons benefit from both singing and hearing these particular melodies in conjunction with the phonetic characteristics of the Latin language. He argues further that the type of auditory environment created in Gothic church spaces bathes people in a generous stream of overtones sounding overhead, drawing the person up vertically.[32] Thus, the principles of listen-

[30] Wilson, "Chant," 17. For a comprehensive, illustrated discussion of scientific research on the sounds, rhythms, and pulses within the organs and systems of the human body, see Jane Redmond, *Sounding the Inner Landscape: Music as Medicine* (Stonington, Me.: Caduceus Publications, 1990) 76–94.

[31] See Wilson, "Chant," 14. See also, Weeks, "The Physician, the Ear and Sacred Music," 47–48; and Campbell, *The Mozart Effect,* 103–06.

[32] See Wilson, "Chant," 24; and Campbell, *The Mozart Effect,* 107–08. Goldman explains the concept of overtones: "[A] string which is struck and vibrates at 256 [hertz] and which we refer to as a C, when we listen to that string we usually hear, first and foremost, the C note. This is referred to as the 'fundamental' tone. However, when that string is vibrating at 256 times a second and that C is sounding, many other notes besides the fundamental tone are also sounding. These are the 'overtones.'" Goldman goes on to explain that overtones are what shape the unique sounds of every musical instrument, as well as the unique speaking and singing qualities of every human voice. *Healing Sounds,* 25–26.

ing and vocalizing, as well as verticality, as these pertain to human health and holiness, come together in Tomatis's narrative of the monks.

Implications for Pastoral Music

While there admittedly are limits to our ability both to review Tomatis's work as a scientist and physician and to the apply the results to the re-formed liturgy of the Church, his practical and theoretical findings do present an opportunity for further reflection on how and why ritual music (and thereby, liturgy itself) makes a difference in the life of faith. We cannot, for example, argue that every voice in the liturgical assembly must necessarily be of a rich timbre or every ear attuned for listening to the degree that Tomatis seeks in healing his patients. The performance of liturgy is not, strictly speaking, a therapeutic activity.[33] Neither could we insist that all liturgical structures be of Gothic design, nor would we promote Gregorian chant as the exclusive form of the Church's ritual music. We can, nonetheless, recognize in Tomatis's work helpful support for the Church's claims about the irreducible value of music in liturgy that pastoral ministers and theologians have been seeking to advance.

Most immediately, we can note that in his assessment and treatment of the ill monks Tomatis drew upon all three categories of Chauvet's concept of human bodiliness.[34] The monks suffered diminished health and vigor in their natural bodies as they refrained from singing and hearing their customary hours of chant. The practice of chanting, moreover, is a social activity, effecting at once the viability of the monastic community as a whole, as well as each of its members. Finally, in their performance of Gregorian chant these monks situate themselves within and, indeed, are supported by a body of tradition, contributing corporately and individually to their comprehensive health and human subjectivity. The triple-bodiliness of the symbolism inherent to liturgy as a human enterprise is exemplified in the narrative. The other crucial element in Chauvet's theory of the person as an *I-body,* namely, the function of desire, also plays a role in the activity of liturgical music under the rubric of *intentionality.* This and several other principles can be explored further by considering some specific aspects of ritual music in contemporary liturgical practice. We shall use the gathering hymn as a base for exploration.

---

[33] See Paul Westermeyer, "Liturgical Music: *Soli Deo Gloria," Liturgy and the Moral Self: Humanity at Full Stretch Before God,* eds. E. Byron Anderson and Bruce T. Morrill (Collegeville: The Liturgical Press, 1998) 197.

[34] See note 3, above.

The performance of an entrance or gathering song not only "charges" the body and mind of those so engaged, heightening their awareness and receptivity to the event of word and sacrament taking place, it also orients the person-bodies assembled in relation to themselves, one another, and God. In its purpose of helping "the assembled people become a worshipping community,"[35] the song orients the people both vertically and horizontally. The posture for this action is one of standing. Commentaries on this liturgical posture tend to describe its sociological meaning as a sign of respect and attentiveness, while explaining its theological significance in terms of the paschal joy and dignity of the assembled in Christ, as well as eschatological expectation of the Lord's return.[36] Tomatis likewise notes the cross-cultural association of verticality with awareness of the divine. His discovery of the "neurological loop" connecting the ear and the voice, however, along with his extensive research on the vestibular function of the ear, provide further insight into why the combined bodily activity of standing, singing and listening heighten the body and mind's awareness of encountering God. The tones and overtones within, around, and above the bodies of worship draw people's consciousness divinely "upward." The ear orients each person-body in standing and singing.

Participation in the gathering song, moreover, orients each person horizontally within the social (and traditional) body of the assembly, the body of Christ. Here the function is one of unifying the group as a corporate body of action.[37] Citing several patristic sources Aimé Martimort asserts, "by its rhythm and melody [song] produces such a fusion of voices that there seems to be but a single singer. As a matter of fact, once there is question of more than a small group of people, song alone makes it possible for an assembly to express itself as one."[38] Given the research of Tomatis and others, we can appreciate more fully the reason for this unifying effect of music. The members of the assembly serve one another by producing the tones and overtones of the music, not only charging each person's body and mind but also producing some degree of synchrony among their bodies as their heartbeats and breath process the entraining rhythm, pulse, and pace of the music. In addition, the potential for this unifying experience in music is a function not only of the ears and voices

[35] *Music in Catholic Worship*, n. 44.

[36] See Aimé G. Martimort, "Structure and Laws of the Liturgical Celebration," Irénée H. Dalmais and others, *Principles of the Liturgy*, The Church at Prayer, vol. 1, ed. Aimé G. Martimort, trans. Matthew O'Connell (Collegeville: The Liturgical Press, 1987) 180–81.

[37] See Foley, "Toward a Sound Theology," 134–35.

[38] Martimort, "Structure and Laws of the Liturgical Celebration," 143.

of the assembly but also of the architectural features of the worshipping space, including the musical instruments therein, as well as the pastoral, technical, and intentional qualities of the liturgical musicians.

The U.S. Bishop's Committee on the Liturgy's *Environment and Art in Catholic Worship,* a set of guidelines to be used in tandem with the committee's *Music in Catholic Worship,* identifies visibility and audibility as the primary requirements for liturgical space to realize its primary purpose: the formation and support of the assembly in its liturgies.[39] That liturgical commissions, pastoral committees, and architectural teams have tended to give greater (and unfortunately, at times, seemingly exclusive) attention to the visible quality of church spaces only confirms the argument of neurological researchers and sound therapists that ours is a culture which underestimates the importance of the ear. While round, square, or octagonal spaces do afford the opportunity for people to visibly perceive one another as members of the assembled body of Christ, the auditory quality of many such spaces has been deeply compromised by the shape and material of the roof or ceiling over them, as well as the upholstered seating and carpeted floors below. The designs of pre-Vatican II houses of worship, of course, pose their own problems concerning both visibility and audibility, and the recourse to extensive carpeting is an unfortunate pattern that seems now to be undergoing a gradual reversal. The crucial issue concerns the ability of all assembled to hear both their own and others' voices, as well as the voices and instruments of the pastoral musicians.

Concerning instruments, *Sacrosanctum concilium's* extolling of the pipe organ[40] finds merit in virtue of its having "breath" in its windchest(s) and resonant, harmonic vibrations in its pipes. The Constitution's openness to other instruments is conditioned by such criteria as their dignity and suitability, but the latter point is best developed in terms of the resonance, pitch, and rhythm that stringed instruments and drums, for example, can provide. The placement of instruments and musicians is, indeed, important as well, but this concern must again be negotiated not only on the basis of visibility in relation to the assembly but also audibility. As the Bishop's Committee's document aptly advises, the electronic amplification of voices is a compromising necessity over against the preferable design of a space that does not require it.[41] This technology needs to be used sparingly, at minimal levels, so as to prevent both the distortion of the resonances in

[39] See *Environment and Art in Catholic Worship* (Washington, D.C.: United States Catholic Conference, 1978) nos. 6, 39–43, 49–51.

[40] See *Sacrosanctum Concilium,* no. 120.

[41] See *Environment and Art in Catholic Worship,* n. 51.

the cantor's or other musicians' voices, as well as an overpowering those of the rest of the assembly.

The acoustical condition of a given space numbers prominently among the several factors that liturgical musicians must take into account in practicing their ministries. An organist must know the reverberation time of the room and take it into account when accompanying a cantor or soloist, especially if the singer is at a significant distance from the organ. This awareness of resonance and sound delay is also essential to successful hymn playing. The organist must set the pace of the hymn and maintain it despite the fact that the sound of the assembly's singing may well reach the organist a few seconds "behind" the notes she or he is playing. For these reasons the conscious intent of the organist is of no small importance to the service he or she is rendering to the worshipping church. Depending on whether a space has a lengthy or short reverberation time, the organist needs to detach the notes or connect them in a more *legato* style, respectively. In addition, the competent organist seeks to make the instrument "breathe" by detaching notes at places where the human voices of the assembly would need to take a breath. Regardless of the space, the organist must focus her or his breathing and through it, bring about the quality of sound, pace, and rhythm she or he intends the assembly to enjoy in singing the particular song. The organist who is privileged to play a fine organ that is well voiced to a particular room, and who does so by drawing his or her consciousness through breath in the body, enjoys over time the experience of the musical instrument teaching the musician.

The integration of the mind's intention and the frequency of sound produced in the body is crucial to the ministry of the cantor as she or he leads the assembly in its gathering song and, of course, the music of the entire liturgy. Sound and music therapist Jonathan Goldman explains that the concept of intention "encompasses the overall state of the person making the sound and involves the physical, mental, emotional and spiritual aspects of that person. . . . It is the consciousness we have when we are making a sound."[42] Goldman suggests that one can readily grasp what he means by the concept if one reflects on the contrasting experiences of being bored when listening to a singer who has an excellent and well-trained voice but being deeply moved when listening to someone whose voice is not nearly of such quality or technical precision. The difference lies in the intention—the admittedly difficult concept to describe, let alone quantify—that each of the two singers brings to the performance of the music. Goldman subscribes to the theory that the intention is usually cre-

---

[42] Goldman, *Healing Sounds,* 18, 138.

ated in the "stillpoint" between our taking breath into our lungs and releasing it in the sound we produce.[43] It is this factor of intention, this joining of mind and body in the practice of liturgical music, that cantors need to examine and nurture within themselves so that they may convey this positive sound to the assembly and enhance the possibility of a yet more full, conscious, and active participation in the liturgy.

Another approach to the concept of intentionality in liturgical music emerges if we consider the choice and performance of a specific hymn in a specific context—such as a gathering hymn for a parish's worship on a Sunday in Ordinary Time. Numerous liturgical theologians and musicians have profitably explored the significance of joining text and tune in the composition and execution of hymnody. In a recent treatment of the topic, E. Byron Anderson describes how the singing of a hymn commits participants in the purposeful intention of producing sound and rhythm in a manner distinct from ordinary speech such that: "The images, themes, and claims of the text [of the hymn] are realized not as text but as a 'writing on the body' in performance."[44] Over time, the assembly's singing of the hymn results in a simultaneously personal and communal experience whereby the hymn "begins, so to speak, to take on a life of its own and to have its way with us. Writing in body and mind, the hymn is no longer only the expressive statement 'This is who I am' but a constituting statement, 'This is who you are coming to be.'"[45]

The notion of intentionality, then, encompasses both productive and receptive action of body, mind, and spirit by all participating in the ritual music of the liturgy. The specific responsibilities of the president, ministers of music, and the other members of the assembly, of course, entail further distinctions of intention and performance, the discussion of which we must forego here. Suffice it to note the pastoral importance of decisions concerning selection of ritual music, styles of musical leadership, the fostering of familiarity and, quite frankly, pleasure in the assembly's singing. All contribute to the quality of communal sharing in divine worship, of proclamation and response to the Word of God living and acting in our midst.

---

[43] Ibid., 139.

[44] E. Byron Anderson, "'O for a Heart to Praise My God': Hymning the Self Before God," *Liturgy and the Moral Self: Humanity at Full Stretch Before God,* eds. E. Byron Anderson and Bruce T. Morrill (Collegeville: The Liturgical Press, 1998) 120. Anderson draws on, among others, the important scholarly work of Teresa Berger and Frank Burch Brown. See Teresa Berger, *Theology in Hymns?* (Nashville: Abingdon Press, 1995); and Frank Burch Brown, *Religious Aesthetics* (Princeton: Princeton University Press, 1989).

[45] Anderson, "O for a Heart to Praise My God," 120.

Suggestions for Further Reading

Campbell, Don, ed. *Music: Physician for Times to Come*. Wheaton, Ill.: Quest
    Books, 1991.
Campbell, Don. *The Mozart Effect: Tapping the Power of Music to Heal the Body,
    Strengthen the Mind, and Unlock the Creative Spirit*. New York: Avon Books,
    1997.
Goldman, Jonathan. *Healing Sounds: The Power of Harmonics*. Shaftesbury,
    Dorset/Rockport, Mass.: Element Books, 1992.
Kubicki, Judith Marie. "The Role of Music as Ritual Symbol in Roman Catholic
    Liturgy." *Worship* (September 1995) 427–46.
The Milwaukee Symposia for Church Composers: A Ten Year Report. Chicago:
    Liturgy Training Publications, 1992.

CONCLUSION

Nonsystematic Reflections on the Practical Character of Liturgy and Theology

Bruce T. Morrill, S.J.

As explained in the preface to this book, and as is hopefully evident in reading the chapters, the two parts of the text have been designed to pursue a theoretical trajectory concerning the multivalent bodiliness of liturgy (Part One) and topical investigations into specific liturgical and bodily practices (Part Two). We can observe across the chapters that while the primary emphasis in the first five is on the theory of liturgy (and the Church, society, anthropology, etc.) and in the last four on practices of prayer and worship, the nature of the subject matter never allows for an exclusive consideration of theory or practice. Neither theological abstraction nor merely pastoral pragmatics will do; rather, the theological character of Christian liturgy requires the mutually informative dialogue between theory and practice. No claim is being made here for a systematic theology of liturgy and body, either in the chapters themselves or the suggestive reflections comprising this brief conclusion to the book. Indeed, the starting point for these several reflections is the question of whether such a systematic theology would be possible at all.[1]

---

[1] Please note that while functioning as a conclusion to this present book, these reflections actually amount to suggestive comments (based on a short review of literature) that I hope to pursue much more rigorously in the reworking and expansion of my dissertation, "Anamnesis as Dangerous Memory: A Dialogue Between Political and Liturgical Theology" (Emory University, 1996).

The profession of trinitarian faith grounded in the confession of the crucified Jesus as risen Lord places narrative and symbol, and thus the
Church's sacramental liturgy, at the center of Christian life. Moreover, the
biblical message that essentially informs the ritual symbols of Christian
faith is, as Johann Baptist Metz has so poignantly argued, utterly practical
in its content.[2] Knowing the message necessarily entails following Christ
in a particular way of life. At the heart of both the Church's narratives and
ritual symbolism, however, is the broken body of Christ—the crucified
Jesus of Nazareth, the eucharistic breaking of the bread, and the broken
lives of the poor and suffering, who come to believers as invitations to
know Jesus by imitating him in messianic service. Thus does salvation
only come through bodies broken in history and redemptively raised up in
the unfathomable love practiced in and by the God of Jesus.[3] Christianity
is not a philosophical system of thought but, rather, in the terminology of
Metz, a praxis of mysticism and ethics.[4] The Church's sacramental liturgy,
and singularly the Eucharist, hold pride of place among its mystical practices, for the liturgy's ritual character forms and nurtures Christ's followers as a body, even as its evangelical content deploys them with joy and
hope to seek the incarnate God emptied out and hidden in the world.

It is this practical character of both the narrative content and ritual shape
of Christian faith that resists the hegemony of any system. As in several
other places in this book, the thought of Louis-Marie Chauvet is instruc-
tive here. In his explanation of the sacraments as acts of ritual symbolism,
Chauvet argues: "Inasmuch as they are rituals, the sacraments are not primarily of the cognitive order, the order of '-ology,' but of the practical
order. Of course, they do communicate information in the areas of doctrine and ethics; but they do not operate at the discursive level proper to
theo-logy."[5] Moreover, in both their ritual nature and their Christian character the sacraments resist a total system of thought.

As Chauvet finds the unity of his massive work in the convergence of
ritual symbolism and trinitarian christology, he notes how the latter also

---

[2] See Johann Baptist Metz, *Faith in History and Society: Toward a Practical Fundamental Theology,* trans. David Smith (New York: Seabury Press, 1980) ix–x, 165, 169.

[3] See Catherine Mowry LaCugna, *God for Us: The Trinity and Christian Life* (San
Francisco: HarperCollins, 1991) 377–82, 400–11.

[4] See Metz, *Faith in History and Society,* 51, 76–77, 111–12, 117–18. See also, Jo-
hannes B. Metz, *Theology of the World,* trans. William Glen-Doepel (New York:
Seabury Press, 1969) 98–99.

[5] Louis-Marie Chauvet, *Symbol and Sacrament: A Sacramental Reinterpretation of
Christian Existence,* trans. Patrick Madigan and Madeleine Beaumont (Collegeville:
The Liturgical Press, 1995) 324.

keeps a fissure open in the metaphysical tradition of theology: "The *indicative* mode of the God crucified in the form of a slave does not tolerate being mastered by a science. Its Word can be expressed only as a 'categorical *imperative* of life and action' which makes it happen among us."[6] It is the executing of this imperative for ethical practice, especially in justice and mercy toward those reduced to various forms of slavery today, that verifies the ritual act of thanksgiving in the Eucharist and "gives a body to this God."[7] Chauvet's sacramental theology strongly resonates with Metz's fundamental theology of Christian faith as a practice of mysticism and ethics (or politics). But can we be more specific concerning what is meant by practice, both in terms of the practical character of Christian (and liturgical) theology and the irreducible role of the body therein?

Rebecca Chopp, a constructive theologian who has for some time been pressing figures such as Metz on just what they mean by practical theology,[8] has come to define *practice* as

> socially shared forms of behavior that mediate between what are often called subjective and objective dimensions. A practice is a pattern of meaning and action that is both culturally constructed and individually instantiated. The notion of practice draws us to inquire into the shared activities of groups of persons that provide meaning and orientation to the world, and that guide action.[9]

Practices are shared activities requiring the participation and interaction of a group or community and, as such, they function as a crucial source of knowledge for the members. Following David Kelsey, Chopp emphasizes the *bodiliness* of practices. While practices bear and lend themselves to ideas, they primarily involve bodily actions, which "hold inner intention and outer behavior together, and thus . . . deny any systematic distinction between the spiritual/intellectual and the physical/material."[10] Shared and acquired bodily, the practices of a community mitigate against such dualisms.

Worship is an exemplary case of Christian practice, Chopp observes, in that it engages all of the bodily senses, places bodies in motion, and includes attention to the affective, cognitive and ethical dimensions of the faith. Crucial to the history of Christian faith, as well, are practices of

---

[6] Ibid., 535.

[7] Ibid.

[8] See Rebecca S. Chopp, *The Praxis of Suffering: An Interpretation of Liberation and Political Theologies* (Maryknoll, N.Y.: Orbis Books, 1986) 79.

[9] Rebecca S. Chopp, *Saving Work: Feminist Practices of Theological Education* (Louisville: Westminster John Knox Press, 1995) 15.

[10] Ibid., 16.

narrativity, for both the entire Christian tradition and the lives of individual believers are works in progress (i.e., process). Through narratives Christian women and men reflect upon, explain, and thereby transform their particular experiences of the life of faith.[11] Thus are narrative and symbol essential to Christianity's being a living tradition. It is concerning this dynamic notion of tradition that Chopp develops one further point on the basis of Kelsey's work: Practices have histories and are socially relative. They both bear traditions and, Chopp infers, bring about their transformation.[12]

As we have seen in numerous passages and bibliographical references throughout this present book, Christians in various times and cultural locations have developed different attitudes toward and practices of the body, whether physical, cultural, or ecclesial. Still, with Chauvet and such eminent predecessors as Alexander Schmemann I would argue that the consistent key to the liturgy's being the source and summit of the Church's life for the world lies in its participants being disposed in body, mind, and spirit to the imaginative, non-utilitarian, and performative realm of symbolism whereby it rehearses the eschatological reign of God.[13] An exploration of the various bodily ways that this tensive symbolic experience of grasping and being grasped by the Spirit of the crucified and risen Christ happens in liturgy has been the burden of these chapters.

[11] See Ibid., 33–34, and 119, n. 42. I find that in elaborating her theory of practice Chopp provides further substance for the three categories Metz proposes for practical theology: memory, narrative, and solidarity. See above, Introduction, p. 5.

[12] See Chopp, *Saving Work,* 17.

[13] See Chauvet, *Symbol and Sacrament,* 338, 533; and Alexander Schmemann, "Symbols and Symbolism in Byzantine Liturgy," *Liturgy and Tradition: Theological Reflections of Alexander Schmemann,* ed. Thomas Fisch (Crestwood, N.Y.: St. Vladimir's Seminary Press, 1990) 126–27.

Index

CPSIA information can be obtained
at www.ICGtesting.com
Printed in the USA
LVHW012244070119
603102LV00018B/991/P